THE MIND AND THE MACHINE
Philosophical Aspects of Artificial Intelligence

THE MIND AND THE MACHINE

Philosophical Aspects of Artificial Intelligence

Editor:

S. B. TORRANCE, B.A.(Hons.), B.Phil., D.Phil.
School of Philosophy
Middlesex Polytechnic

ELLIS HORWOOD LIMITED
Publishers · Chichester

Halsted Press: a division of
JOHN WILEY & SONS
New York · Chichester · Brisbane · Toronto

First published in 1984 and
Reprinted in 1986 by

ELLIS HORWOOD LIMITED
Market Cross House, Cooper Street, Chichester, West Sussex, PO19 1EB, England

*The publisher's colophon is reproduced from James Gillison's drawing of the
ancient Market Cross, Chichester.*

Distributors:

Australia, New Zealand, South-east Asia:
Jacaranda-Wiley Ltd., Jacaranda Press,
JOHN WILEY & SONS INC.,
G.P.O. Box 859, Brisbane, Queensland 4001, Australia

Canada:
JOHN WILEY & SONS CANADA LIMITED
22 Worcester Road, Rexdale, Ontario, Canada.

Europe, Africa:
JOHN WILEY & SONS LIMITED
Baffins Lane, Chichester, West Sussex, England.

North and South America and the rest of the world:
Halsted Press: a division of
JOHN WILEY & SONS
605 Third Avenue, New York, N.Y. 10158, U.S.A.

©1984 S. Torrance/Ellis Horwood Limited

British Library Cataloguing in Publication Data
The mind and the machine. —
(Ellis Horwood series in artificial intelligence)
1. Artificial intelligence
I. Torrance, S.
001.53'5'01 Q335

Library of Congress Card No. 84-12845

ISBN 0-85312-712-3 (Ellis Horwood Limited)
ISBN 0-470-20104-5 (Halsted Press)

Typeset by Ellis Horwood Limited
Printed in Great Britain by R.J. Acford, Chichester

Contents

Foreword

John Campbell

Forewords seem to be a matter of culture: in some cultures they are near-universal, but in others one hardly ever sees a book that begins with a short contribution from anyone except an author or an editor. Artificial Intelligence (AI) is now generally a foreword-less culture while philosophy is not. This raises the question of how to treat a collection of primarily philosophical papers in a book which is published in a series on AI: should content or location have the final say?

Having raised the question, I shall avoid it by finding another type of justification for a foreword in this case. While there are not yet any definitions of the subject of AI that are both simple and convincing, specialists in AI are in general agreement on most of the topics which belong within their subject. These topics need no preliminary explanations when they are treated in books or series on AI. Others, which include issues in philosophy at present, deserve a special welcome.

One of the achievements of computer science, which is at least a foster-parent of AI, is that it has converted the status of parts of other subjects, notably mathematics, from 'pure' to 'applied'. For example, the applied mathematics taught to computer scientists under the headings of finite or discrete mathematics is algebra, of a kind which is usually otherwise reserved for final-year undergraduate or early postgraduate programmes for students specializing in pure mathematics. Nor is this an effect confined to algebra; thanks (if that is the word) to computer science, some passages of G. H. Hardy's classic *A Mathematician's Apology* on the purity of pure mathematics now read very strangely indeed. Lately, AI has begun to show that it has inherited similar powers of conversion from its ancestors, in offering the same service to other subjects, including philosophy. The present book is by no means the first book to make the point implicitly, but the variety of questions related to philosophy which its different chapters consider demonstrates probably more effectively than any single-author presentation can do that the influences of AI and philosophy on each other should be beneficial for the future of both.

On the philosophical side, 'mind and machine' issues are changed in detail from what they were even as recently as 15 years ago because philosophers are now relieved by progress in AI from the additional duty of having to devise their own plausible 'machine' situations as tests or examples for philosophical work that touches on such issues. On the side of AI, the good news which philosophy brings to AI specialists is that there are problems for which they do not need to spend time re-inventing hexagonal approximations to the wheel because specialists in a much older branch of knowledge, with many more man-years invested in the effort, have succeeded in finding good dodecahedral approximations to the same wheel already.

The organizers of the meeting of the Anglo-French colloquium on philosophy from which the contributions that follow have been drawn, and Dr Torrance in particular, are to be congratulated on the timeliness of their choice of topic. The plan of bringing together workers in AI and philosophy with overlapping concerns was clearly successful. The evident aim of the present book is to make the fruits of the success available to a wider audience in both subjects, and therefore to stimulate further work of the kind that is published here. I hope that this collection will add significantly to the trend towards closer communication between the subjects, and to a general appreciation that AI properly includes parts of applied philosophy and that philosophy properly includes the study of applied AI.

Exeter, March 1984   J.A.C.

Preface

The chapters in this volume are based on presentations at a weekend meeting between philosophers, AI researchers, computer scientists and workers in related fields, held in London in April 1983, under the title 'The Mind and the Machine'. This was the Second Anglo-French Philosophy Colloquium organized jointly by Middlesex Polytechnic Faculty of Humanities, and by the Université de Lille III U.E.R. de Philosophie. The Colloquium was held at Middlesex Polytechnic, Trent Park.

The Anglo-French Colloquia have owed their existence and success largely to the guiding inspiration and energies of Noël Mouloud, formerly Professor of Lille. It was with great sadness that we learned of his death in Paris, in April 1984, just one year since the Trent Park Conference. We dedicate this book to him, as a monument to his endeavours.

I am indebted to my friend and colleague Jean-Michel Vienne, of the Université de Lille, without whose organizational powers and hard work the Colloquia would not have come to fruition. Thanks are also due to Roger Waterhouse and to Gérard Simon, who arranged necessary material and institutional support for the conference, from Middlesex and from Lille respectively. Additional financial support came from the Centre de Recherche sur l'Analyse et la Théorie des Savoirs at Lille, under M. Mouloud's direction. I am also indebted to the following for assisting me in a variety of ways over the planning or the running of the conference: Janet Blackler, Margaret Boden, John Cornish, Richard Ennals, Peter King, David Kirsh, Helen Loughlin, Aaron Sloman, Grenville Wall, Masoud Yazdani, as well as many others.

John Campbell and Michael Horwood guided me enormously in the preparation of this volume. In writing the Introduction I benefitted from conversation or correspondence with Pascal Engel, Mark Fisher, André Gallois, Keith Lehrer, Karen Neander and Philip Pettit; as well as from having the opportunity to read drafts of it to the Philosophy Departments at Hong Kong University, the University of East Anglia and Middlesex Polytechnic. (But the usual exclusions about responsibility for errors apply.)

The Editor would like to record his gratitude to the following publishers for their kind permission to reproduce items as listed below:

D. Dennett, 'Artificial intelligence as philosophy and as psychology', first published in M. Ringle, Ed., *Philosophical Perspectives in Artificial Intelligence*, Atlantic Highlands, N.J.: Humanities Press, and Brighton, Sussex: Harvester Press; reprinted in D. Dennett, *Brainstorms*, Cambridge, Mass.: Bradford Books, and Brighton, Sussex: Harvester Press. Excerpts reprinted in Chapter 2 below.

G. Ryle, 'Review of A. Quinton, *The Nature of Things*', first published in the *New Statesman*, 6 April 1973, Statesman and Nation Publishing Co. Excerpt reprinted in Chapter 2 below.

J. Higginbotham, 'Chomsky's linguistic theory', *Social Research,* vol. 49, no. 1, Spring 1982, The Graduate Faculty, New School for Social Research, New York. Entire article reproduced with minor additions below as Chapter 8.

M. Boden, 'Methodological links between AI and other disciplines', first published in *The Study of Information: Interdisciplinary Messages,* Ed. F. Machlup and V. Mansfield, New York: John Wiley and Sons. Copyright © 1984, John Wiley and Sons. Reprinted by permission as Chapter 9 below.

London, May 1984   S.B.T.

Editor's Introduction

Philosophy and AI: Some issues

Steve Torrance

I

Ever since Alan Turing's influential paper 'Computing machinery and intelligence', published in 1950 (Turing 1950),[1] and the birth of the research field of Artificial Intelligence (AI) in the mid-1950s, there has been considerable interest among computer scientists in theorizing about the mind. At the same time there has been a growing feeling amongst philosophers that the advent of computing has decisively modified philosophical debates, by proposing new theoretical positions to consider, or at least to rebut. Important early landmarks here were a series of papers by Hilary Putnam, starting with his 'Minds and machines' (1960), in which the notion of a Turing machine was used as a tool of criticism of established theories in the Philosophy of Mind, and as the basis for a new, 'functionalist' approach;[2] and J. R. Lucas's paper 'Minds, machines and Gödel' (1961), which appealed to Gödel's incompleteness proofs to argue that computer programs would necessarily fail to model the human mind.[3] Philosophical critics like J. R. Lucas, Hubert Dreyfus and John Searle[4] have provided many grounds for doubting that genuine mental qualities could ever inhere in computers or their programs. But it is clear that, whatever else computers are or might one day be, they are undeniably mind-*like*. Within the last two or three decades, research in AI has had remarkable success in producing in machines performances which hitherto were thought to lie exclusively in the domain of human mentality, such as chess, backgammon (a computer beat the winner of the 1979 World Backgammon Championship), theorem-proving, conversations in English (at least of limited, rudimentary kinds) and a host of other simulations of human cognitive, perceptual and motor performances.[5] Some of these simulations may have the air of magician's acts — Joseph Weizenbaum's Eliza program being the most famous example (Weizenbaum 1966, 1976). But most aren't so easy to dismiss, and it is obvious that, taken cumulatively, they pose important problems for adherents to traditional views of the nature of mind.

At all events, AI has been one major focus of the growing interdisciplinary activity which has come to be known as 'Cognitive Science', an activity which has involved linguists, psychologists and brain scientists, as well as philosophers and AI researchers. Two other foci are worth mentioning. First there is the influence of Noam Chomsky: his critique of behaviourism in psychology and in philosophy (Chomsky 1959), and also his positive method within generative grammar. This latter showed how mental (specifically linguistic) activities can and should be investigated independently both from behavioural performance patterns and from neural underpinnings (see Higginbotham, Chapter 8 below). Second, there is the move away from the 'ordinary language' philosophical approach associated with Gilbert Ryle (1949) and Ludwig Wittgenstein (1953), which saw the philosophy of mind primarily as a second-order subject (if a 'subject' at all) whose primary aim was the negative one of clearing away conceptual confusions. An alternative conception of the subject has emerged within the last two decades, which sees the philosopher as contributing to the same theoretical tasks as the empirical psychologist, but from a different direction. A notable illustration of this latter approach is Jerry Fodor's *The Language of Thought,* (1975) where evidence is adduced from work in psychology and linguistics to buttress philosophical considerations in favour of postulating an internal representation code to which all human cognitive activity is computationally related (see below, Engel, Chapter 3 and Jacob, Chapter 4).

II

A traditional theme of Western philosophy was that the essence of humanity — what distinguished us from the brutes and from purely inanimate objects — was our intellectual capacities. Aristotle said that the specific function — the *telos* — of a human being was 'rational activity of the soul'. Descartes proclaimed that his existence was knowable from the mere fact of his thinking, and that accordingly his essence was that of a ratiocinating soul — a *res cogitans* — only continguently linked to a physical body. Intellectual properties of mind have consistently been appealed to by philosophers in order to provide a principle of distinguishing between the spiritual and the material, between the 'higher' and the 'lower'. It was their lack of language, and hence of an ability to engage in logical or mathematical reasoning, which allowed Descartes to conclude of non-human animals that they were mere automata. Despite a refinement of theory which has naturally taken place since Descartes, the association of linguistic and logico-mathematical abilities with rationality, responsibility, moral dignity, and so on, and the contrasting of such 'essentially human' traits with the 'merely animal' or the 'merely mechanical', are themes which still permeate our philosophical culture. So it is of interest to see how subversive of such assumptions were the early results in AI. For it was precisely the most abstract 'achievements' of the intellect — mathematical calculation, theorem-proving, natural language production (of sorts at least) etc. — which most easily succumbed to replication by electronic automata. The difficult things to stimulate have proved to be precisely those qualities which we share with the brutes — capacities such as visually processing, manipulating and moving through our physical environment. A corollary to this has been the discovery that even the lowly housefly (for example) must embody quite phenomenally complex *cognitive* processes.[6]

Of course philosophers have been quick to reprove the artificial intelligentisia for too glibly passing off their creations as the real thing, when they were merely simulations, or models, and only partial and often not very good ones, at that. To some extent these reproofs are deserved. Hubert Dreyfus has catalogued some of the early over-optimistic predictions, and subsequent climbdowns, of AI researchers, and Drew McDermott has drawn attention to the tendency of workers in the field to resort to 'wishful mnemonics' and other theoretical obfuscations.[7]

III

Daniel Dennett has observed that the philosophical literature on minds and machines has moved away from early preoccupation with the simple-minded question 'can computers think?' (1978c). Nevertheless it's still important to examine the different possible positions on the issue of whether and when mental properties (or mind, or personhood)[8] might literally and veridically be ascribed to machines. There seem to be four positions here: *This year* — existing programs already display genuine mentality; *Next year* — current state-of-the-art programs are too crude, but it won't be long before programs which are complex and comprehensive enough have been developed; *Some time* — nothing achievable within currently envisaged research programs is remotely rich enough to instantiate genuine mental properties, but there's no reason in principle why such a result shouldn't be obtained one day; *Never* — the computer instantiation of mental properties is *a priori* impossible.

In his paper 'Minds, brains and programs' (Searle 1980), John Searle distinguishes between weak AI — the view that AI programs can be useful and powerful tools in the study of the mind, but not necessarily anything more; and strong AI — which roughly covers the this year/next year/sometime combination of views outlined above. Searle's paper is a critique of strong AI, one which raises some important challenges to workers in the field and to their philosophical sympathizers. Searle usefully distinguishes between four questions: Could a machine think? Yes he answers, because *we* are machines and we can think. Could a man-made machine think? Yes: if it can exactly replicate all the *physiological* causes of consciousness, then perhaps an artificially built biological replica might indeed possess genuine mental states. Could a digital computer think? Yes, because human beings instantiate any number of computer programs, and therefore are *eo ipso* digital computers. Could something think *solely* in virtue of instantiating a computer program (of the appropriate sort)?

This is the question which Searle takes to be at the heart of the 'strong' AI project, and his answer is, roundly, No.[9] We shall be examining his reasons below.

Many people would claim that the question of the genuineness of thinking in computers present or future, is a purely conventional one, or at least that it's pointless to suppose that there's some 'essence' to having a mind which computer replication may or may not be able to capture. Aaron Sloman, for example, argues forcefully for a variant of this view (see Chapter 1 below, and Sloman 1978a). It might be argued that, if I can play a tolerably good game of chess with my home computer it would be otiose to quibble about whether the computer was or wasn't 'genuinely' thinking about the moves. On the other hand there do seem to be cases where such an issue does not matter: if someone claimed to have a machine that really could feel pleasure and pain, for example. Suppose the machine displayed all the appropriate behavioural responses in the appropriate situations: surely it would be important to be clear whether or not it was *genuine* pain. A machine which gave howsoever lifelike an imitation — but only an imitation — of pain would not be adding to the sum total of misery in the universe, would not merit our *concern*, in the way that would a behaviourally indistinguishable machine that really was in agony. (But no doubt, if the former machine showed every indication of *believing* itself to be in pain, one might not wish to take on the task of telling it that it wasn't!)[10]

IV

It would be tempting to argue that there is a distinction between two types of mental state: cognitive states, such as believing, etc., which lend themselves readily to implementation in computer programs; and qualitative, or experiential states, such as pains, which don't. (See below, Engel Chapter 3, Section 3.) Perhaps one might concede that these latter experiential states — *qualia*, as they have come to be called — are not the kind of mental state which can be captured in a purely information-processing model such as is provided by a computer program, but that all cognitive states can, in principle, be fully captured by some appropriate set of programs. But such a view generates a curious anomaly, at least if interpreted as the view that *all* beliefs, and other cognitive states, are genuinely computer-realizable. For suppose you had a very detailed and lifelike computer simulation of a human being, lifelike enough for one to be prepared to say that it *genuinely* did have beliefs, even though it did not undergo any genuine experiential states — any qualia — for all its convincing behavioural manifestations of such states. We would then seem to be committed to saying that, even though it genuinely *believed* it was in pain, etc., it wasn't. Such a position is highly counter-intuitive, especially for *intense* pains![11]

To return to Searle: his arguments against strong AI address the position that cognitive states (at least) are genuinely computer-realizable. Take a human cognitive capacity — say that of an average native Chinese speaker to produce and understand written sentences of that language. Consider a program P which accurately replicates the *behaviour* of such a person. The success of this behavioural imitation is not put into question: the program can win an 'imitation game' of the sort proposed by Turing (cf. his 1950) and fool native Chinese speakers into thinking they are talking to a human being. Adherents of strong AI would want to say that such a program would *genuinely* understand Chinese. But now, says Searle, consider an individual S, who understands only English, and who is locked in a room, following the steps in program P written out in English, responding to a set of (meaningless to S) Chinese symbols given to him as input, with another set of (equally meaningless) such symbols as output, as determined by the program. (We will have to stretch our imaginations somewhat, and endow S with miraculous abilities of operational speed, and/or extraordinary longevity.) Searle's point is simple: if a computer implementing program P genuinely understands Chinese *in virtue of being a P-implementer,* then so would S. But clearly S doesn't understand Chinese, since *ex hypothesi* the symbols which form the input and output of program P are meaningless to S, identifiable by *form*, but not by content.

There are a number of possible responses to Searle's argument — to all of which he claims to have replies.[12] One possibility would be to argue as follows. (A) in order for P to replicate genuine understanding of Chinese, it would have to incorporate more than some narrowly defined set of linguistic competences, it would have to incorporate some elaborate system of knowledge representation, and no doubt much else besides, with the result that P would really have to be an entire person, an understand*er*, rather than just understand*ing*. (B) But this resulting person (call her T) who is constituted by P when run by S is not identical to S. T, not S, would understand Chinese, S being just the engine which drives P. (Compare: it's not the washing-machine *motor* which washes my clothes, but the washing-machine.) It will be noted that such a reply already involves an enormous concession by many adherents of strong AI, who would wish to claim that existing AI programs embody genuine understanding, at least within limited domains.[13] Condition (A) above would rule out any AI program achievable within our lifetimes, certainly.

Another sort of reply, which avoids the extravagant supposition that one person can somehow inhabit another person, would be to challenge Searle's claim that S fails to understand Chinese in virtue of implementing P. Searle is appealing to our intuitions here, which are partly fed by the fact that S will, of course, assert complete ignorance of Chinese. Surely I am the ultimate authority on whether or not I understand Chinese. Or am I? Suppose I was 'taught' to play chess while under hypnosis. Subjects can be induced, through post-hypnotic suggestion, to open umbrellas at an alloted time, while offering some spurious ad hoc justification for the act, quite unrelated to the hypnosis. I might sit at a chess board and say, 'I've no idea how these pieces are supposed to be moved, but I think I'll put this piece here'. In such a way I might perhaps make a series of legal and appropriate moves, and even win, all the time assured of the fact that I had no idea how to play chess, but that I was just arranging the board in ways that looked pretty. Wouldn't this be a case of my possessing genuine understanding of playing chess, if only at an unconscious or tacit level, despite my strongest denials of such a fact? Could not S possess an understanding of Chinese, in a similarly tacit way?

Well, perhaps Searle would say that in such a situation I *wouldn't* have an understanding of how to play chess, even though I was able to 'go through the motions' of playing it, and that the same thing would go for the Chinese example. But the trouble is, our pre-theoretical intuitions seem to be stretched in two ways here. On the one hand we would want 'understanding Chinese', 'knowing how to play chess' to be attributions on which the subject had some authority (see below, Engel, Chapter 3, Section 4); on the other hand we would want to say that a subject's systematic success in going through the appropriate input— output behaviours for chess-playing, etc., were constitutive of the possession of the appropriate understanding, despite all the subject's protestations to the contrary.

V

But it's not at all clear how conclusive such a reply to Searle could be. How would matters be affected, for instance, if we imagined S to be a *committee*?[14] In any case there is a deep issue underlying Searle's argument which has to be addressed. This concerns the relation between syntax and semantics and the relation of both to what philosophers call intentionality.

A chess-playing computer (for example) operates according to purely formal algorithms, specified in purely syntactical terms. The semantic content of the machine's output — the interpretation of the purely formal symbols *as* moves in chess — is something which is applied to the output by us, on the basis of a happy fit, and a consistent one over time, between the sequence of formal operations engaged in by the machine and the chess interpretation. Transport that machine to some community in the region of Alpha Centauri, and it might, by chance, be able to star in some totally fresh role — an intergalactic religious ritual, perhaps — where the formal operations of the program were this time interpreted in some quite new, but equally appropriate fashion. Semantic content is thus relative to a given scheme of interpretation.[15]

Now Searle insists that it is of the essence of human cognitive states — intentional states — that semantic content is self-ascribed. When we play chess the formal symbol-manipulation which we engage in is *meant* by us to be chess, rather than an Alpha Centauran religious ritual. What gives it its character as chess is our *intending* it to be chess, within the context of a certain set of social practices. It is this self-ascription, this 'intrinsic' nature of human intentional states, that seems to be absent in any purely computational simulation. The program operator S knows no semantic interpretations, having recourse only to syntactical operations. Syntax cannot miraculously generate semantics. Of course it's always in principle possible to embed any given computationally realized formal system in a wider computational context that applies a semantic interpretation to the tokens of the embedded system. But then the same problem of interpretation will now apply to the *embedding* system. No solution of this sort will avoid an infinite regress.

There are at least two other kinds of solution to this problem. The first consists of denying that there is anything like 'intrinsic' intentionality in the way Searle suggests, insisting that all mental contents have to be fixed by reference to some contextually applied scheme of interpretation or translation (see Churchland and Churchland 1982, and below, Engel, Chapter 3). A second approach is to be found in the writings of Jerry Fodor, in particular his claim that any mental attitude displaying intentionality will exemplify a particular computational relationship to some formula of an internal 'Language of Thought'. This internal code is supposed by Fodor to be directly implemented by a human being's neural 'hardware', the relation between it and the person's conscious thoughts and outward linguistic productions being supposed to be analogous to that obtaining between a computer's machine code and the high-level language in which the computer interfaces with its environment (Fodor 1975, 1981, 1983. See also below, Engel, Jacob. Critiques in Dennett 1978a, Chapter 6, and Heil 1981.)[16]

VI

Searle's arguments are targetted, not merely against claims made by AI workers, but also against a certain philosophical approach, which often makes a direct appeal to computational ideas, an approach which goes under the name of *functionalism*. Functionalism, as a philosophical theory of mind, may be contrasted with such other theories as dualism, behaviourism and physicalism. Dualists claim that mental states are the operations of some non-physical substance, which in some way influences and is influenced by, or at least accompanies, the operations of the physical body. Behaviourism is the view that mental states are nothing other than our dispositions to behave in certain ways in the appropriate situations. Physicalism claims that mental states are in fact identical with physical states of an organism's central nervous system. Each of these positions has notorious difficulties, which functionalists claim their theory surmounts — although on certain construals, functionalism is a species of, or a development from, physicalism, rather than a rebuttal of it. One problem with simple versions of physicalism is this: If X and Y are identical then any predicate attaching to X will necessarily attach to Y. A rose, by any other name, will satisfy as well the predicate 'smells sweet'. But then it would seem, according to physicalism, that if my memory of a certain rose is *poignant*, there will have to be a corresponding physical process in my brain which is poignant too; and that does seem counter-intuitive. Then there is a problem of multiple realizations: by tying mental states down too closely to states of the central nervous system, physicalists have difficulty accounting for the logical possibility of there being creatures — round Alpha Centauri, for example — who have mental states, but who have a completely different kind of bodily make-up.

Functionalist theories have been offered as a way of surmounting problems such as these and others. Some philosophers have proposed functionalist approaches as ways of defending physicalism, identifying mental states, not with neurophysiological states directly, but with the causal or functional *roles* occupied by those states and potentially by other kinds of states as well. David Armstrong and David Lewis were early defenders of such views. (See Armstrong 1968; Lewis 1966, 1972.) Others have proposed functional theories as critiques of physicalism: for example Hilary Putnam's invocation of the notion of a Turing machine in order to raise general problems with identity theories (Putnam 1960, 1967a). Philosophers who in developing functionalist theories put great weight on analogies with computers might be called machine-functionalists. When Searle claims (as he does) that anything, and only such, that has the same *causal powers* as the human brain may exhibit mentality, he is, perhaps, proposing a view which is compatible with functionalism in the broad sense of the term. It is machine versions of functionalism against which his critique is primarily directed.

In order to understand machine functionalism, consider a homely pocket calculator. This contains a set of keys for input, a display for output, and electronic circuitry inside to perform the necessary transformations between input and output. Now as well as input and output devices and actual physical circuitry — the hardware — there is also what might be called the functional organization of the calculator. There are two things that are important about this functional organization. First, it can be described and understood totally without reference to the underlying electronic hardware. Thus it's possible to to produce a flow chart of the various operations of the calculator, making reference to various storage locations, flow of control, etc., but without mentioning the actual electronic parts which perform these operations. The second point — really a consequence of the first — is that the same functional organization can be 'realized' by totally different underlying hardwares. Thus my calculator might be filled with little gremlins whose collective behaviour exactly mimics a normal calculator's electronic circuits. So functional organization is neutral as between different underlying realizations. Indeed one doesn't even have to be a physicalist about the calculator. It could be angels, made of pure Cartesian mind-stuff, who constitute the calculator's 'hardware'; as long as their actions exhibit the appropriate functional organization (and also provided they can interact causally with the key-pushes, and with the liquid crystal display). As Aaron Sloman has remarked, 'it's not the stuff, but the structure that counts'. (But in fact functionalism indirectly supports the view that only material stuff exists, on grounds of economy. For, given the truth of functionalism, why *should* one believe in mind-stuff, since one doesn't have to in order to explain minds?)

VII

William Lycan makes a distinction between machine versions of functionalism and 'homuncular' functionalism. (Lycan 1981; see also his 1979.) A machine functionalist holds a view approximating to the following, with respect to mental states: 'To be in mental state M is to realize machine program P and be in functional state S relative to P.' A homuncular functionalist, on the other hand, operates with a wider notion of function which is not so directly tied to computation (but may be indirectly so). On Lycan's version of the view – a view which is also attributable to Daniel Dennett – we should 'view a *person* as a sort of corporate entity which corporately performs many immensely complex functions – functions of the sort usually called "mental" or "psychological"'. Each of these functions will be performed by some sub-personal agency or 'homunculus', which will in turn delegate powers to sub-sub-personal agencies, and so on. Now although this version of functionalism is not explicitly computational it still takes its cue from AI research or from programming generally, where a given procedure is defined in terms of simpler sub-procedures.[17] (Dennett's homuncular view is criticized below by Palmer, Chapter 2.) Now Dennett hints, and Lycan stresses, that the homuncular conception of function is teleological in character: that is, 'we identify mental entities (as a first step in the direction of structural concreteness) by reference to the roles they play in furthering the goals and strategies of the systems in which they occur or obtain'. (Lycan 1981).

It is possible that homuncular functionalism, and other versions of functionalism that do not seek to define mental states directly in computational terms, are not vulnerable to many of the criticisms levelled against machine versions of functionalism, in particular to Searle's argument considered above. But there is at least one other major kind of objection to functionalism to which both machine and homuncular functionalists seem vulnerable, and to which other kinds of functionalists are also no doubt vulnerable. This concerns the 'inner', qualitative aspect of mentality. Thomas Nagel has argued that we can characterize human subjectivity, and the subjectivity of non-human organisms, in terms of the following formula: there is something *which it is like to be* that organism (Nagel 1974, and see below Narayanan Chapter 6.) Even in the case of organisms very different from us, such as bats, we are constrained to recognize that there is some point of view, some subjectivity, which that organism really possesses: not something which we imaginatively construct, but rather something that is there independently of our construction. Now theories which seek to explain mentality in terms of functional organization relating inputs to outputs are liable to the objection that they are unable to account for the viewpoint which constitutes any particular organisms's mentality, for the fact that there is something which it is like to be that organism. There is also the objection, mooted earlier, that functionalists have difficulty accounting for the 'felt' quality of certain specific mental states, pain states being the most obvious examples.

There are a variety of difficulties raised along these lines (see Churchland and Churchland 1982 for a review). Part of the general worry underlying such objections is that it is indeed difficult to imagine what it is like to be (for instance) an electronic digital computer, even one which is programmed in the appropriate manner. (But suppose one woke up one day to be told (and it be true!) that one's entire brain had been replaced by electronic components — would this not be a case of one's having *become* (in the appropriate sense) a machine? Indeed, perhaps one could even imagine such a changeover happening piecemeal over a period of time, with the modifications always occurring while one was awake, so that there was no loss of continuity of consciousness.)[18] But there are graphic ways of putting *qualia* objections to functionalism which don't revolve around difficulties with electronic implementations of the relevant functional organization.

VIII

Ned Block has proposed the following, now famous, thought experiment: imagine the entire nation of China dedicated to realizing a Turing machine which was functionally equivalent to someone's mental organization for, say, an hour. Each individual person was responsible for obeying one machine-table instruction of the form: 'When in state S_j, and on receipt of input I_j, emit output O_k, and switch into state S_1.' Imagine the inputs being a series of flashing lights connected by radio to neurons from the sensory organs of (something which is externally just like) a human body, and the outputs being a series of buttons connected in like manner to the motor-output neurons of that body. Satellites visible from all over China beam down the relevant machine table states, so that everybody knows when it's his or her turn to act. Block's conclusion: no such corporate being, whatever its functional organization, could possibly be *genuinely* in pain (etc.) (Block 1980c).

Patricia and Paul Churchland (1982) have pointed out that Block has seriously underestimated the number of distinct machine table instructions that would be necessary in order for a Turing machine to be functionally equivalent to anything approaching the complexity of our neural organization. In fact, say the Churchlands, 'a spherical volume of space centred on the sun and ending at Pluto's orbit packed solidly with cheek-to-cheek Chinese (roughly 10^{36}) homunculi would still not be remotely enough . . .'. A one-person/one-instruction Turing machine which was equivalent to the neural organization of an entire human being, while abstractly possible, would be physically too enormous to be 'constructable in this universe' (pp. 133ff.) But surely this complaint can be replied to by Block either by imagining a much, much larger universe, or by replacing the Turing machine program with a far more computationally efficient program which realizes the same functional organization, but which requires fewer people to operate it.

One possible response to Block's objection is just to brazen it out. Lycan, who seems to take quite seriously the idea that each of *us* is a group person, offers a counter-challenge to Block: why shouldn't such a homunculi-headed giant be capable of being *genuinely* in pain? We would, after all, be able to engage in philosophical discussion with her, and we would observe her emphatic and impatient denials when we explained that there was nothing which it was like to be her. But it seems to me that these can at best be only rather weak counter-intuitions to Block's. The unshakable belief of the giant that she is in pain may be simply unshakable pseudo-belief.

Block's example appeals to our strong feeling that, contrary to Lycan's suggestion that we view people as hierarchially organized corporations, there is something radically *non*-personal about the processes that underlie mentality. Selfhood, we feel, like lightening, should strike only once: there should be no sub-personal persons. But can we not, then, propose an alternative, *anti*-homuncular version of functionalism, suggesting that mentality can be characterized in terms of functional organization (and indeed, as homuncular functionalists suggest, can be somehow teleologically characterized), but that a constraint upon any actual functional realization of mentality is that none of the underlying functional processes be themselves the product of the intention or design of some *separate* mentality? Such a modified functionalism would, perhaps, be able to offer a reply to the challenges of both Searle and Block, to the extent that both objections are based upon the difficulty of making sense of situations in which one or more persons deliberately set out to *realize* some further person.

Block considers a modification along these lines outlined by Putnam (in his 1967a). Block offers several objections to it, appealing to our intuitions to support the view that there are cases where a 'high-level' person may be constituted by one or more distinct 'lower-level' persons. His strongest counter-example is the following. Imagine a region of space where microscopically small people in spaceships simulate the behaviour of the molecules found in the solar system. Human travellers to the region come, through molecular transfer, to have bodies entirely composed of such micro-people, with mental continuity preserved throughout. Here, it seems, is a case of one person made up of separate sub-persons — yet it is clear that we would not wish to deny genuine personhood to the travellers when their bodies came to be composed of the micro-people.

But it seems to me that a supporter of the modified kind of functionalism I have been envisaging can distinguish this sort of case from the objectionable kinds of 'person-in-a-person' cases, as follows. In the case of the space travellers, what the micro-people who come to make up their bodies are reproducing, is the physical or chemical, or perhaps physiological, organization of their bodies, rather than their psychological or *personal* organization. It is only *per accidens* that the bodies that the micro-people come to be a part of are the bodies of persons at all — it might have been earthworms. There's surely an important difference between a low-level person's contributing to the physical constitution of a high-level person, and his contributing to that high-level person's subjectivity. It is surely the latter process and not the former which is envisaged both in Searle's 'Chinese Room' example and in Block's 'Chinese Nation' example. So perhaps it may be possible after all to defend a view which allows one to attribute genuine personhood or consciousness to certain computer realizations without falling foul of those and other similar objections.

IX

The foregoing theoretical speculations are somewhat removed from the practical concerns of AI researchers. No-one's going to be in the business of producing a simulation of a whole, live, human being for a long time. And in any case, while workers in AI might like to think that they are constructing genuine replications of certain isolated mental operations, they would be happy, for the most part, to rest with the more modest claims that they are merely simulating certain limited aspects of these operations, aspects which, however, are still highly relevant to understanding how *our* minds are organized. But even this more modest conception of AI has been strongly challenged. Hubert Dreyfus has claimed, at some length, that accounts of the mind underlying current and forseeable work in AI is based on radically misconceived philosophical assumptions (Dreyfus 1972, 1980, 1981).

Dreyfus concentrates particularly on the comparative difficulties AI research has had in capturing everyday cognitive capacities. Programs like Terry Winograd's SHRDLU showed that AI could cope relatively easily with producing sensible English conversation with respect to a highly circumscribed sub-domain, a 'micro-world' of differently coloured and shaped blocks (Winograd 1972). It has often been supposed that all one needed was to produce more comprehensive programs along the same lines to produce ever closer approximations to genuine human linguistic abilities. Dreyfus claims such an enterprise is quixotic. The common sense knowledge which informs our linguistic productions is essentially open-ended, in a way that it is impossible to capture within the pre-defined limits of any computer program. The procedures underlying human knowledge representation are not just exceedingly difficult to formulate, they are unformulable. According to Dreyfus, the approach to knowledge which underlies AI research is that of an inadequate metaphysical tradition which has dominated much of Western Philosophy, an inadequacy identified by Heidegger and by Wittgenstein.[19] According to this tradition, everything we know can be explicitly expressed in some proposition. But, Dreyfus argues, this is an entirely inappropriate model for knowledge. Our understanding of what a chair is, or of what is involved in going into a restaurant (for example) involves *skills*, such as knowing how to sit, how to order food, rather than knowing distinct propositional items. Skills, whether practical or cognitive, are acquired through repetition and practice, and it seems difficult to see how that kind of process could be reproduced in computer programs, even ones that 'learn' in the way that modern AI programs do.

Dreyfus continually insists on the necessity of *context* for cognition, stressing, with Merleau-Ponty (1962) the essential role played by the fact of our *embodiment* in our perception of and interrelation with the world, and also stressing, with Heidegger (1962) and Wittgenstein (1953) the importance of social and cultural surroundings.

Marvin Minsky, in his work on frame analysis (1974), is at pains to overcome the epistemological limitations of earlier approaches to cognition in AI, and to show how the contextuality, the open-endedness, the concreteness exhibited by everyday human understanding can be enshrined within a conceptual framework amenable to an AI treatment. Minsky's frames are a special kind of data-structure, which has the form of 'a network of nodes and relations' whose top levels 'are fixed, and represent things that are always true about the supposed situation' (Minsky 1974, pp. 1–2, quoted in Dreyfus 1981), but whose lower levels can be filled out in different and changing ways. Minsky believes his notion of frames lies in the same tradition as Thomas Kuhn's 'paradigms' (Kuhn 1970), which latter are invoked by Kuhn to explain development and changes in scientific understanding. But Dreyfus is emphatic that Minskyan frames do not have the explanatory power of Kuhnian paradigms. For the former are 'descriptive schemes' (Minsky's term) which must necessarily represent the various features of their subject-matter in an explicit fashion, albeit ones which can accommodate property-clustering and open-texture. Kuhn's paradigms, on the other hand, revolve around concrete illustrative cases, 'exemplars', which 'group objects and situations into similarity sets which are primitive in the sense that the grouping is done without an answer to the question "similar with respect to what?" ' (Kuhn 1970, p. 200).

Dreyfus's analysis of the theoretical difficulties which beset the claims made by researchers on behalf of AI, are clearly challenging, but occasionally at least, quite excessive. On the subject of Roger Schank's work on 'scripts' to conceptualize behaviour in restaurants, Dreyfus recalls the *faux pas* depicted in the film *Annie Hall*, of ordering pastrami on white with mayonnaise in a New York delicatessen, citing this as an instance of an abnormal and *unpredictable* way in which activities in restaurants may break down. 'When we understand going into a restaurant we understand how to cope with even these abnormal possibilities', he writes (1981, p. 189). Plainly, if *this* is what is involved in understanding the activity of eating in a restaurant then most human non-New Yorkers will fail to possess the understanding, let alone computers. One feels constantly that Dreyfus views the contexts of common sense understanding through too fine a grain, proposing impossibly stringent criteria of adequacy. And there is a constant elision, in his criticism, between stressing limitations in current and immediately foreseeable AI research (limitations which are for the most part acknowledged at least by its more sensitive practitioners), and drawing general conclusions about any conceivable such research.

Nevertheless I do think that Dreyfus has succeeded in formulating some formidable *a priori* difficulties for the AI research paradigm. It could be that AI workers have come, over the last few decades, to occupy an epistemological and metaphysical terrain that many philosophers have some time been struggling to move out of. Might it be that AI theorists are simply reliving the doomed positivistic vision that informed Russell's dream of a logically perfect language, or Carnap's *logische Aufbau*, with the aim not, this time, of establishing firm epistemological foundations for scientific knowledge, but rather of modelling the human mind? The computer is, after all, a tool which can represent powerful logical structures in spectacular and hitherto undreamt-of ways. The 'moving' formalisms of the computer provide a logical resource which has allowed a far greater degree of flexibility and imagination that the 'still' typographical formalisms of previous logical systems, in their applications to the phenomena of actual human thinking and reasoning (cf. Chouraqui, below, Chapter 11). Dreyfus has perhaps identified important limits to any such research activity, limits which are bound up with the nature of formalism itself, and its relation to concrete lived reality. It is at least incumbent upon AI workers to consider such a possibility, rather than simply to dismiss Dreyfus's criticisms with the excuse that AI is a young science, and that one cannot predict in advance its long-term possibilities.

X

There is, however, a crucial ambivalence which infects Dreyfus's criticisms, and the philosophical perspective informing them. But this same ambivalence is to be found running right through the brief history of AI. This is to do with whether AI research is concerned with the analysis and modelling of specifically human mentality, or of mentality *as such*. People in the field have sometimes represented themselves as doing the former and sometimes as doing the latter. Now it seems to me that accounts of knowledge or experience that stress the importance of human embodiment and of human cultural practices in the way that Dreyfus does (not to mention Wittgenstein, Merleau-Ponty and Heidegger, etc.), run a certain danger. This is the danger of supposing that accounts of knowledge and experience which have to do with non-human kinds of mentality — both those to be found in actual biological species, and those to be found in artificial or merely thinkable, mentalities — are somehow uninteresting or invalid.[20] It is certainly tempting to argue, as Dreyfus seems to, that previous theorists of the mind had proposed an unduly formalistic or propositional or rule-bound picture of human mentality and understanding, thereby ignoring the concreteness of actual human experience, immersed as it is in cultural contexts, physically embodied activities, etc. It is also tempting to claim further that all conceivable mentality has to operate within such constraints, and that these constraints set the limits to any philosophically adequate understanding of anything whatsoever. But clearly such a strong position is not warranted. It may well be the case that the major contribution to be made by AI research will lie in its contribution to expanding our ideas of possible forms of mentality, rather than in its contribution to empirical theory building in psychology — or at least that the former, more speculative, role will be as important as the latter one.

Aaron Sloman, in the opening chapter to this volume, provides an eloquent statement of the view that the 'space' of possible minds is multi-dimensional. Indeed he invokes Wittgenstein in arguing against an essentialism with regard to the mental — an essentialism in which theorists such as Dreyfus risk being trapped, in laying too much stress upon the particularities of the human context in their accounts of mind.

Further, one might point out that, precisely because our understanding is conditioned by cultural context, notions of mentality are themselves continually in a process of change – and, one might have thought, increasingly so because of the recent developments in science and technology in which research in AI and in computing generally has played a substantial part. (An additional, and related point is that such developments have also changed our conception of mechanisms, and of the relation between mechanical processes and 'natural' human processes. This is a major theme of Boden 1977.)

Current AI programs, and the machines that run them, provide a pretty poor match for human cognitive abilities in all sorts of ways. But there are also various ways in which computer performances outstrip human cognitive performances. An all-too-chilling testimony to the potentialities of artificial intelligence for providing mind-like control capabilities in situations where human control would be inadequate for the given purposes, is provided by reports of President Reagan's plans for 'Star Wars' laser weapons systems, centred around advances in hardware and software which will build a high-speed decision-making facility 'in the range of one billion to one trillion instructions per second' to which all powers for directing strategic response (the *whether* as well as the *how*, it seems) will be delegated (Mangold 1983). More generally, it should be borne in mind that many of the special features of human cognitive capacities are dependent upon *limitations* imposed on us by our physiological and evolutionary situation – limitations of recall, for example, which require us to use mnemonic devices, or our propensities to muff our executions, or to lapse rapidly into boredom. So there's surely a lot of point in seeing computers as the source, not so much of mock-mental abilities, mechanical analogues for, and poor substitutes for the real thing, as of new forms of the real thing.

NOTES

1. All bibliographical references are listed at the back of the book.
2. See also Putnam (1964, 1967a, 1967b, 1975c). The notion of a Turing machine is due to Alan Turing (1937). It refers to a class of idealized computing devices which have the following characteristics: an *input–output device,* classically a tape, of unlimited length, from which symbols may be read, and upon which symbols may be printed, by a read–write head, which can move along the tape in either direction; and a set of instructions, called a *machine table,* which completely determine the movement of the read –write head, in conjunction with the symbols on the tape. Each machine table instruction (or 'square') refers to one of a finite number of *logical states* into which the machine can pass, and to one of the finite alphabet of input–output symbols. An instruction will have the conditional form: 'if you have just read symbol S_i and you are in logical state Q_j then emit output O_k, and shift into logical state Q_1.' Possible output actions are: to move the read–write head one position to the left or to the right along the

tape; or to overwrite the symbol at the current tape position with another one; or alternatively to halt execution. One of the major theses of modern mathematical logic — the so-called Church—Turing thesis — is that any effectively computable procedure can be translated into a Turing machine table. Further, Turing proved that there is a class of *universal Turing machines* which can imitate any other Turing machine. Putting these two ideas together, it follows that it is possible to describe devices which are computationally powerful enough to perform any formal operation (any determinate sequence of symbol manipulations) whatsoever. Thus any proposed computer representation of human mentality can be given a standardized description in terms of a Turing machine table.

3. For criticisms of Lucas,, see Whiteley (1962), and Dennett (1978a, Chapter 13). An elaborate, multi-layered, not to say fugal, celebration of the wonders of the computational approach to mind, which takes Lucas's argument as a central challenge, is to be found in Hofstadter (1979).

4. See Dreyfus (1972, 1980, 1981); and Searle (1980).

5. A source of stimulating accounts of research in AI is to be found in the writings of Margaret Boden (1972, 1977, 1981a), where a large variety of AI successes (and failures) are discussed in the light of issues within philosophy and pyschology. For other surveys or anthologies, see Feigenbaum and Feldman (1963), Haugeland (1981), Hofstadter and Dennett (1982), Ringle (1979), Sloman (1978a), Winston (1977). See also the *Machine Intelligence* series, edited by Donald Michie and others.

6. Consider, for example, the enormous difficulties encountered in the computer simulation of vision. See Winston (1975), Marr (1982).

7. See Dreyfus (1972), etc.; McDermott (1981). See also Weizenbaum (1976).

8. On personhood, see Chapter 14 of Dennett (1978a) for an interesting discussion relevant to this context.

9. '. . . [A] project at IBM to wire and program an intelligent robot would probably be AI, whereas a project at DuPont to brew a mold a synthetic–organic android probably would not. But . . . the crucial issue is not protoplasm versus semiconductor ("wetware" versus "hardware"), but rather whether the product is designed and specified in terms of a computational structure'. (Haugeland 1981, Introduction, p. 2).

10. Cf. Lycan 1981, pp. 36–7.

11. One of the most celebrated attempts to face up to *qualia* objections concerning computers and pain is Daniel Dennett's 'Why you can't make a computer that feels pain' (Ch. 11 of Dennett 1978a). Ned Block has characterized Dennett's account of pain as having 'the relation to qualia that the U.S. Air Force had to so many Vietnamese villages: he destroys qualia in order to save them' (Block 1980c). One hardly has to be a Dennettian to think this an unfair dig. But clearly there is a good deal of force in supposing that qualitative mental states are, as Block goes on to say, more likely to be 'determined by the physiological or physico-chemical nature

of our information-processing . . . than by the information-flow *per se*' (pp. 290–1).

12. See the Peer Commentaries to Searle's paper in its original printing, and Searle's responses to them.

13. Searle specifically mentions claims made on behalf of programs developed by Roger Schank and his colleagues at Yale (Schank and Abeslon 1977).

14. See our discussion of Ned Block's 'Chinese Nation' example, below.

15. See the Introduction to Haugeland 1981, sections VI–VIII; also Haugeland 1978, section 4. In the latter place Haugeland relates the possibility of multiple interpretations to Quine's thesis of the Indeterminacy of Translation (Quine 1960). See also Dennett (1982a, Section III), who, however, relays an observation of John McCarthy to the effect that the possibility of alternative *non-trivially* different interpretations of, say, an entire book, is strongly limited by 'the cryptographer's constraint': patterns of pure repetition and co-occurrence of strings of symbols (ibid., fn. 7). Similar constraints will apply to the chess case, discussed above, and indeed the more complex the case the stronger the constraint. But this presumably does not affect the point that different but equally coherent interpretations are always *in principle* possible.

16. There are several other problems concerning the notion of intentionality, one of the foremost of which is the problem of 'methodological solipsism'. See Fodor (1980), and the discussions in Woodfield (1982). The issue is discussed below by Engel, Chapter 3, and Jacob, Chapter 4.

17. Lycan (1981) quotes the following passage from *Brainstorms:* 'The AI researcher *starts* with an intentionally characterized problem (e.g., how can I get a computer to *understand* questions of English?), breaks it down to sub-problems that are also intentionally characterized (e.g., how do I get the computer to *recognize* questions, *distinguish* subjects from predicates, *ignore* irrelevant parsings?) and then breaks these problems down still further, until finally he reaches problem or task descriptions that are obviously mechanistic' (Dennett 1978a, Chapter 5, p. 80).

18. There may be formidable *empirical* obstacles to such a change-over, but the Nagelian difficulty is surely supposed to be a conceptual one.

19. For a general critique of this philosophical tradition, along similar lines, see Rorty (1980).

20. Thus Dreyfus considers the work done in recent years by Terry Winograd and colleagues on KRL, a knowledge representation language, which seems to offer more flexible modes of description in order to capture our common sense understanding (Winograd 1976). Dreyfus comments that such an approach depends upon the fact that any current context of current focus has to be explicitly specified, whereas human beings 'are, as Heidegger puts it, already in a situation which they constantly revise'. Dreyfus says of any KRL program that, 'even if it represents all human knowledge in its stereotypes, including all possible types of human situations, it represents them

from the outside like a Martian or God' (1981, p. 198). But even if this is a valid criticism of aspirations of people working with KRL or similar languages to represent actual human understanding, they may nevertheless still be representing a *kind of understanding*, albeit of a non-human variety.

About the contributions

The conference from which the following chapters are drawn addressed itself to a wide range of issues, encroaching on psychology and linguistics, as well as philosophy and computing. In preparing the present volume I have tried to arrange a certain degree of coherence in the ordering of the chapters which wasn't present in the original discussion – a coherence which is not too spurious, I hope. The papers in the first part of the volume address issues which relate fairly clearly to mainstream questions in the philosophy of mind, in particular with issues dealt with by writers such as Dennett and Fodor. The papers in the second part of the volume have a more explicit emphasis on work within computer science and AI.

The opening chapter, by Sloman, proposes a broad conception of what it is to have a mind, based on both computational and philosophical considerations. Palmer's paper (Chapter 2) is concerned with Dennett's homuncular version of functionalism, particularly with regard to intentionality: a general critique of functionalist and AI claims within philosophy is developed. Engel (Chapter 3) discusses a number of different issues surrounding functionalist and other theories, with particular reference to the analysis of belief. Jacob (Chapter 4) discusses Fodor's views on the role of an internal Language of Thought in explaining our mental contents. Narayanan (Chapter 5) replies to the Nagelian complaint made against AI approaches to the mind, to the effect that there is nothing which it is like to be a computer. Mouloud (Chapter 6) provides a general survey of philosophical issues concerning functionalism, with particular reference to Putnam, and some French writers. Tiercelin's paper (Chapter 7) studies the views of C. S. Pierce, showing some surprising anticipations of recent views on machines and mentality. Higginbotham (Chapter 8) surveys some philosophical and methodological issues arising out of Chomsky's linguistic theory, which has been deeply influential both upon AI research and upon cognitive science in general.

Boden (Chapter 9) discusses some of the ways in which AI research has contributed to other fields, particularly empirical psychology, and also logic, epistemology and education. Ennals and Briggs (Chapter 10) review recent developments within Logic Programming — a field which has recently been given a lot of attention in relation to the Japanese 'Fifth Generation' programme. The origins of Logic Programming are situated within the philosophical tradition of logical theory stemming from Aristotle. Chouraqui (Chapter 11) also discusses the relation between logic and computation, tracing some of the ways in which recent work within AI and computer science has led to more flexible and lifelike accounts of human reasoning. Bundy's paper (Chapter 12) relates work done on meta-level inference rules in producing 'intelligent' equation solving systems, to discussions on the nature of consciousness. Kayser (Chapter 13) provides some insights drawn from AI work concerning the nature of knowledge and meaning, suggesting that meaning can best be studied by linking it to the notion of plausible inference. Creativity is an attribute of human mentality which presents a particular challenge to AI: Yazdani (Chapter 14) discusses recent research on the problem, stressing the difficulties in ascribing creativity to the programs themselves as opposed to the programmers. Kodratoff and Ganascia (Chapter 15) discuss an algorithm incorporating simple learning processes, which supports generalization from particular descriptions of features in a Winogradian blocks world.

S.B.T.

About the contributors

AARON SLOMAN took his first degree in Maths and Physics in Cape Town in 1956, and the D.Phil. in Philosophy in Oxford in 1962. He has taught at Sussex University since 1964, and in Spring 1984 he became Professor of Artificial Intelligence and Cognitive Science. He is the author of *The Computer Revolution in Philosophy*, and has developed with others the POPLOG system, a user-friendly AI programming environment.

ANTHONY PALMER took a B.A. in philosophy and Psychology at Hull, and a B.Phil. in Philosophy at Oxford. He is a Senior Lecturer in Philosophy at the University of Southampton. He has published articles in *Mind, Philosophy,* and other journals.

PASCAL ENGEL studied philosophy at the Sorbonne and at the University of California at Berkeley. He has a doctorate in Philosophy, on Proper Names, with the University of Paris I. He has published articles on philosophy of language and philosophy of mind, and is currently working on a study of Herbrand and a Doctorat d'Etat on the semantics of natural language. He is maître assistant de philosophie at the University of Grenoble.

PIERRE JACOB received his agrégation de philosophie in 1972. He studied at Harvard 1973–78, receiving his Ph.D. there. He has been attaché de recherche in Philosophy at the C.N.R.S. in Paris since 1980. He is editor of *De Vienne à Cambridge, l'héritage du positivisme logique,* and author of *L'Empirisme logique, ses antécédents ses critiques*.

AJIT NARAYANAN was born in Madurai, India. He took a degree in Communication Science and Linguistics at Aston University in 1973, and a Ph.D. in Philosophy at Exeter University in 1975. He was a Lecturer in Philosophy and Data Analysis Officer at Aston University between 1976 and 1980. Since then he has been a Lecturer in Computer Science at Exeter University.

NOEL MOULOUD was born in 1914 and died in 1984. He was a disciple of Gaston Bachelard. He taught at the Universities of Lyons II and Lille III, as Fellow and as Professor in Philosophy, and as Director of various research Centres. He published several books, including *La peinture et l'espace, Les structures, la recherche at le savoir; Langage et structures;* and *L'analyse du sens.* His most recent work was on the logic and philosophy of evolutionist knowledge.

CLAUDINE TIERCELIN studied Philosophy at the Sorbonne and at the University of California at Berkeley. She has a doctorate on Peirce's early Metaphysics with the University of Paris I. She has articles on Peirce forthcoming in French and German journals, and is working on a Doctorat d'Etat on Peirce and the Problem of Universals. She teaches philosophy in a lycée in Grenoble.

JAMES HIGGINBOTHAM is an Associate Professor of Philosophy at the Massachusetts Institute of Technology, in the Department of Linguistics and Philosophy. He has written on the philosophy of language and linguistics, and on syntactic and semantic theory.

MARGARET BODEN is Professor of Philosophy and Psychology at the University of Sussex. She has an M.A. in Medical Sciences and Philosophy from Cambridge and an A.M. and Ph.D. in Cognitive Psychology from Harvard. She is the author of *Purposive Explanation in Psychology, Artificial Intelligence and Natural Man, Piaget,* and *Minds and Mechanisms.* She is a Fellow of the British Academy.

RICHARD ENNALS was English scholar at King's College Cambridge where he read Philosophy and History. After some years teaching History he is now Research Fellow in the Department of Computing at Imperial College, working in the Logic Programming group, on the 'Logic as a Computer Language for Children' project.

JONATHAN BRIGGS is a graduate in Computer Science from Imperial College. He is now a Research Associate at Imperial College, supported by Sinclair Research, and working on child-oriented interfaces to PROLOG, as part of the 'Logic as a Computer Language for Children' project.

EUGENE CHOURAQUI is a Docteur d'Etat ès-science. He is a Senior Researcher at the Laboratoire d'Informatique pour les Sciences de l'Homme, C.N.R.S.,

Marseille, and he lectures in AI at the University of Aix-Marseille and the Architecture School of Marseille-Luminy. He researches into knowledge representation and expert systems, and has developed the ARCHES reasoning system.

ALAN BUNDY studied Mathematics at the University of Leicester, receiving a B.Sc. in 1968, and a Ph.D. in Mathematical Logic there in 1971. Since then he has been a Research Fellow and then a Lecturer in the Department of Artificial Intelligence at the University of Edinburgh. He is editor of *Artificial Intelligence: An Introductory Course,* and the 1983 IJCAI Proceedings; and author of *Computer Models of Mathematical Reasoning.*

DANIEL KAYSER taught Computer Science at the University of Paris VI, from 1968 to 1975, and, since then, as Associate Professor, at the Technology Institute of the University of Paris XI (Orsay). His research areas include Natural Language Understanding, Computer-aided Instruction, Learning, and Knowledge Representation.

MASOUD YAZDANI published children's stories in Iran before coming to England in 1975. He took a B.Sc. in Computer Science at Essex University and has since been working on a Doctorate at Sussex on story writing by computer. He is a Lecturer in Computer Science at Exeter. He is editor of *New Horizons in Educational Computing,* and has other books forthcoming on novel educational uses of computers.

YVES KODRATOFF obtained his Doctorat d'Etat in 1967 in the field of paramagnetic resonance applied to chemistry. He is now a maître de recherche at the C.N.R.S., working in the Laboratoire de Recherche en Informatique, Université de Paris-Sud, Orsay. He heads a small group who are working on inference and learning.

JEAN-GABRIEL GANASCIA obtained a degree as Docteur Ingénieur in 1983. He is now Assistant Professor at the Université de Paris-Sud, Orsay, where he is working in the Laboratoire de Recherche en Informatique. He is completing a Doctorat d'Etat in Computer Science, his field being rule learning as applied to Expert Systems.

1

The structure of the space of possible minds

Aaron Sloman

Describing this stucture is an interdisciplinary task I commend to philosophers. My aim for now is not to do it — that's a long term project — but to describe the task. This requires combined efforts from several disciplines including, besides philosophy: psychology, linguistics, artificial intelligence, ethology and social anthropology.

Clearly there is not just one sort of mind. Besides obvious individual differences between adults there are differences between adults, children of various ages and infants. There are cross-cultural differences. There are also differences between humans, chimpanzees, dogs, mice and other animals. And there are differences between all those and machines. Machines too are not all alike, even when made on the same production line, for identical computers can have very different characteristics if fed different programs. Besides all these *existing* animals and artefacts, we can also talk about theoretically *possible* systems.

One common approach to this space of possible 'behaving systems', to coin a neutral phase, is to seek a single sharp division, between those with minds, consciousness, souls, thoughts, or whatever, and those without. Where to draw the line then becomes a major problem, with protagonists of the uniqueness of man, or of living things, or champions of machine mentality, all disputing the location of the boundary, all offering different criteria for allocating things to one side or the other.

The passion accompanying such debates suggests that more than a search for truth motivates the disputants. To a dispassionate observer such debates can seem sterile.

Both sides assume that there is some well-defined concept of 'mind', 'consciousness', or whatever, whose boundaries are to be discovered, not created. But these are complex and subtle concepts of ordinary language, not designed for scientific classificatory precision. When using them of our fellow men, or animals, we don't first check that certain defining conditions for having a mind or being conscious are satisfied. Rather we take it for granted that concepts are applicable, and then we make distinctions between quick and slow minds, conscious and unconscious states, feeling of various sorts, etc. Equally we take it for granted (most of the time) that such concepts and distinctions cannot be applied to trees, lakes, stones, clouds. (However, not all cultures agree on this.) But we don't discriminate on the basis of any precise shared definition of the *essence* of mind, consciousness, or whatever. For there is no such precise shared definition.

One traditional way to seek an essence is through introspection. However, nothing learnt in this way about the nature of mind or consciousness could help us distinguish *other* beings with and without consciousness.

Another approach is to seek behavioural definitions of mental concepts: but these founder on the objection that behaviour merely provides evidence or symptoms and does not *constitute* what are essentially internal states.

The only alternative until recently has appeared to be to locate mind in brain matter – but this ignores important category distinctions: although neuronal states, events or processes may correlate with my being conscious, they are not themselves consciousness. Consciousness is not anything material.

Yet any other attempt to identify a referent for 'mind', 'consciousness', 'pain' etc. has, until recently, looked like an attempt to populate the world with mysterious, inaccessible metaphysically unjustified entities.

What is different now is that Computing Science has provided us with the concept of a *virtual machine*, within which computational states and processes can occur. A virtual machine has much in common with the kind of formal system studied by mathematicians or logicians. It is an abstract structure which can undergo various changes of state. A virtual machine can be embodied in a physical machine without *being* that machine. The same virtual machine can be embodied in different physical machines. Different virtual machines can be embodied in the same physical machine. Different virtual machines can have very different abilities. Work in Artificial Intelligence has shown that some virtual machines can produce behaviour which previously had been associated only with minds of living things, such as producing or understanding language, solving problems, making and executing plans, learning new strategies, playing games. By studying the space of possible virtual machines we can replace sterile old boundary drawing disputes with a new, more fruitful, more objective investigation.

First we must abandon the idea that there is one major boundary between things with and without minds. Instead, informed by the variety of types of computational mechanisms already explored, we must acknowledge that there are *many* discontinuities, or divisions within the space of possible systems: the space is not a continuum, nor is it a dichotomy.

Secondly, we can combine the advantages of both behaviourist and mentalist approaches to the study of the mind. The main strength of behaviourism, in all its forms, is that minds are not static things – it's what they *do* that is so important. But emboldened by the computational analogy we can see that some doings are external, and some internal: operations within a virtual machine. It is even quite possible for the internal processes to be too rich to be revealed by external behaviour, so that in an important sense external observers cannot know exactly what is going on. For instance, a computer program may be able to print out 'tracing' information reporting some of its internal states, but the attempt to trace the internal processes which produce trace printing can lead to an infinite regress. A more interesting example is a computing system with television camera performing complex and detailed analyses on large arrays of visual data, but with limited capacity 'output channels' so that any attempt to report current visual processing will inevitably get further and further behind. Here perhaps is the root of the sense of a rich but inaccessible inner experience which has been the source of so much philosophical argument.

TWO LEVELS OF EXPLORATION

We can attempt a two level exploration of the space of possible minds, one descriptive the other explanatory, though with some overlap between them.

The *descriptive* task is to survey and classify the kinds of things different sorts of minds (or if you prefer behaving systems) can do. This is a classification of different sorts of abilities, capacities or behavioural dispositions – remembering that some of the behaviour may be internal, for instance recognizing a face, solving a problem, appreciating a poem. Different sorts of minds can then be described in terms of what they can and can't do. The *explanatory* task is to survey different sorts of virtual machines and to show how their properties may explain the abilities and inabilities referred to in the descriptive study.

These explorations can be expected to reveal a very richly structured space – not one-dimensional, like a spectrum, not any kind of continuum. There will be not two but many extremes. For instance one extreme will be simple servo-mechanisms like thermostats or mechanical speed governors on engines. Another kind of extreme may be exemplified by the simplest organisms.

EXAMPLES OF DIVISIONS IN THE SPACE

Among the important divisions between different sorts of virtual machines are the following.

- Some systems, like a thermostat, have only quantitative representations of states, processes etc. For instance, a very simple organism may be able to measure temperature, or the density of useful chemicals in the surrounding medium. Others, like some computer programs and people, can build structural descriptions, like parse-tree representations of sentences or chemical formulae.
- A closely related distinction can be made between systems whose internal

processing consists only of continuous variation of quantitative measures and systems which in addition can perform a variety of discrete operations on discrete structures, e.g. matching them, rearranging them, storing them in a memory etc. (This should not be confused with discontinuous jumps in values of scalar variables, as in catastrophe theory.)

- Some systems (unlike a thermostat, for instance) have the ability to store complex sequences of symbolic instructions. Different sorts of instructions provide different sorts of behavioural capacities. For instance conditional instructions are crucial for flexible, context sensitive performance. Instructions for modifying stored instructions may play an important role in learning processes.

- Some systems, like conventional digital computers, can essentially do only one thing at a time, albeit very quickly in some cases. Others are parallel machines. The study of different sorts of parallelism and their properties is now in its infancy. One consequence of certain sorts of parallel architecture is the ability to monitor (internal or external) behaviour while it is being produced. It also permits 'postponed' conditional instructions of the form 'If ever X occurs do Y'. This seems to be crucial to many features of human and animal intelligence. When combined with the ability of some sub-processes to interrupt or modify others, we find the beginning of an explanation of certain characteristic features of emotional states.

- Some parallel systems are composed of a network of serial machines whereas others are massively and fundamentally parallel in that they consist of very large collections of processing units, no one of which performs any essential computing function. What would normally be thought of as a computational state is distributed over large portions of the network. The implications of this sort of distinction are at present hardly understood, though it seems clear that at least the more complex animal brains are of the massively parallel type. The gain seems to be that for certain sorts of task, including pattern recognition, very great speed can be achieved, along with the ability to generalize from old to new cases and to degrade gracefully as input information degrades. Other sorts of task, for instance long chains of deductions, may only be achievable on this sort of machine by indirect, clumsy and unreliable strategies. We see here an echo of the current fashion for distinguishing left and right brain activities: except that both halves of the human brain seem to be massively parallel systems.

- Some systems merely perform internal manipulations, except possibly for receiving some input to start things off and producing some output at the end. Others are linked to sensors which continuously receive information from the environment, which affects the pattern of internal processing. The 'environment' may include the physical body in which the virtual machine is instantiated.

- Some systems are embodied in a complex physical machine with many sensors and motors which are controlled to perform complex actions in the environment. Others must merely passively react to what the environment offers, like a paralysed person.

- Some perceptual mechanisms essentially only recognize patterns in the sensory input. Others interpret the input by building descriptions of *other* things which may have produced the input. Thus two-dimensional images may be interpreted as produced by three-dimensional structures, and various forms of observable behaviour may be interpreted as produced by unobservable mental states in other agents. Thus some systems can represent only observable or measureable properties and relations between things, whereas others can construct hypotheses which go beyond that given. In particular, some can postulate that other objects may themselves be agents with internal programs, motives, beliefs, etc., and take these internal states into account in their own planning, perception, etc.
- Some computational systems can construct formulae of predicate calculus and perform logical inferences. Other systems lack this ability.
- Some systems have a fixed collection of programs, whilst others have the ability to reprogram themselves so as radically to alter their own abilities — possibly under the influence of the environment.
- Some systems, especially AI programs, are essentially presented with a single goal at a time, from outside, and all they can do is pursue that goal and sub-goals generated by it. Other systems, notably living organisms, have a motley of motive-generating mechanisms so that current motives, preferences, principles, constantly need to be re-assessed in the light of new ones which may have nothing to do with previous ones. This seems to be another of the computational properties underlying the ability to have emotions.
- Some systems have a fixed set of motive generators, whereas others may have motive-generator-generators. Can this hierarchy be extended indefinitely?
- Some systems can select goals for action, yet postpone action because there will be better opportunities later. Others can only act immediately on selected goals. The former need databases in which postponed goals and plans are stored, and monitors which can react to new opportunities. This ability to postpone intended action would seem to be one of the differences between more and less sophisticated animals, and perhaps between human infants and adults.
- Some systems, once they have begun to execute a plan or program cannot do anything else, whereas others can, where appropriate, interrupt execution, and switch to another plan if necessary, and then continue execution of the original later, if appropriate. This requires mechanisms for storing what has been done so far and some indication of where to continue an interrupted plan.
- Some systems can monitor only the subsequent effects of their actions, e.g. a thermostat. Some can monitor the behaviour itself, e.g. placing a paw

carefully on a potentially dangerous object. Some can monitor internal as well as external processes, for instance a computer checking which of its routines are used most frequently, or a person detecting and classifying some emotional state. Different kinds of monitoring provide different opportunities for self-assessment, self-modification, self-understanding.

These are merely examples of some of the more obvious discontinuities in the space of possible explanatory mechanisms — virtual machines. Although the descriptions are general and vague, it is already clear how we can design machines which illustrate both sides of each of these distinctions. We don't yet have a full understanding of all the different ways of doing this, nor what their implications are. Moreover, many more detailed distinctions are being explored by computer scientists — distinctions between sorts of languages, sorts of operating systems, sorts of algorithms, sorts of data-structures. Eventually we should have a far clearer grasp of the structure of this space, with some sort of global, generative, description of its contents.

In terms of such mechanisms, we can begin to account for different abilities found in human beings and other animals, as well as constructing machines which display such abilities. What we still need to do is explore which combinations of mechanisms are required to account for the characteristically human abilities which have puzzled philosophers and psychologists and provide much of the motivation for research in AI. A tentative list of such characteristics in need of explanation follows:

SALIENT FEATURES OF THE HUMAN MIND
(The order is not significant)

- Generality, including:

    (a) the ability to cope with *varied* objects in a domain
    (b) the ability to cope with a *variety* of domains of objects
    (c) the ability to perform a *variety* of tasks in relation to any object.

'Object' here is a neutral term, covering such diverse things as physical objects, spoken or written sentences, stories, images, scenes, mathematical problems, social situations, programs, etc. 'Coping' includes such diverse things as perceiving, producing, using, acting in relation to, predicting, etc.

- Being able to co-ordinate and control a variety of sensors and manipulators in achieving a task involving physical movement or manipulation.
- Coping with messy, ill-defined problems and situations, and incomplete or uncertain information; and degrading *gracefully* as the degree of difficulty/ complexity/noise/incompleteness etc. increases, rather than merely crashing, or rejecting the problem.

Degrading gracefully may involve being slower, less reliable, less general, less accurate, producing less precise descriptions, etc.

- Various forms of development, learning, or self-improvement, including:
  - increases in speed of performance, complexity of tasks managed; qualitative extensions to new domains, new kinds of abilities, etc.

Important special cases include the creation of new domains, and the novel combination of information about several different domains to solve a problem. The more complex examples overlap with what we ordinarily refer to as 'creativity'.

- Performing inferences, including not only logical deductions but also reasoning under conditions of uncertainty, including reasoning with non-logical representations, e.g. maps, diagrams, models.
- Being able to answer hypothetical questions about 'What would happen if . . .?' in order to make plans, make predictions, formulate and test generalizations.
- Using insight and understanding rather than brute force or blind and mechanical execution of rules, to solve problems, achieve goals, etc.
- Being able to communicate and co-operate with other intelligent agents, or take their beliefs, intentions, etc. into account.
- Coping with a multiplicity of 'motivators', e.g. goals, tastes, preferences, ethical principles, constraints, etc. which may not all be totally consistent in all possible circumstances.
- Coping flexibly with an environment which is not only complex and messy, but also partly unpredictable, partly friendly, partly unfriendly and often fast moving. This includes the ability to interrupt actions and abandon or modify plans when necessary, e.g. to grasp new opportunities or avoid new dangers. It also includes the ability to behave sensibly when there is no time to collect or analyse all possibly relevant evidence or perform relevant inferences.
- Self-awareness, including the ability to reflect on and communicate about at least some of one's own internal processes. This includes the ability to explain one's actions.
- The ability to generate, or appreciate, aesthetic objects.
- The ability to experience bodily sensations.
- The ability to enjoy or dislike experiences, to be amused, angry, excited, irritated, hopeful, disgusted, etc.

Although there is no artificial computing system which combines more than a few fragmentary versions of these features, and there is no chance of combining all in the foreseeable future, work in AI suggests that provided suitable hardware and software architectures are used, most or all of these features can be explained in computational terms. (This is by no means established, however). There is still a lot more to be done to discover precisely what sorts of computational and representational mechanisms are capable of accounting for what sorts of abilities.

CONCLUSION

Instead of arguing fruitlessly about where to draw major boundaries to correspond to concepts of ordinary language like 'mind' and 'conscious' we should analyse the detailed implications of the many intricate similarities and differences between different systems. To adapt an example of Wittgenstein's: there are many ways in which the rules of a game like chess might be modified, some major some minor. However, to argue about which modifications would cause the *essence* of chess to be lost would be a waste of time, for there is no such thing as the essence. What is more interesting is what the detailed effects of different modifications would be on possible board states, possible strategies, the difficulty of the game etc. Similarly, instead of fruitless attempts to divide the world into things with and things without the essence of mind, or consciousness, we should examine the many detailed similarities and differences between systems.

This is a multi-disciplinary exercise. Psychologists and ethologists can help by documenting the characteristics of different types of systems to be found in nature, including the many detailed differences between humans of different ages, and the results of various types of brain damage, which produce systems not normally found in nature. Anthropologists can help by drawing attention to different sorts of minds produced by different cultural contexts. Linguists and other students of the structures perceived and produced by human minds can help to pin down more precisley what needs to be explained. Computer scientists can help by proposing and investigating detailed mechanisms capable of accounting for the many kinds of features of human minds, animal minds, robot minds. Philosophers can help in a number of ways. They can analyse the many complex implicit assumptions underlying ordinary concepts and thereby help to indicate what exactly it is that we need to explain: for instance those who start from an over-simplified analysis of emotion concepts will over-simplify the explanatory task. More generally, a philosophical stance is needed to criticize conceptual confusions and invalid arguments, and to assess the significance of all the other work. For example, does a computational model of mind really degrade us, as some suggest, or does it reveal unsuspected richness and diversity?

By mapping the space of possible mental mechanisms we may achieve a deeper understanding of the nature of our own minds, by seeing how they fit into a larger realm of possibilities. We may also hope to get a better understanding of the evolutionary processes which could have produced such minds. We will learn that there is neither a continuum of cases between ourselves and a thermostat or amoeba, nor an impassable gulf either.

So much for exhortation. The hard work remains to be done.

2

The limits of AI:
Thought experiments and
conceptual investigations

Anthony Palmer

On page 117 of his book *Brainstorms* Daniel Dennett writes the following.

> Some AI people have recently become fond of describing their discipline
> as 'experimental epistemology'. This unfortunate term should make a
> philosopher's blood boil, but if AI called itself thought-experimental
> epistemology (or even better: *Gedanken*-experimental epistemology)
> philosophers ought to be reassured. (Dennett 1978b).

The idea here is that computational techniques provide us with a way of solving
philosophical problems. It is not unusual to hear philosophers say that they have
turned to AI because it seemed to them to present a way of doing systematically
what until then in their philosophical researches they had been doing in an
unsystematic way. The aim of this paper is to show that such views are confused.

Dennett himself offers the following example of a philosophical problem
to which work on AI has provided a solution. He calls it Hume's problem. First
of all he argues for the importance of internal representations with regard to
psychology. He then reminds us of the role that these have played in the history
of thinking about the mind, and brings out a problem associated with them.

> For the British Empiricists, the internal representations were called
> ideas, sensations, impressions: more recently psychologists have talked
> of hypotheses, maps, schemas, images, propositions, engrams, neural
> signals, even holograms and whole innate theories . . . [However]
> nothing is intrinsically a representation of anything; something is a
> representation only for or to someone; any representation or system
> of representations thus requires at least one *user* or *interpreter* of the

representation who is external to it. Any such interpreter must have a variety of psychological or intentional traits: it must be capable of a variety of *comprehension* and must have beliefs and goals (so it can *use* the representation to *inform* itself and thus assist itself in achieving its goals). Such an interpreter is then a sort of homunculus . . . Therefore psychology without homunculi is impossible by psychology with homunculi is doomed to circulatory or infinite regress, so psychology is impossible.

He then proceeds to give what he considers to be AI's solution to the problem. First of all he points out that homunculus talk is ubiquitious in AI but that far from it being harmful there it turns out to be extremely beneficial. The reason why this can be so, he argues, is that they are not invoked to explain abilities wholesale.

Homunculi are *bogeymen* only if they duplicate *entire* the talents they are rung in to explain. If one can get a team or committee of *relatively* ignorant, narrow-minded, blind homunculi to produce the intelligent behaviour of the whole, this is progress. A flow chart is typically the organisational chart of a committee of homunculi (investigators, librarians, accountants, executives); each box specifies a homunculus by prescribing a function *without* saying how it is to be accomplished (one says in effect: put a little man in there to do the job). If we then look closer at the individual boxes we see that the function of each is accomplished by subdividing it via another flow chart into still smaller, more stupid homunculi. Eventually this nesting of boxes within boxes lands you with homunculi so stupid (all they have to do is to remember whether to say yes or no when asked) that they can be, as one says, 'replaced by a machine'. One *discharges* fancy homunculi from one's scheme by organising armies of idiots to do the work.

Now it is easy to see that this solution is no solution at all. For it is clear that the Hume's problem remains even at the level of the stupidest homunculus. The problem was from the start one of intentionality. Indeed, Hume's problem is just one way of stating the problem of intentionality. One criterion of an intentional verb is that propositions containing it do not retain their truth value through changes in correct characterizations of their objects. They do not go through the hoops of what Peter Geach has called Shakespearian inference. While that which we call a rose by any other name would smell as sweet that which we think about or worship or intend would not be thought about or worshipped or intended if its characterization were altered even to something which is true of what is thought about or worshipped or intended. The Greeks worshipped Zeus, Oedipus thought about Jocasta and intended to make love to her, but given that it is true that Zeus is nothing but a collection of sticks and stones and Jocasta was the mother of Oedipus it will not necessarily be true that the Greeks worshipped sticks and stones and that Oedipus thought about his mother and intended to go to bed with her. For this we need the way in which the Greeks represented Zeus to themselves and the way in which Oediupus represented Jocasta to himself. If Hume's problem of internal representations is one of intentionality from the start then we will not solve it by merely restricting the range of intentionality.

There are, I think, very strong parallels here to the solution which Descartes produced to the mind—body problem when he sought to avoid the difficulties in his conception by suggesting that mind only acted upon a very little bit of body, the pineal gland. The problem, though, (as I suspect he himself recognized) was not one of size. Similarly, if Hume's problem is that of intentionality, it will not be solved by making the range of its application smaller and smaller. Hume's problem really does require that homunculi are dispensed with altogether for *remembering* to *say* yes or no provides us with just the same problem from a logical point of view as remembering that two bishops are more powerful than a knight and a bishop in a restricted end game, or remembering to say check at the appropriate moment. There is also a striking parallel here to the way in which many philosophers of the 1950s and 60s suffering from what has been called the Routledge and Kegan Paul Syndrome sought to answer the question 'What must be added to (mere) bodily movements to turn them into fully fledged human behaviour?'. Correctly suspicious of supposing that the answer was to add a bit of mental stuff, they argued, (over-influenced, I suspect, by the pressure the analogy with games and in particular the game of chess was exerting on philosophical speculation) that what was needed was for bodily movements to be set in the background of a society with its rules, conventions, institutions etc. The following passage from A. I. Melden's book *Free Action* is typical.

> [T]he child needs to be trained . . . to recognise *this* bodily movement of its mother in *this* transaction in which it engages, as *this* action, *that* bodily movement in *that* transaction as *that* action. Only in the context of the specific activities which it has been trained to perform . . . is it possible to understand the bodily movements of those participating . . . as the actions they are . . . So one could go on to explore the manner in which the concepts of action and agent are enriched by relating to the wider scenes of social intercourse in which in divers ways various social and moral institutions, conventions, statutes etc., are relevant to the background activities against which bodily movements are understood as the actions they are. (Melden 1961, p. 190).

However, it is clear that setting bodily movements in the background of rules and conventions could not possibly have the effect of turning it into human behaviour. The model does indeed provide us with a way of showing how something which is an action can have a different force or become a quite different action if set in different backgrounds — raising one's arm on the starting grid of a grand prix is to do something quite different from raising one's arm before serving in a game of tennis — for raising one's arm is already an action. However, a model which serves well to explain how one action can become another will be a non-starter when used to explain how something which is not an action becomes an action. To use the former as an explanation of the latter is really only an unargued assertion that the latter is no problem. Moreover, if we permit ourselves the luxury of thinking of intentionality as being unproblematic, i.e. if we permit ourselves homunculi in our explanations, then (as Eliot Sober has argued in 'Why must Homunculi be so Stupid' (Sober 1982)) there is no reason from a logical point of view why the homunculi we import to explain the abilities of human beings should be less intelligent than the human beings whose behaviour they are brought in to explain. It would indeed be an explanation of why I behave in the ways that I do, or of how I am able to do the things that I do, if it were discovered that inside my skull were a miniature genius who for purposes of his own moved my limbs around. This is no doubt not very likely but there would be nothing wrong with it as an explanation. What it would not serve to explain is the problem which Dennett calls Hume's problem.

The upshot of all this is that if we think of AI as thought experimentation within the constraints of a new technology, namely computers, then Hume's problem or any similar problem is not going to be resolved by workers in AI. What we need to do, then, is to ask ourselves what is there about Hume's problem which makes it insoluble by computational means.

Before doing this, however, it is worthwhile considering a prior question. Why given that the computational psychologist's solution is manifestly no solution could it possibly have been thought to be so? I think that the right answer to this question is that the AI solution would be a proper solution to something which looks like Hume's problem but is not. The computational approach is dependent upon the assumption that philosophical problems about mind and body have been solved in advance. If minds are brains, i.e. if the thesis of contingent identity of mind and body is correct, then we no longer have Hume's problem. For the thesis of contingent identity is just the thesis that there are no logical problems with regard to the postulation of that identity. It is precisely for that reason that the term 'contingent' is contained in the statement of the thesis. Hume's problem might be stated by saying that we cannot dispense with intentionality. The identity thesis might well be stated by saying that ultimately there are no logical problems which stand in the way of dispensing with intentionality, even though it may empirically be the case that we cannot. Moreover, if the contingent identity thesis is stated in a particular way an added impetus is given to the use of an intentional terminology which is integral to the AI approach. If instead of saying (a) there are brain states that for any person are identical with states of mind, we say (b) for any person there are brain states that are identical which states of mind, this leaves open the possibility that such brain states may differ from person to person, and indeed that they may be different in the same person at different times. If such were the case then the AI approach would be the only sensible approach. Hence given that there are no logical problems in dispensing with intentionality we can reconstruct something that looks like Hume's problem and use a computational approach to solve it for us. We set ourselves the problem of how a very large-scale ability whose characterizations would involve intentional descriptions could be a consequence of a series of smaller-scale abilities whose descriptions also involved intentional characterizations and so on until we have reached the smallest possible abilities. We then add the reminder that we have shown in advance that there is no logical reason why such abilities will not turn out in the end to be identical with certain brain states. Showing how they turn out to be so will be the point at which the so called computational or top-down approach meets up with the physiological or bottom-up approach. If you are sceptical of the contingent identity thesis then the philosophical problems of which Hume's problem is an illustration remain untouched. The AI approach has solved no philosophical problems, on the contrary its adoption presumes that the philosophical problems have been solved.

I am not in this chapter going to give the grounds for my scepticism about the cogency of the contingent identity thesis. Since I have, however a good deal of sympathy with the views expressed by Gilbert Ryle when he reviewed Anthony Quinton's book *The Nature of Things*, (Ryle 1973), and since I understand that that review is not very widely known I provide an extract from it in a way in which he would certainly not have approved, i.e. in a footnote! (See the end of the chapter.)

I now return to the question of why Hume's problem is not soluble by computational means. My suggestion here hinges upon the terminology with which I began, i.e. the idea that work done in AI is correctly characterized as the conducting of thought experiments. Dennett's view was that while the phrase 'experimental epistemology' smacks of confusion (the confusion of supposing that epistemological problems can be solved by empirical means), if we can envisage a form of experimentation which is not empirical then the possibility of an experimental epistemology opens up. It is here that the notion of thought experiments comes into play. Thought experiments are experiments all right but they are precisely not empirical experiments. They deal not so much with what is the case but with what might be the case, not so much with actualities as with possibilities. Possibilities may be unactualized but actualities are at least possible. *Ab esse ad posse valet consequentia*. What the computer enables us to do is to be systematic in our exploration of possibilities. The discipline of the computer enables us to turn our *a priori* speculations into thought experiments, computation standing to speculation about possibilities in the way in which experimentation stands to speculation about actualities. Computers are the 'prosthetic regulators' of our *a priori* speculation. Hence to philosophize without the computer is to unreasonably deny ourselves the use of such regulators.

With such a characterization of thought experiments we can now turn to

Hume's problem. We have seen how that problem turns out to be insoluble by even prosthetically regulated thought experiments. It follows from this that in so far as Hume's problem is correctly thought of as a problem about the possibility of a psychology which utilizes the idea of internal representations then such a possibility is not one which will be capable of being explored in a prosthetically regulated way. Similarly, if Hume's problem is correctly thought of as a conceptual problem it will follow that we shall need to distinguish between conceptual investigations and thought experiments even though both might be correctly characterized as explorations of possibilities. Such a distinction, although not put in this way, has been central in philosophical logic since the time of Bradley and Frege, and yet is one which is permanently in danger of being overlooked. Bradley pointed to it when he argued that ideas were from the point of view of logic parasites cut loose, or adjectives divorced, but it is more familiar to us nowadays as Frege's insistence that concepts are not objects. Hume's problem is a problem about the nature of concepts. He called them ideas. But because he thought of them as peculiar sorts of objects (mental objects) he found himself ensnared in the problem which we have given his name to in this paper. Hume's problem is best thought of as the name we give to the difficulties that ensue when we treat concepts as objects. The characteristic form which such difficulties take is that of an infinite regress.

Hume's talk of impressions and ideas is an attempt to explain the ways in which they think about the world, and we like him can ask how it is possible to think of the world in the ways in which we do. We can, for example, ask how it is possible for us to think of it in terms of cause and effect given that necessary connections are never observed. Or we might wonder how it is possible to think of rights and obligations given that these are never observed. We know that Hume's response to these and similar questions was to point to the role of the passions in human affairs. We might produce different solutions. But when in the Appendix to the *Treatise* he raises the question of the self, i.e. when he raises the question we have labelled Hume's problem he raises a question which he himself recognizes is unanswerable in that way. The first two questions do indeed ask us to experiment in thought but the question in the Appendix does not. It cannot do so for it raises quite a different problem about ideas or about the perceptions of the mind, or, to use Dennett's terminology, about internal representations. And this question arises from treating them as objects, a view to which he can see no alternative.

> In general the following reasoning seems satisfactory. All our ideas are borrowed from preceeding perceptions. Our ideas of objects therefore are deriv'd from that source. Consequently no proposition can be intelligible or consistent with regard to objects which is not so with regard to perceptions. (Hume 1955, p. 634).

The trouble is, as Hume saw, that if ideas are thought of in that way, i.e. if they are thought of as objects then it is difficult to see how they could play the role that they were invoked to play. How could objects give us the way in which we represent objects (the world) to ourselves? Hence Hume's search for the self which regressed to infinity.

This all important, but difficult to articulate, distinction between concepts and objects might serve to illuminate the remark at the end of Wittgenstein's *Philosophical Investigations* which has generated so much work in philosophy and which has at the same time served to alienate philosophical research from psychological research. I refer to the remark in which he compares work in psychology to work in mathematics.

> The confusion and barrenness of psychology is not to be explained by calling it a 'young science'; its state is not comparable with that of physics for instance, in its beginnings. (Rather with that of certain branches of mathematics. Set theory.) For in psychology there are experimental methods and *conceptual confusion* (As in the other case conceptual confusion and methods of proof.) (1953).

On my reading of this remark it is not so much that psychology presents us with muddled thinking which needs philosophical expertise to sort out (as though philosophers had somehow managed to corner the market in clear thinking), a philosophical expertise that will be greatly enhanced by the prosthetic regulation of computer simulation, but rather that in psychology, as in the area of mathematics to which Wittgenstein refers, we are likely to become confused about concepts. In mathematics when thinking about concepts there is an inclination to confuse them with sets or classes, and this is an example of the same sort of error as Hume made when he thought of concepts as mental objects. If Wittgenstein's remark had been read in that way at the time of the publication of the *Philosophical Investigations* then a great deal of what was written about philosophical psychology in the late 1950s and through the 1960s would have remained unwritten (there would have been no Routledge and Kegan Paul Syndrome) and in the 1970s and early 80s we should have been able to see more clearly the limits of AI.

FOOTNOTE: RYLE ON THE CONTINGENT IDENTITY THESIS (Ryle 1973)

Quinton, who treats the veteran Mind/Body as a serious difficulty for his materialism, intrepidly champions the so-called Contingent Identity Thesis. As the Morning Star and the Evening Star have turned out, against early expectations, to be, not two planets, but one planet; as the convivial party at which John met Jane happens to have been the very same party as the party at which Tom met Sarah; and as Doctors are at least agreed that the infection from which Henry suffered last week was the same infection as, and not a different infection from, the infection from which he is suffering today, so it is vicariously promised neurologists are going one day to establish that William's surprise, anxiety or ambition on Boxing Day 2073 AD is (or else is *not*) one and the same what-have-you as one of synchronous states, conditions, processes, events or modifications of a brain — and, it is assumed, William's own brain. That they will thus establish also the idealistic inverse identity is hushed up.

Worryingly over William's case our planetary, convivial and clinical examples of identity-or-non-identity throw no light. Our same 'what-have-you' is to be encashed neither by 'same emotion' nor by 'same brain event', but only by such neutral because blank-cheque nouns as 'entity', 'condition', and perhaps 'set-up', 'circumstance', and 'thingummy'. These will surely start our future neurologists wondering, even before their diagnostic identity-parade begins. 'Yes but only one *what*? — or else two *whats*?' They will find out, but not by surgery, that William's surprise, anxiety or ambition had been neither a numerically different [   ] from, nor yet the numerically same [   ] as, this or that recorded modification in a brain, any more than this edge of this tea-table is either a different [article of furniture?] from, or the same [configuration?] as, the table's centre of gravity or its pattern.

Seventeenth-century Occasionalism is resurrected in our century with its Divine Juggler thinly disguised as the very scientific Principle of Contingent Identity of (some) Hetero-categorials.

3

Functionalism, belief and content

Pascal Engel

1. INTRODUCTION: BELIEFS AS PSYCHOLOGICAL STATES AND BELIEFS AS CONTENTS

Philosophers, psychologists and researchers in Artificial Intelligence aim at producing theoretical models for beliefs. My intention in this chapter is to show that there are constraints on the ordinary, commonsensical notion of belief which weigh on the theoretical, sophisticated notion as well, and which no account, whether philosophically or AI inspired, can ignore.

There is a common distinction in the philosophical literature about belief, between belief as a psychological state and belief as a propositional attitude. On the one hand beliefs are said to be mental occurrences or states, to be characterized, like other states, in terms of a certain psychological theory; on the other hand beliefs are said to be the contents of propositional attitudes, the counterpart of linguistic expressions embedded within the 'that-clauses' of propositional attitude attributions using certain 'propositional attitude verbs' (X believes that p; X desires that p, etc.). This distinction is well entrenched within our 'Commom sense' or 'folk' psychology: we say that people perform certain actions *because* they have such and such beliefs, desires or other attitudes, and we explain these actions by specifying *what* they believe – the *content* of their attitudes – in such and such circumstances. But very often we are unable to say more than that: we say that beliefs have a certain causal role to play in the production of behaviour, but are at a loss when we want to spell out this role. Part of the reason for this is that we need a more refined psychological theory of the mechanisms which underlie the production of beliefs, but it is also partly that we do not know exactly what the contents of beliefs are. This is no surprise since the content of a belief is said to be what is expressed or represented by the sentences occurring in the 'scope' of propositional attitude verbs (the *p*'s and *q*'s that a person believes) and such sentences, according to philosophers, have a particular sort of 'referential opacity' (for instance, if X believes that *the milkman* has come, it does not imply that he believes that *John* has come, when in fact John = the milkman: we can't exchange the two expressions *salva veritate*). Opacity of reference seems to parallel opacity of belief. For example we ascribe beliefs to animals, saying that these have beliefs in connexion with desires on the basis of our observation of their behaviour. But when asked *what* they really believe we encounter a difficulty, since obviously a dog or a cat can't believe that today is Saturday or that John has left the house, for he does not have the concept of what day it is, or can't use proper names the way we do. Because of the linguistic phenomenon of referential opacity we meet similar problems for language speaking creatures.[1]

The main problem for an account of belief seems to be: how are we to reconcile the two features of belief, the matter of causal role and the matter of content? Some argue that the first is essential to an elucidation of the second; others that we have to follow the inverse strategy; others that we can't reconcile the two at all. In what follows I want to stress the various shortcomings of these alternative strategies. Locating their sources can improve our understanding of the very notion of belief. My own answer, however, will be inspired by the last alternative.

2. FUNCTIONALISM

Functionalism, conceived broadly as the thesis that psychological states are individuated by the abstract causal roles they play among internal states mediating environmental inputs and behavioural outputs, seems to be the right sort of psychological theory for such states as beliefs. For one thing 'folk psychology' seems to be 'functionalist' in the sense alluded above, that beliefs interact with desires and other states to cause actions. A functionalist psychology would be a refinement of this rough scheme, describing further the causal roles played by the psychological states, proceeding from 'top' (beliefs in the ordinary medium) to 'bottom' (the inner workings of the 'hardware'). In short there may be different levels of functional organization and the causal roles may be more or less abstract, according to the level of description. This squares well with the common assumption of most functionalists in the philosophy of mind, that there may be different realizations of these roles or 'programs' which mental states such as beliefs and desires are said to consist in. The main appeal of functionalism in the philosophy of mind seems to be that it can be taken as a general doctrine about mental states, inducing a common 'research program' for psychologists, cognitive scientists and philosophers, in the task of drawing a map of our minds and their workings.

There are of course several versions of this general picture,[2] but they all share the conception of belief as a state having certain causal relations to perceptions and to behaviour. This scheme is by no means new: Ramsey invoked it in support of his 'pragmatic' conception of belief and truth, and it may be called behaviouristic as well — having a belief is a matter of having certain dispositions to act, given certain relations to other states.[3]

3. THE QUALIA OBJECTION

The standard objection to functionalism is the so-called 'qualia objection': we could be in such and such a state, defined functionally, but feel quite different things at the same time, thus being in a quite different mental state as far as the *qualitative* aspects of our feelings are concerned. Two persons may be functional twins, instantiate the same causal roles, but yet not be *qualia* twins, so to say. Here too, there are many versions of the argument, from *qualia inversion* (you might experience the smell of a hamburger when I experience the smell of a violet, functional properties notwithstanding) to *absent qualia* (nothing is felt, but the functional properties are there), and different ways to answer this question. Whatever these answers may be, no such objection can be raised in the case of belief, for belief is not, unlike a sensation such as pain or colour vision, a feeling. If you believe that London is pretty, it does not matter what feeling is attached to your belief. You may have a number of feelings and qualitative impressions to call to your mind with this belief, but you will believe the same thing even if different feelings occur. This does not imply, however, that we cannot become *aware of*, or *be conscious of*, the contents of our beliefs, and that in this case belief is accompanied by a state of conscious awareness that we may call qualitative. But one should not confuse having a belief with being conscious of the content of belief. The first may be ascribed to dumb creatures like animals without the second, whereas a disposition to be conscious of one's beliefs (believing that one believes, having 'second-order beliefs') is characteristic of humans. So a 'dispositional' account of belief does not imply that all beliefs are kinds of latent states of the subject, incompatible with conscious awareness of them, any more than having this awareness is necessary in order to be in a state of believing *something*. To acknowledge the validity of the distinction between belief and assent or between belief and opinion or judgement, does not commit us to saying that this state of conscious awareness is infallible or incorrigible.[4] So we can't make it a *criterion* of belief.

Granted that belief belongs to this class of mental states which are 'program receptive', while sensations are 'program resistant' on a functionalist hypothesis,[5] one may object to their *over-sensitiveness* to programs on such a view: if the causal roles of our functional theories are abstract, we may fear that they could be applied to the description of systems which lack the appropriate mental characteristics. For instance we may take a chess-playing computer to be 'really' believing that X is the best strategy. In other words our programs may be too loose or too liberal to capture mental representation as such. On the other hand, if we characterize our inputs and outputs too physiologistically, we run the risk of 'chauvinism' that any kind of identity theory runs (i.e. we will be forced to withold mental properties from systems that might in fact have them — such as possible extra-terrestrial beings with very different physical constitutions from ours).[6] Here the appropriate answer seems to be that which is offered by Dennett and Lycan, defenders of the 'homuncular' version of functionalism: functional description, they would say, affords different levels of abstraction: some areas of our 'flow charts' may be more physiological, others more 'structural', without there being any preeminence of one level over others, since all cooperate together.[7] It remains true, however, that in the case of beliefs, we stay at a relatively general level of abstraction. For instance, even if a box labelled 'perceptual analysis' interacts with another one labelled 'belief' in our flow chart, it seems that we can understand the workings of this latter box without appeal to physiological descriptions of perception. However, some have argued that even if it were the case, our whole system would lack *intentionality*, and so the functionalist picture would also be too naroow.

4. THE APPEAL TO INTENTIONALITY

A version of this objection has been given by Searle (1980). Imagining the case of a monolingual English speaker locked in a room and receiving a number of instructions to apply transformational rules to a number of Chinese symbols which he does not understand, Searle claims that the speaker could in principle perform all the operations of a native Chinese speaker without being able to speak or understand Chinese. Commenting in this thought experiment, P. and P. Churchland remark that it is a mistake to try to meet Searle's challenge by showing that we can impose various conditions to the system in order to endow it with the appropriate amount of intentionality. For Searle would reply (and did reply to his AI objectors) that we thus fail to distinguish between *intrinsic* intentionality and *observer-relative* intentionality ascriptions. The latter are 'ways that people have of speaking about entities figuring in our activities but lacking intrinsic intentionality'[8] They cover the whole range of our ordinary third-person attributions of attitudes, for instance when we ascribe intentional states to a robot 'from the outside'. For Searle, the paradigm case of *intrinsic* intentionality are first-person attributions of intentionality, when we ascribe intentional states to ourselves. In the case considered, *I* understand my own tongue, and *I* know what it is to mean anything in it. As such it looks like a 'privileged access' (Ryle) criterion of the mental. Searle has other criteria for intentionality and mentality of a 'genuine' kind, but they are more obscure.[9] Moreover, he claims that observer-relative ascriptions of intentionality are dependent on intrinsic ones, namely on the intrinsic intentionality of the observers.

We may grant Searle's point: even on observer-relative grounds, the speaker does not understand Chinese.[10] But to grant that does not show that understanding, meaning, and other states belong to the kind of intrinsic or genuine intentionality that Searle wants us to acknowledge. It is true that we make

attributions of attitudes (extrinsic) to others on the basis of attributions to ourselves, but it does not imply anything 'substantial' about the latter ones. In the
case at hand, a key constraint on understanding is not that we understand
others in the light of our own states, but that we can discern a network of beliefs
linked with the ones we are considering. Let's call it the *holistic constraint*.
Searle's case is not very different from ordinary cases of translation of alien
utterances in our native tongue. We do not attribute content to such utterances
on the basis of isolated utterances paired with isolated beliefs, but assign specific
contents to beliefs on the basis of our evidence that it plays a certain role in an
economy of other, related beliefs and representations which matches our own
economy of beliefs and representations. If this whole intentional *structure* is
'a matter of the inferential/computational relations to all the rest of the speaker's
representations',[11] this does not mean that intentionality is only extrinsic or
relative to observers' having operational criteria of intentionality; but it is nevertheless *relational*. There is nothing 'substantial' or 'intrinsic' in Searle's sense,
but intentionality is nevertheless *real*, as displayed by this relational network.
'Our own mental states are just as innocent of "intrinsic intentionality" as are
any states of any machine simulation'.[12] The holistic constraint is the real problem that we have to meet when we ask whether computers can understand
fragments of natural language.[13]

   This relational character of belief ascription seems to me essential, and what
is overlooked in each of the two main concurrent accounts of belief proposed
in the recent years by philosophers. Let us call them the language of thought
hypothesis and the causal theory of thought respectively. Each of them is an
attempt to solve the problem of the dual aspect of belief — as psychological
state and as content. I shall briefly examine them in turn.

5. THE LANGUAGE OF THOUGHT HYPOTHESIS

What would be the task of a psychological theory of the contents of beliefs
according to the language of thought hypothesis? It would be an attempt to re-
state the particular representations that are linked to the use of certain words
and which account for the opacity of the propositional contents of beliefs as
reported in our attributions. It would have to specify what 'modes of presentation' are linked to these expressions that (for instance) would refer to particulars
in the mind of the subject. If we knew what is thus represented, we would know
what the sentences reported in belief ascriptions mean.[14] We could then have a
functional theory of meaning itself, as a matter of *cognitive role:* what determines *meaning*, and thus *content* as a property of sentences, is a state of the
head — our knowledge of the mode of presentation of objects and properties
designated in sentences — a state characterized by the causal links it entertains
with other states, and with the behavioural manifestations it produces.[15] Such is
the story, as it is ordinarily told. Not every belief, of course, is given in words.
Language is not the only medium of representation, but at least there is a repre-

sentation of some kind.[16] We may not be committed to the strong version of the 'language of thought hypothesis', according to which *every* representation is language-like, and all mental states of a computational kind are written in the brain in a 'mentalese language' of which our spoken and written linguistic expressions are but a particular translation in an outer garment. But there is nevertheless a strong tendency among functionalists to endorse this version, since it fits so well with the picture they advocate.[17]

I do not want to enter any detailed criticism of this picture.[18] I will only put emphasis on two points, which show that it is very difficult, on this theory, to have *both* the psychological account of belief *and* the account of the content right. Again these two points have to do with the holistic constraint, with the relationship between belief and inference, between having a belief and having other beliefs connected with it.

First, according to the holistic constraint, beliefs do not come as separate items, so that we could draw up lists of them or count them. If I believe that a cloud is passing before the sun, it seems that I must also believe that there is a sun, there are clouds (some of our beliefs are existential, others ascribe properties and relations),[19] maybe I must also believe that an opaque body interfering between a source of light prevents the light from coming out, and so on. But how far should this list be extended? Here it is not only that there are relations and links, most of them the products of inferences, between our various beliefs, as noted earlier. It's also that we may fail to know *how far* these relations pertain, how many interrelated beliefs there are. If we had to *write* into our brains some belief-sentences instead of reading them, we would have to take into account many such cohering beliefs, perhaps an indefinite number of them. So even if we could say what a person means when he or she has a belief by locating the appropriate psychological state responsible for this belief, we would not be sure that we have fixed the very *content* of this belief.[20]

The second point is independent as such of the language of thought hypothesis, and involves a distinction between what Stephen Stich has called *sub-doxastic states,* and beliefs.[21] Roughly the distinction is that between beliefs as such, i.e. as states having a propositional content, and the mechanisms that underlie the production of beliefs. For example the depth perception mechanisms which underly our ability to judge the relative distance of objects in our visual field constitute a complex psychological set of factors which do not figure in reports of our visual perceptions, as when we say that we have a perceptual belief that such and such an object is further away in our visual field than this other one. To quote Stich directly:

> Contrast, for example, the *subdoxastic state* representing the information that a dot on a certain part of the left retina is displaced five seconds further toward the nose than the similarly situated dot on the right retina, with the *belief* that the dot in that part of the retina is displaced five seconds further towards the nose than the similarly

situated dot on the right retina. The subdoxastic state can lead directly only to the restricted class of beliefs about the apparent relative depth (and perhaps some other aspects of the visual field). By contrast the belief, if supplemented by suitable additional beliefs, can lead to just about any belief. There is also a striking contrast in the way other beliefs can *lead to* either the subdoxastic state or the belief. A subject might inferentially acquire the belief (that a dot on a certain part of the left retina . . . etc.) in numerous and diverse ways. He may be told that the dot is thus displaced by a person he takes to be trustworthy, and infer that on the basis of this belief about what his informant believes. Or he may infer it from other beliefs formed by observing the readings of certain test instruments.[22]

The point of the story is that if we want to say that a subdoxastic state *is* a belief, we would be unable to say *what* belief it was. True, the subdoxastic state is supposed to store the very information that leads to the belief that *p*. But the paths leading to the informations conveyed by the belief, the mechanisms of perception for instance, certainly differ from the belief issued, so that we cannot say that they have a content in the way belief itself has content. One solution, advocated by Harman, would be simply to identify the sensory stimulations that provide the input to the information processing system compounded of brain and nervous system with beliefs.[23] Inference from stimulations to beliefs would be on the same footing as inference from beliefs to beliefs since sensory stimulations just *are* beliefs. But even if we grant that there are inferential relations between, for example, retinal stimulations and beliefs that such and such an object is to the left of the visual field, it does not follow that these subdoxastic states *are* beliefs. If they were, what would be their content? It could not be expressible in words, since the process of retinal stimulation is not something to which the subject can have access, nor any propositional content to which we can assent. One way out could be to claim that a number of subdoxastic states involve a kind of representation which is semi-linguistic or symbolic in some way, but Harman himself admits that these are not linguistic representations at all. Harman seems to take us back where we started, and is led to admit that the pure psychological states, even if they convey some information, cannot convey the same kind of information as that conveyed by beliefs, since they don't have any definite *content.*[24]

6. THE CAUSAL THEORY OF THOUGHT

The contrast between psychological state and content is even more obvious on the so-called causal theory of reference and of thought, which was propounded by philosophers mostly inspired by semantical matters.[25] The gist of this theory is the remark that we can conceive a person's psychological states (and in the context of this discussion functional states) as fixed, while his propositional attitudes vary. To show this, one devises certin thought experiments, called, after Putnam, 'Twin Earth Cases', of the following kind. On a certain planet (Twin Earth), exactly identical to ours save in one respect, people encounter samples of a certain substance, which looks exactly like an ordinary substance on Earth (water, milk, or whatever), but different in its internal structure (atomic composition for instance). These people, being identical to us, have the same psychological (here, functional) states as we have, so that in *this* sense they believe the *same* things about the substance considered, refer to the *same* stuff. But the substance being different, their beliefs *as propositional contents* are not about the same substance, so that a judgement that 'water is H_2O' for instance is *false* on Twin Earth, whereas it is *true* on Earth.[26] Cases of this kind involve typically what philosophers call *de re* beliefs. These are beliefs which, unlike *de dicto* beliefs, bear a certain *direct* relation to the environment. *De re* beliefs issue in such belief ascriptions as 'About X, Jones believes that he is a coward', while *de dicto* beliefs correspond to such ascriptions as 'Jones believes that the man with such and such characteristics is a coward' (where the man is not a particular person Jones 'has in mind').[27] *De re* beliefs are specifiable only if we take into account the *semantical* relation of 'aboutness', signalled by the indexical component of the corresponding belief-sentences ('he', 'this', 'the' on demonstrative readings, proper names in most uses). This relation is, it is said, irreducible to any kind of explanation in terms of the functional states relating to the *syntactic* representations of sentences, as on the language of thought hypothesis. This latter hypothesis is tied to what Fodor has called 'methodological solipsism' (after Putnam), and claims that the inner workings of the representations can be investigated separately from what constitutes the surroundings and environment of the speakers. On the causal account, however, the contents of beliefs depend on what objects and properties exist outside the subject's mind. As Dennett puts it, we could be psychological twins, while not being propositional attitude twins. Here too, I can't enter a detailed discussion of this theory. Its main difficulties are that it relies on intuitions about reference and about the *de re/de dicto* distinction which are too fragile. What is it to be 'about' something? I may think about you in many ways, which are in some cases very 'conceptual' (or *de dicto*) even though my thinking has you as its particular object. The pretendant to marriage who puts an ad in the newspaper thinks about his future love in a way which is neither general or conceptual ('blue-eyed girl') nor particular or non-conceptual ('*that* very girl').[28] Moreover it is highly improbable that the *whole* content of our beliefs is determined by the outside environment and our relations to it. If this were so, then it's not the mind which has a natural tendency to spread over objects in the world, but the world which spreads over the contents of the mind. By giving too much importance to the *semantical*, world-oriented, content of our thoughts, we lose grip on their psychological content. The causal theory of thought, however, by insisting on the causal relations to the environment and the indexical features of many beliefs, has a merit: it reminds us that any attempt to 'model' beliefs will have to take such relations into account. This is known, among AI researchers, as the 'frame problem': how are we to adjust the relationships of some abstract, context-independent sets of beliefs, to the various changes of perceptual inputs occasioned by any contact by a system with concrete situations and 'the world'?[29]

7. DOUBLE ASPECT THEORIES

I have been envisaging various versions of the same difficulty. It seems that you can't get the functional role of beliefs right without getting the propositional content wrong, and conversely. A solution would be to rest content with that, and say that belief just is a double-aspect concept, or that there are two kinds of roles that beliefs may perform, or a 'bifurcation of content'. Field for instance defines belief in this dual way:

> X believes that p if and only if there is a sentence S such that X believes* S and S means that p . . .
>   I believe* a sentence of my language if and only if I am disposed to employ that sentence in a certain way in reasoning, deliberating and so on . . . On the other hand, everyone impressed with the problem of explaining what it is for a sentence to mean that p invokes a semantic relation (of *meaning that* . . .).[30]

This would amount to the claim that we can never specify the whole content of a belief since X's believing* S and S's meaning that p might tell us different stories, as our previous discussion of subdoxastic states shows.

Some time ago, Donald Davidson came through the same difficulty in the course of his attempt to build what he calls a theory of interpretation:

> A central source of trouble is the way beliefs and meanings conspire to account for utterances. A speaker who holds a sentence to be true on an occasion does so in part because of what he means, or would mean, by an utterance of that sentence, and in part because of what he believes. If all we have to go on is the fact of honest utterance, we cannot infer the belief without knowing the meaning, and have no chance of interpreting meaning without the belief.[31]

The solution, Davidson argues, does not rest on an attempt to break this circle, and define belief as psychological state in terms of sentence-meaning or the contrary, or split the very notion of belief in two components, but to deliver simultaneously a theory of both. And he shows that it is possible by drawing an analogy with the case of decision theory, when we have to compute the relative values an agent places on the outcomes of a bet, given his choices and given his subjective probabilities (his beliefs, in the terms of the theory of subjective probability).[32] The point here is that we can only interpret subjective probabilities and values, or beliefs and meanings, in the light of a *normative* theory that would tell us in each case what an ideal agent or believer would do or believe.

In the case of decision theory, Davidson defends Ramsey's solution[33] and in the case of the theory of meaning, he works out the standards of his theory of interpretation.

Without taking sides on the issue of whether Davidson's theory of interpretation is the best, I would claim that any elucidation of the contents of beliefs rests upon *some kind* of normative theory setting the standards of the rationality of beliefs and actions. Some of these standards can be principles of charity, laws of logic, principles of decision making under uncertainty etc. In the case of belief and the interpretation of attitudes, Dennett's concept of an 'intentional system' seems to me the best candidate for these canons of rationality. But whatever they may be, the important point to notice is that we cannot ascribe contents to the beliefs of other creatures, or indeed to our own, *independently* of these canons of rationality. Dennett argues this forcefully:

> Suppose I find a mechanism in Jones that reliably produces an utterance of 'It is raining' whenever Jones is queried on the topic and it is raining in Jones' epistemically accessible vicinity. It also produces 'yes' in reponse to 'Is it raining?' on those occasions. Have we discovered Jones' belief that it is raining? That is, more circumspectly, have we found the mechanism that subserves this belief in Jones' cognitive apparatus? Maybe — it all depends on whether Jones believes that it is raining when (and only when) this mechanism is 'on'. That is, perhaps, we have discovered a weird and senseless mechanism . . . that deserves no intentional interpretation at all, or at any rate not this one: that it is the belief that it is raining. We need a standard against which to judge our intentionalistic labels for the illata of subpersonal cognitive theory: what we must use for this standard is the system of abstracts that fixes beliefs and desires by a sort of hermeneutical process that is the best, most rational, story that can be told.[34]

8. CONCLUSION: RELATIVITY AND INDETERMINACY OF BELIEFS ASCRIPTIONS AND TWO KINDS OF HOLISM

Because of this necessary relativity of ascriptions of beliefs to some interpretive standard, there is an indeterminacy of the content of beliefs. Quine was right when he stressed the indeterminacy of the intentional idiom (although he was wrong to discern it only against the background of behavioural standards). This fact is overlooked by what I have called purely psychological theories of belief: they are commited to the claim that if we were not to find the relevant functional structures responsible for the productions of beliefs, we would have to say that *there are no beliefs at all*, that there are no such states as beliefs, or that these occupants of our mental lives are just posits of folk psychology bound to disappear in the light of an evolved psychology.[35] But partisans of the strong intentionality thesis, who insist that there are no beliefs where there is no intrinsic intentionality, are committed to saying that there are no beliefs where there is no 'genuine' intentionality. Both are reluctant to admit that where there is representationality or intentionality, there is a vagueness of some kind. In both cases our answer has been to invoke a holistic constraint operating upon ascriptions of beliefs. But there are two varieties of holism here: on the one hand we may say that beliefs are interrelated *real* entities bearing functional links with one another; alternatively we may say that beliefs are interrelated only in the light of a normative theory that is used to interpret their content. In this latter case, we may also say that there are no beliefs at all, since beliefs are just theoretical *posits*, having a purely instrumental character.[36] Although we must recognize the relativity of belief ascriptions, I think we must resist the temptation to consider beliefs as pure 'illata' of our psychological theories. From the fact that beliefs are vague entities we should not infer that there are no beliefs at all, or that any kind of functional theory of them is doomed to failure.

Research in Artificial Intelligence encounters many similar difficulties.[37] Success in this field will be attained by satisfactory modelling of our ordinary notions of mental processes or states. But any theoretical venture pays the price of its increasing distance from the ordinary idiom. This of course is true of the philosophical speculations as well. Although these cannot pretend to the experimental advantage that the effective building of models and systems provides, they somewhat indicate the nature of the holes we have to fill.

NOTES

1. Similar but not identical, since in this latter case, the question is: *what* concept is involved in such and such an utterance, and not whether there is any concept at all. Cf. Stich 1979. For an elaborate study of the common sense concept of belief, see Morton 1980.
2. I shall ignore the fact that functionalist theories differ in the strength of their respective claims and ontological commitments, and that we can distinguish 'Turing machine functionalism' from 'carburettor functionalism' and from 'homuncular functionalism' respectively. For an account of such distinctions, see Block 1980c, Dennett 1978a, and Shoemaker 1982; cf. also note 7 below.
3. Cf. Ramsey 1978, and the various articles in Mellor 1980b, for a comparison. Of course the difference between this theory and behaviourism properly so-called is that it does not attempt to *reduce* beliefs to dispositions to act, and that it defines it in connexion with other *mental* states. In a broad sense we can call it a 'dispositional' theory if we are to allow a 'liberal' sense of the term 'disposition' such as the one in Mellor 1974.
4. As Mellor puts it, 'insight, like eyesight, is fallible' (Mellor 1980a, p. 151). For another account of the distinction between belief and assent, cf. Dennett 1978a, Chapter 10.
5. The distinction is due to Keith Gunderson (Gunderson 1971).
6. Block 1980c, p. 270 and 291–6. I take Kripke to be alluding to this difficulty in his 1982, p. 36–7.

7. Briefly summarized, Dennett's position is that an 'intentional system' (a program for answering various questions, for instance) breaks down into an organization of subsystems, where a fictitious 'homunculus', 'a bogeyman' operates. A flow chart is a committee of such little men, all more and more 'stupid' in the tasks they perform, but which, *together*, perform at a sub-level the operations ascribed to the system as a whole. Cf. Dennett 1978a *passim*, and especially p. 124–6, and his 'program for pain' in 1978a, Chapter 11. (See also Palmer, Chapter 2 in this volume.)

8. Searle, *Author's response's*, in Searle 1980, p. 451–2 of the original printing. Cf. also Searle 1981. I borrow most of this discussion from Churchland and Churchland 1982, p. 121–45.

9. He seems to believe that there is intentionality when a creature has some 'causal power' to produce intentional phenomena (Searle 1980, in Haugeland 1981, p. 299), but this seems circular.

10. Here I'm much indebted to Steve Torrance.

11. Churchland and Churchland 1982, p. 140.

12. Ibid. We may construe the 'What it is like' test offered by Thomas Nagel (1974) as a mark of real intentionality and consciousness in this way: we say what it is like to be others on the basis of our knowledge of what it is like to be us, because we can discern an isomorphic intentional structure.

13. Cf. Haugeland 1979, pp. 619–32 for an exploration of various versions of this constraint.

14. See Schiffer 1978 for an account of these 'modes of presentation'.

15. Cf. Harman 1973 for instance, and of course Fodor 1975.

16. As Fodor puts it, 'No representations, no computations. No computations, no model' (1975, p. 31).

17. Harman and Fodor are notable examples, See also Lycan 1981, p. 85.

18. For such criticisms, cf. Dennett 1978, Chapters 3 and 6, and 1982a. There are also critics of Wittgensteinian inspiration, such as Heil 1981, unlike Dennett, believe that their views imply a general scepticism about AI and functionalism.

19. For an account of this distinction, see Unger 1981.

20. This indefinite link is what Davidson calls the 'holism of the mental'. It is not only a feature of beliefs, but of beliefs together with wants, desires, and other states (and constitutes the main reason for the failure of definitional behaviourism). Cf. Davidson 1980 *passim*, Dennett 1978a, p. 46, Dennett 1982a, pp. 30–1.

21. Stich 1978, pp. 499–519.

22. Ibid., p. 509.

23. Harman 1973, pp. 185–6.

24. Stich 1978, pp. 516–17.

25. Putnam (1975a) first espoused such a theory. Burge (1979 and 1982) is another proponent.

26. Putnam 1975a. We can find less *recherché* cases such as this one: Snow

White believes of the apple she saw yesterday that it is good; when a witch brings her another apple, identical in appearance but poisoned, she believes that this, too, is good. She is in the same belief state in the two cases, but she does not have the same belief as content, since 'This apple is good' is true in one case and false in another (cf. Burge 1982). (But someone who was sceptical about the distinction between *de dicto* and *de re* beliefs may find this sort of example less than compelling.) (See also Jacob, in this volume, Chapter 4, Section 3, for a related discussion [Editor's note].)

27. I can't enter here into the precise distinction, which may be confused in itself. Cf. for instance, Burge 1979.

28. For a detailed criticism of the distinction see Dennett 1982a, and the various articles in Woodfield 1982. Cf. Fodor 1980 in Haugeland 1981, p. 333.

29. Cf. Dennett 1978a, p. 125.

30. (I have slightly modified the quotation) Field 1978, p. 13. Cf. also McGinn 1982 for another defence of this 'dual' role.

31. Davidson 1974, pp. 310–11.

32. Ibid., pp. 313–15.

33. Ramsey 1978.

34. Dennett 1982b, p. 71. On intentional systems, cf. his 1978b.

35. Stich (1982a) seems to advocate this position; cf. also his 1982b.

36. Dennett seems to be a defender of the latter kind of holism, when he says that 'beliefs are not good theoretical entities' (Dennett 1978a, p. xx). But in other places he says that he does not want to deny that there *are* beliefs (Dennett 1980). Notice also that the first kind of holism implies that it may be the case that most of our beliefs are false, while the second kind of holism is committed to such postulates of interpretation as the principle of charity, according to which most, or a large number, of our beliefs must be true.

37. In the course of this discussion, I have tried to indicate some of them: modelling of beliefs and other intentional states, the frame problem, and understanding of natural languages.

I would like to thank Steve Torrance for his numerous and useful remarks on this paper.

4

Remarks on the language of thought

Pierre Jacob

J. A. Fodor has forcefully argued that a good deal of work in cognition (psychology, AI, linguistics, philosophy of mind) implies or presupposes the existence of a 'language of thought' or mentalese. According to him, mental computations, as required for example by language-acquisition, would be carried out in that 'private code'. Furthermore, the language of thought, though different from any natural language, would share various features with natural languages – particularly as far as its expressive power is concerned.

In the present chapter, I would like to make three related points about what Fodor says about the language of thought. These will be questions or criticisms, although I don't myself have an alternative to Fodor's point of view. My first point has to do with the role of the language of thought in the process of language acquisition as envisaged by Fodor, in his 1975 book. My second point will deal with the bifurcation between two aspects of beliefs, the mental or psychological aspect, and the propositional or content aspect. That point has been extensively discussed in recent times by Fodor himself (in his 1981 book) as well as by Dennett (1982a) and a wealth of other people. The problem emerges from the tension between two assertions: on the one hand, one needs a notion of belief as one of the attitudes or states that will play a causal role in the explanation and prediction of observable behaviour. On the other hand, many of the natural language sentences that will be used to report the content of the belief will contain indexical expressions. More of that later. Finally, I want to point out that one of Fodor's frequently iterated assertions might have undesirable consequences, that is his claim that for an organism to have a given propositional attitude is for that organism to bear a proper relation to a formula of the language of thought – in the sense that for a psychologist to ascribe to an organism a given propositional attitude is to ascribe to it a relation to some given formula of the language of thought. I will argue that there are ascriptions of propositional attitudes (e.g. beliefs) to a person in which, contrary to Fodor's view, no single formula seems to adequately represent the content of the attitude.

1. IS LEARNING A LANGUAGE LEARNING ITS TRUTH-CONDITIONS?

As one of the most eloquent advocates of functionalism, Fodor (1975) explicitly and heavily relies on the analogy between the following two relations: the relation between the brain and the mind, and the relation between the physical structure of a computer and its computational states. More precisely, Fodor says that real computers characteristically use two different languages: an input–output language and a machine-language. In the former they (computers) communicate with their environment (particularly the human person who programs them). In the latter 'they talk to themselves'. The role of compilers being that of 'mediating' between the two languages by providing a translation between them. The translation will in turn consist of 'biconditionals whose left-hand side is a formula in the input–output language and whose right-hand side is a formula in the machine code' (Fodor 1975, pp. 65–6).

On the other hand, Fodor not only accepts the Davidsonian view that for a human to understand his language is to know a truth-definition of that language but, as he says (p. 81), *learning* it is learning its truth-conditions. Now a truth-definition for a language (in the Tarski–Davidson tradition) will be a recursive construction that will provide for each of the infinitely many sentences of that language L a truth-condition, where a truth-condition for the open sentence 'Fx' will be a meta-linguistic formula of type (T):

(T) 'Fx' is true if and only if Gy

In formula (T) it is crucial to note that the predicate F (which is a consituent of the open sentence on the left-hand side of the biconditional) is *mentioned* while G is *used*. This simply means that what appears on the left-hand side is the metalinguistic name of F.

Now what Fodor does is to combine the two views mentioned: the view that computers use two different languages and the view that learning a language is learning its truth-definition. To combine them, he notices that the only model of learning that is available is the view according to which learning is a matter of hypothesis-formation and testing. As James Higginbotham put it at the Conference, referring to Chomsky's characterization of the task of generative linguistics, i.e., to account for the child's acquisition of language on the basis of his linguistic experience, the child is 'a theory-constructor'. According to Fodor, nobody has ever proposed an alternative to that view. Perhaps Chomsky's recent talk of 'the growth' of language might be seen as an alternative (cf. Chomsky 1975, 1980).

Let us suppose that any learning is literally the formation and the confirmation of hypotheses. Then the child who learns (e.g. his language), like any scientist, needs a 'language' (a medium or a system of representation) in which to express his hypotheses. Since learning a language is learning a truth-definition for that language and since learning consists in formulating hypotheses and checking them, then learning a language will consist in putting forward hypotheses about the truth-conditions of the sentences of that language and testing them. The language in which the child who is learning say French will express his truth-conditional hypotheses will not be French (by hypothesis); it will be the language of thought. But now let us go back to the implication of our (T) formula. In such a formula, F stands for any predicate of the language to be learnt. So what is true of F will *ipso facto* be true of any predicate of the language. Psychologically interpreted, F stands for a predicate of the natural language that the child is learning (let us say a predicate of French). As I said before, in (T) F is mentioned. G stands for a predicate of the metalanguage. Interpreted psychologically, that means that G is a predicate of the language of thought. But for (T) to be true, G and F must at least be *coextensive*. What this means psychologically is for that child to be able to learn the semantic properties of F, he must be able to use or understand a formula like (T) which in turn implies or presupposes that he has available in his language of thought the predicate G coextensive with F. Since the predicates of the language of thought are not learnt, they must be innate. Since the argument applies to any predicate, for the child to learn any predicate he must already have innate knowledge of its mentalese counterpart. Therefore for every predicate of French that the child will come to learn there exists a coextensive mentalese predicate that he knows innately. Thus (assuming that mentalese predicates *are* concepts) all concepts are innate, or some boolean function of innate primitives.

Fodor sometimes writes as if *this* conclusion proved the untenability of some of his assumptions:

> I admit that these conclusions really may seem scandalous. I should be inclined to view them as a *reductio ad absurdum* of the theory that learning a language is learning the semantic properties of its predicates, except that no serious alternative to that theory has ever been proposed. Consonant with the general methodology of this study, I shall endure what I don't know how to cure. In particular, I shall continue to   assume that learning a natural language is learning the rules which determine the extensions of its predicates. (Fodor 1975, p. 82).

But he nevertheless uses those assumptions (very effectively) against the Piagetian general picture of conceptual development. That picture includes the three following claims: (i) the development of the child's cognitive abilities exhibits an orderly transition between stages; (ii) each stage reflects the child's conceptual competence; (iii) as every later stage is conceptually richer than any of its predecessor, learning mediates the transition from one stage to the next (cf. Fodor 1975, p. 87). Crucial to Fodor's discussion of that picture is the Piagetian assumption (approximately (ii)) that the development of the child's intellectual capacities as inferred from his behaviour can directly be mapped onto (or fundamentally reflects) an evolution of his intellectual or logical competence. If a stage n child can do better and more things than a stage $n-1$ child, this is not because he has more computational memory to work with, or because his attention span is longer, or because he has more knowledge of the world. Rather it is because the expressive power intrinsic to his conceptual repertoire is richer or more powerful.

But if we keep in mind the assumption that learning a concept is formulating and testing hypotheses about the semantic properties of that concept, then we get the following dilemma. Consider a stage 1 child who is trying to learn a stage 2 concept. Either he can represent the semantic properties (say, the satisfaction conditions) of that stage 2 concept or he cannot. If he can, then he does the representation within his stage 1 conceptual system. In which case, there is no point in saying that his stage 1 conceptual system is inherently weaker than stage 2. If we say that he cannot do the representation for we want to insist on the fact that stage 2 is intrinsically richer in expressive power than stage 1, then we have to admit that the child has no way of representing at stage 1 the semantic properties of any stage 2 concept. In which case, any stage 2 concept would be unlearnable by a stage 1 child. So the dilemma is between keeping a picture of conceptual development according to which each successor stage is intrinsically richer and more powerful than any predecessor stage and assuming that learning is a matter of hypothesis formation and testing.

Fodor's own choice is quite clear and drastic: he keeps the latter view and gives up the former. According to him, one learns the semantic properties of *words* (or predicates) of *natural languages* by formulating mentalese hypotheses about them. But one does *not* learn the semantic properties of *concepts*, i.e. of mentalese predicates, Those are innate.

I once thought of an objection to Fodor's picture that now seems wrong to me.[1] The objection was that Fodor cannot both have the truth-definitional approach to language-acquisition and the analogy between minds and machines. Here was the argument. According to Fodor's analogy between minds and machines, the machine uses a machine-language to compute ('to talk to itself') and an input—output language to communicate with its environment; the mind uses mentalese (which is the brain's machine-language) to compute (or to think) and a natural language to communicate with other minds. According to the truth-definitional approach to language-acquisition, the child who is learning French represents to himself a set of truth-conditional formulae of type (T) expressed in mentalese. So, in virtue of the analogy between minds and machines, for the machine to 'understand' a statement in its input—output language it must represent to itself in its machine-code a truth-conditional formula of type (T). Now, according to my now given up line of thought, there is a major difference between the two following relations: the relation between an object-language and its metalanguage (as required by truth-conditional semantics in order to avoid the semantic paradoxes, among other things); the relation between a computer's input—output language and its machine-code. The object-language is a proper subset of the metalanguage (in other words, the natural language to be learnt has to be a proper subset of mentalese) for the metalanguage will contain all the symbols of the object-language, plus naming devices and semantic predicates like 'satisfies' and 'is true' not contained in the object-language. On the other hand, although instructions in the machine-code of the computer will be coextensive (or extensionally equivalent) to statements in the input—output language, the latter will not be a proper subset of the former. Predicates contained in the input—output language will not occur, even in quotation marks, in the machine-code, which will contain numerical instructions such as 'Go to address K; store digit L'.

So for this argument to establish that Fodor cannot both hold on to a truth-definitional approach to language-acquisition and to the analogy between minds and machines, it is crucial that there be a sense in which the coextension between symbols of the metalanguage and symbols of the object-language and the co-extension between symbols of the machine-code and symbols of the input—output language be significantly different. Or, to put it differently, it is crucial that something like convention (T), according to which to say of a sentence 'S' that it is true is just to assert 'S', be inapplicable to the relation between the two languages of the computer. Obviously, as was pointed out to me,[2] the combinatorial power of the machine-code of a computer will allow it to match a vast quantity of strings of the input—output language and hence will permit the correspondence between instructions in the machine-code and statements from the input—output language. But if it were true that the coextension between predicates from the object-language and predicates from the metalanguage required for a truth-conditional formula to hold were different from the coextension required for machine-code instructions to match input—output language statements, then the fact that the machine-code had the combinatorial power that it has would not suffice to reconcile a truth-definitional approach to language-acquisition and the analogy between minds and machines. The presumed difference between the two kinds of coextensionality now seems to me to be immaterial: suppose an input—output language contains the 'concept' of multiplication and the machine-code has the concept of addition but does not contain multiplication as a primitive concept. To each higher-level statement in terms of multiplication, there will correspond a lower-level statement in terms of addition. That kind of computational extensional equivalence is all that is needed. The proper inclusion relation is just one among many possible ways to ensure extensional equivalence between two languages.

2. THE BIFURCATION BETWEEN BELIEF-STATES AND BELIEF-CONTENTS

As Fodor says in 'Methodological solipism' (in Fodor 1981), both folk psychology and presumably scientific psychology appeal (and will appeal) to propositional attitudes to explain and predict observable human behaviour. So, for example, I see that Bill is drinking a glass of water. Characteristically, I shall explain this by the following type of reasoning: Bill is thirsty; Bill wants to quench his thirst; he believes that water quenches one's thirst; he believes there is water in the glass; therefore he drinks what is contained in the glass. The 'explanation' of Bill's behaviour typically contains two statements of propositional attitude: a statement which ascribes a belief to Bill and a statement which ascribes a desire to him. Typically those statements are made of sentences containing a verb of propositional attitude (like 'believe') followed by an embedded clause that expresses the content of the belief (or of the attitude), i.e. what the relief is about. So, as Fodor puts it, psychological explanations of that sort have two degrees of freedom to play with: the attitude and the content. As far as Bill is concerned, he may be ascribed a desire, or a fear, or a wish, or a belief, and so on; and his attitude might be about various propositions (p, q, etc.) expressed by the embedded sentence.

When we consider beliefs as causal factors entering into the explanation of observable behaviour, we view them as unobservable states that are mental causes. Furthermore we typically invoke two kinds of such mental states, beliefs and desires. Because by combining such attitudes, we make sense of behaviour. We say that Bill did such and such because he believed that p and he wanted q. More precisely, we assume that the agent has preferences over various states of affairs, that he believes that by accomplishing action such or such he will bring about his preferred state of affairs, and that the therefore picks among the possible action open to him the one he thinks will help him realize his most favoured state of affairs.

Several people have observed the following. Consider first the now legendary science-fiction example due to Putnam (1975a). Suppose there exists a planet identical to Earth. Call it 'Twin Earth'. On Twin Earth, everything is a counterpart of something on Earth. So every English-speaker on Earth for example has a copy on Twin Earth. The only difference between the Earth and Twin Earth is that on Twin Earth the liquid that is called 'water' by English speakers, that fills oceans, lakes, quenches thirst and so on does not have the molecular structure H_2O by ZYZ. So consider my twin on Twin Earth. When I think (say to myself) 'I want to drink a glass of water', he thinks exactly the same. Let us assume that the English sentence goes through both our heads and that we compute the same mentalese sentence. As Putnam says, my twin and I are in exactly the same mental state. But in the token of his mentally uttered sentence the word 'water' refers to a liquid whose molecular structure is XYZ, whereas in the token of the sentence as mentally processed by me the same word 'water' refers to a liquid whose molecular structure is H_2O. This difference between the references or the extensions of both occurrences of 'water' in the two utterances induces a difference in the content of what is said or thought in each case: the proposition expressed by the sentence he thinks is different from the proposition expressed by the same sentence (-type) I think. So we can perfectly be in the same mental state while processing the same English sentence and nevertheless express different propositions.

The same point can be made by switching to more obvious indexicals, as has been observed by Kaplan (1977), Perry (1977, 1979) and Fodor (1981). Suppose Jerry Fodor and I both think that we are thirsty. So we both tell ourselves 'I am thirsty'. The same English sentence or perhaps the same mentalese sentence goes through our heads. We again are in similar mental states and we are likely to exhibit relatively similar behaviour — thirst-extinguishing type of behaviour. So as far as the notion of a state conceived of as a mental cause of observable behaviour is concerned, the same mental state can be ascribed to both of us. However, when Fodor mentally utters 'I am thirsty' he refers to himself (Fodor) by using 'I', while I refer to myself by my use of the personal pronoun. Since we are two different persons, we express two different propositions by uttering two tokens of the same sentence-type. But now if both Fodor and I think that he is thirsty, he tells himself 'I am thirsty' and I tell myself 'He is thirsty'. In that case, we use two different sentence-types — one contains the indexical 'I', the other the indexical 'he'. But with those two different sentences we express the same proposition. Interestingly, the following correlation emerges: when we use the same sentence-type containing only one indexical, we express two different propositions *and* we are likely to exhibit similar types of behaviour. When we use two different sentences containing two different indexicals, we can express the same proposition *and* we are likely to exhibit different kinds of behaviour — *he* (not I) is likely to exhibit drinking behaviour. Perry has more dramatic examples: if you and I both think that each of us is about to be attacked by a bear, we each tell ourselves 'I am about to be attacked by a bear': same sentence; same type of behaviour (we roll onto ourselves and stay as still as we can); different propositions expressed. If you and I both think that I am about to be attacked by a bear, you tell yourself 'He is about to be attacked by a bear': different sentences; different types of behaviour (you go and look for help; I roll onto myself and stay as still as I can); same proposition expressed.

When Putnam coined the phrase 'methodological solipism' (Putnam 1975a), he wanted to discredit the very view that Fodor is advocating. In 'Methodological solipism', Fodor distinguishes between what he calls the 'representational view of the mind' and the 'computational view of the mind'. The former seems to be quite uncontroversial: it amounts to assuming that psychological theorizing (about human behaviour) cannot do with fewer than two degrees of freedom. If John believes that p, then he does not fear that p nor does he believe that q. The two parameters of psychological theorizing are the attitude expressed by the verb of propositional attitude and the proposition expressed by the embedded sentence. This is not yet methodological solipism. Methodological solipism amounts to the computational view which requires the acceptance of the 'Formality condition': the condition that mental processes 'apply to representations in virtue of (roughly) the *syntax* of the representations' (Fodor 1981, p. 116). The computational view is patently stronger than the representational view of the mind: it is more restrictive since by claiming that the relevant mental processes are *syntactic* it denies that they can be semantical. As Fodor recognizes,

> 'accepting a formality condition upon mental states implies a drastic narrowing of the ordinary ontology of the mental; all sorts of states which look, prima facie, to be mental states in good standing are going to turn out to be none of the psychologist's business if the formality condition is endorsed . . . Take, for example, knowing that such-and-such, and assume that you can't know what's not the case. Since, on that assumption, knowledge is involved with truth, and since truth is a semantic notion, it's going to follow that there can't be a psychology of *knowledge* (even if it is consonant with the formality condition to hope for a psychology of belief)'. (Fodor 1981, pp. 227–8).

Actually, the computational view and the formality condition are again evidence of Fodor's enthusiasm for the analogy between mental computations and computers' computations. It is a point made by a number of philosophers (Fodor himself, Putnam 1981, Searle 1980) that semantic predicates like 'to refer to' are *intentional* (there is a sense emphasized in particular by Strawson in which words don't refer to anything, only speakers can refer to things by using words). Since computers lack intentionality they literally cannot be said to refer to anything. It is thus inappropriate if not meaningless to ascribe semantic properties to them. It is not surprising therefore that, assuming the analogy between mental computations and computers' computations, Fodor would urge the acceptance of the formality condition and the computational view of the mind. What might be more surprising, in view of his 1975 defence of the claim that learning a language is learning a truth-definition for that language, is his endorsement of the claim that computers cannot be said to refer, for reference implies or presupposes 'organism/environment transactions' which computers, as opposed to *programmers*, lack (Fodor 1981, pp. 232–3). The reason it is surprising is this: Fodor's 1975 picture seemed to imply that he wanted both the analogy between the mind and the machine (which he obviously still wants in his 1981 book) and the assumption that learning a language is learning a truth-definition for it. But, it could be said, that view of learning does not seem to fit the computer, for the machine-language does not seem to be the metalanguage in which truth-conditions of the input–output language could be expressed. *If* learning a concept was, for computers too, learning a satisfaction-condition for that concept, it would follow that computers have semantical capacities. So the very fact that Fodor 1981, while advocating a *syntactic* view of the mind, admits that computers have no semantical capacity, contradicts the 1975 combination of (a) the view that all learning involves hypotheses about the semantic properties of concepts, and (b) the analogy between minds and computers.

So faced with the above-mentioned dilemma, Fodor 1981 firmly chooses to keep the analogy between minds and machines and drops the view that for a computer to learn a concept is for it to learn the semantic properties of that concept. Since he keeps the analogy, he needs a purely syntactic taxonomy of mental states as required by psychological theorizing, a taxonomy 'according to which Misha and Sam are in the same mental state when each believes himself to be ill' (Fodor 1981, p. 239). As computers, when they carry out computations in the machine language, follow syntactic instructions, the mind, according to the formality condition (and the computational picture), goes from state to state, as states are syntactically defined. 'Truth, reference and the rest of the semantic notions aren't psychological categories' (Fodor 1981, p. 253).

As a consequence, mental states posited by psychological theorizing will be syntactically identified. Sam and Misha will be psychologically in the same mental state when both think that they are sick. Again, similarity of behaviour can be expected from such an identification of mental causes. But when Sam thinks that he is sick and Misha thinks that he (Misha) is sick their thoughts are different since one thought is *about* Sam and the other is *about* Misha. So Fodor's individuation of beliefs as required by psychological theorizing implies a bifurcation between the psychologically relevant aspect of belief (the state) and the propositional aspect of belief (the content). The content will be out of reach of a psychological theory syntactically defined along the lines of the formality condition and methodological solipsism.[3]

3. CAN BELIEFS BE FORMULAE OF THE LANGUAGE OF THOUGHT?

Fodor 1975 asserted that 'the computational states ascribable to organisms can be directly explicated as relations between the organism and *formulae*: i.e. formulae in the internal code . . . for any propositional attitude of the organism (e.g. fearing, believing, wanting, intending, learning, perceiving, etc., that *P*) there will be a corresponding computational relation between the organism and some formula(e) of the internal code such that (*the organism has the propositional attitude iff the organism is in that relation*) is nomologically necessary' (Fodor 1975, p. 75). I shall ignore Fodor's reference to perceiving as one of the attitudes (which contradicts methodological solipsism as defined in 1981 insofar as one cannot perceive what is not there). The same claim is made again in 'Propositional attitudes': 'propositional attitudes are relations to propositions — viz., they are *mediated* relations to propositions, with internal representations doing the mediating' (Fodor 1981, p. 200).

Fodor has several arguments for the claim that propositional attitudes are or correspond to relations to sentences but these sentences cannot be *public* sentences of a natural language (otherwise we could not ascribe propositional attitudes to higher mammals or non-speaking children, which for a variety of reasons he assumes we must do). They have to be private sentences of the language of thought. I will not review those arguments but take them for granted.

The arguments reviewed in the preceding section establish the bifurcation between belief-states and belief-contents. They crucially rely on the existence of indexicality in natural language. In a sentence used to report somebody's belief (the sentence embedded within the scope of the verb of propositional attitude) there might be an indexical. It is an open question whether an advocate of the language of thought hypothesis would want to maintain that sentences of the language of thought might contain indexicals too. This question is related to the difference between 'propositions' and sentences of the language of thought. If in some sense internal formulae are supposed to provide translations for sentences of natural languages (in the sense of yielding their meaning – on whatever view of meaning), then it would seem that they are more similar to propositions than to sentences of natural language. In which case, formulae of the language of thought would not be indexical. This seems to be Fodor's 1975 view. But in his 1981 book he writes as if formulae of the language of thought were decidedly different from propositions: 'my main reason for not saying "propositional attitudes are relations to propositions. Punkt." is that I don't understand it. I don't see how an organism can stand in an (interesting epistemic) relation to a proposition except by standing in a (causal/functional) relation to some token of a formula that expresses the proposition' (Fodor 1981, p. 201). In that case, internal formulae might contain indexical features.

Whatever the view one takes of the difference or identity between propositions and internal formulae, the claim that propositional attitudes are relations to formulae of the internal code has a definite consequence. And I want to question that consequence. If propositional attitudes are relations to internal formulae then presumably the objects of propositional attitudes are internal formulae. So for example the objects of beliefs (or belief-contents) will be internal formulae. Whatever such formulae are, what that view presupposes is that belief-contents are well-defined entities whose identification does not depend on the perspective, the goals or the aims of the person who is reporting the beliefs. This is questionable.

Whatever else might be used to identify and individuate beliefs, truth-conditions will presumably come into play. So while it is perfectly possible that beliefs having identical truth-conditions might nevertheless differ in other respects, it seems plausible that beliefs having different truth-conditions cannot be identical, so far as their content is concerned. Now the problem emerges of whether truth-conditions may be ascribed to beliefs (or to sentences expressing them) independently of the reasons why the person who is ascribing the belief wants to identify it. I shall explain with an example due to C. Travis in a paper to appear.

Imagine that I have a swan. Let us call it Humphrey. Suppose I dye it black. Suppose Bill sees Humphrey and thereby comes to believe it to be black. So he tells his friend Bob what he believes. Perhaps he simply expresses his belief by uttering the English sentence. 'Humphrey is black' (combined with other English sentences about who is Humphrey). Now Bob might want to check whether what Bill told him was true. It is possible that in recent times many people have dyed their pet swans, following a fad. Bob might have noticed that the most popular colour has been dark blue, a colour that can easily be misperceived as black. So Bob checks and finds out that Humphrey's colour is not dark blue but black. So he decides that Bill's belief is correct. Now Bill tells another of his friends, Joe, about Humphrey's colour. But according to Joe, naturally (genetically) black swans (non-dyed swans) are extremely infrequent and consequently very valuable. So Joe wants to know whether Humphrey is one of those. So he checks and finds out that Humphrey is dyed. So he takes Bill's belief that Humphrey is black to be incorrect. Therefore both Bob and Joe are correct in ascribing to Bill the belief they ascribe to him. But according to Bob, Bill's belief is true (or correct); according to Joe it is false (or incorrect). Bob ascribes to Bill a belief that is true if Humphrey is dyed. Joe ascribes to Bill a belief that is false in the same circumstances. So fixing the circumstances, Bill's belief as ascribed by Bob is true and as ascribed by Joe it is false. It would seem to follow therefore that Bill's belief as ascribed by Bob cannot be the same as Bill's belief as ascribed by Joe, since the belief Bob ascribes to Bill and the belief Joe ascribes to Bill do not have the same truth-conditions.

If we assume that, in the context of the above story, the sentence 'Humphrey is black' expresses a belief (of Bill's) (assuming, that is, that we know which Humphrey is referred to by the token of 'Humphrey' in the sentence), then such a sentence does not by itself possess definitive truth-conditions. As used by Bob to report Bill's belief, the sentence might be assigned the value True; but as used by Joe to report Bill's belief, the sentence might be assigned the value False. Now, in itself the fact that a sentence might be assigned different truth-values on different occasions of use does not seem surprising, for different tokens of the same sentence are often given different truth-conditions. But the generally recognized source of variation in truth-conditions lies in the indexicality of the referring device contained in the sentence. Here the indexical referring device might be 'Humphrey'. But as we already noticed, in the present case, 'Humphrey' is not the source of the variation in truth-conditions since we assumed that by 'Humphrey' both Bob and Joe are referring to Bill's pet swan. The source of the variation rather lies in the difference between what Bob takes to satisfy his use of the predicate 'is black' and what Joe takes to satisfy his use of the predicate 'is black'. For Bob's use of the predicate, something will count as black if it is not perceived as dark blue or any other colour but black, whether or not it is dyed. For Joe's use of the predicate, something will count as black not only if it *looks* black but also if it turns out not to be dyed. So what counts in each case as satisfying the predicate 'is black' cannot be determined independently of Bob's and Joe's background assumptions. Those assumptions differ and they reflect the different purposes Bob and Joe have for discovering Bill's belief. Bob wants to determine the content of Bill's belief in the light of his own assumption that many swans have been dyed dark blue. Joe wants to determine the content of Bill's belief in the light of his own assumption that non-dyed black swans are very rare. If it is true that belief-contents cannot be determined but in the light of such assumptions, then belief-contents cannot be formulae of internal sentences any more than they can just be sentences of a natural language.

At this point one could do one of three things. One could turn to holism; one could keep trying to ascribe truth-conditions to Bills' belief independently of Bob's and Joe's background assumptions; or one might hold the view that the predicate 'is black' is ambiguous. In the present context what turning to holism would mean is this:[4] of course, a holist would say, Bill's belief that Humphrey is black cannot just by itself be assigned either definite truth-conditions or a definite truth-value. For no isolated belief ever possesses definite truth-conditions. But if we combine Bill's belief that Humphrey is black with his other beliefs, then we should be able to fix the truth-conditions of Bill's belief that Humphrey is black.

Then the problem becomes: which other of Bill's beliefs should the holist conjoin with Bill's belief that Humphrey is black for the latter to be ascribed definite truth-conditions? If Bill believes that Humphrey is black and he does not suspect that Humphrey is dyed, then given the fact that Humphrey is dyed black, no wonder why Bob (who wants to check whether Humphrey is black as opposed to dark blue) takes Bill's belief to be true and why Joe (who wants to check whether Humphrey is dyed or not) takes Bill's belief to be false.

But to say this raises at least two problems. First of all, it begs the question of how we decide among all of Bill's beliefs which is (or are) relevant to determining the truth-conditions of his belief that Humphrey is black. How are we to decide that we should consider Bill's lack of presumption that Humphrey is dyed as opposed, for instance, to Bill's belief that the Earth is a sphere? What we need is a notion of Bill's *relevant* auxiliary beliefs. But Bill's relevant auxiliary beliefs themselves cannot be determined but in the light of Bob's and Joe's interests. Bill's lack of presumption about Humphrey's being dyed will contribute to the determination of the truth-conditions of his belief that Humphrey is black *if* we make Bob's and Joe's assumptions about other swans. Bob and Joe are trying to determine the content of Bill's belief. They are doing the investigation. They will assign both content and truth-value to Bill's belief. But they cannot do it without making assumptions about the context and without having interests and purposes for doing the investigation. What the holistic move does is build inside Bill's head what can only be provided by appealing to the purposes and interests of the person (or persons) who is (are) ascribing the belief, not the person to whom the belief is ascribed.

Furthermore, in our case, Bill's relevant auxiliary belief has been ascribed as a 'lack of presumption' (about Humphrey's being dyed). But if we can do better than describe Bill's relevant auxiliary belief as something missing, this confirms the hypothesis that the truth-conditions of Bill's belief that Humphrey is black can only be fixed relative to the assumptions of the belief-ascribers. For it makes sense to 'lack a presumption' only in the light of some positive counterpart. One can lack a presumption only where someone else has the lacking presumption.

A second move to open to Fodorism would be the following.[5] When Bill tells Bob and Joe that he believes that Humphrey is black, he does so by means of his use of the English sentence 'Humphrey is black'. Let us call the belief expressed by Bill's use of the above-mentioned sentence B_1. For B_1 to be true, it might be said, Humphrey must simply be black, not genetically black — merely black. Such is the truth-condition of the English sentence 'Humphrey is black' used by Bill to express B_1. It is perfectly conceivable that Bill has thought of none of the questions Bob and Joe have in mind. For example, Bill might not have thought about whether Humphrey's colour was genetically determined. Still, on the view presently under discussion, Bill would be ascribed a *bona fide* belief B_1 to the effect that Humphrey is black.

On that view, B_1 would be different from both Bob's belief, B_2, that Humphrey is dyed black (as opposed to dark blue), and Joe's belief, B_3, that Humphrey is dyed black and is not genetically black. Bill's belief, B_1, though it will count as an individual belief with its own truth-conditions, will not be specific enough to enable Bill to answer Bob's and Joe's worries: Is Humphrey really dyed black rather than dark blue? Is Humphrey naturally (genetically) black or is he dyed?

Now, the question raised by the view under discussion is this: it is generally recognised that a sentence-type such as 'Humphrey is black' which contains a referring device that can be used to refer to different individuals in different contexts of use does not have truth-conditions. Only a token such that the reference of the indexical singular term is fixed has a truth-condition. Now, we have seen that even when the reference of 'Humphrey' is fixed, the truth-conditions of the sentence 'Humphrey is black' might change according to how the predicate 'is black' is interpreted. But for Bill to be said to hold a belief B_1 (expressed by his use of the sentence 'Humphrey is black'), different from both B_2 and B_3, while Bill will be held to be incapable of answering Bob's and Joe's questions, one must assume that there exist truth-conditions of B_1 which will be truth-conditions of the sentence 'Humphrey is black'. If only a particular use of 'Humphrey is black', one in which 'Humphrey' is used to refer to a particular swan, can be said to have truth-conditions, what state of affairs will be considered as satisfying Bill's use of the predicate 'is black'? What must the world be like for Bill's use of the predicate 'is black' to be satisfied?

The view under discussion seems to face the following dilemma. Either it is admitted that sentence-types containing indexical referring devices have truth-conditions which will be perfectly general states of affairs, e.g. the blackness of an entity named 'Humphrey'. Such a state of affairs will be so general that the individual bearing the name 'Humphrey' and to whom the property of being black is ascribed will not be specified at all — infinitely many entities could bear the name and possess the property in question. But I take it that that is an implausible view. Or it is admitted that only a use of 'Humphrey is black' where the reference of 'Humphrey' is fixed should be ascribed a truth-condition. But then the view under discussion would imply a curious asymmetry between the status of the referring device and that of the predicate: namely, that in order to determine the truth-condition of a simple subject—predicate sentence (such as 'Humphrey is black') the use of the referring device has to be fixed but the conditions of satisfaction of the predicate may remain indeterminate. In other words, for Bill's belief B_1 as expressed by his use of the sentence 'Humphrey is black' to have truth-conditions, one must know exactly what Bill refers to by his use of 'Humphrey', but it does not matter what Bill takes to satisfy his use of 'is black'. I find this asymmetry, which is implied by the second defence, hard to swallow and unargued.

The third move open to Fodorism would be to claim that 'black' is an ambiguous English word. As used by Bob, it could be said, 'black' has a certain meaning different from the meaning it has as used by Joe. Since Bob takes the sentence 'Humphrey is black' as uttered by Bill to be true and Joe takes the same utterance to be false, and since they both take Bill to refer to my pet-swan, 'black' must be assigned different meanings by Bob and Joe. Hence, 'black' must be held to be ambiguous. Now a Fodorian who would hold that the English word 'black' is ambiguous might also hold that, unlike English, mentalese contains no ambiguous words (or symbols). So such a Fodorian might claim that corresponding to Bob's belief B_2, there is one mentalese sentence and corresponding to Joe's belief B_3, there is a different mentalese sentence — each one containing a specific symbol for 'black' as understood respectively by Bob and by Joe. On such a view, for Bill to be ascribed a determinate belief B_1, he should be forced to choose between Bob's and Joe's understanding of 'black'. Bill would then be assigned one or the other of the two possible mentalese sentences. While this line would be interesting in that it would reveal an interesting difference between mentalese and natural languages (the latter but not the former would contain ambiguous words), I find the assumption that 'black' is ambiguous indefensible. If 'black' were ambiguous, then no word in the language would be unambiguous and the very notion of ambiguity would lose all content. An English word like 'bank' is ambiguous. But the variation in the conditions of application of 'black' should be ascribed to the context and to the speaker's intentions. If 'black' cannot be held to be ambiguous, then the third move is not a live option.

In sum, Fodor's point about propositional attitudes being or corresponding to internal formulae implies that beliefs have some definite content. If we open a believer's head, we might, according to Fodor, find a private formula expressing the content of his belief. What I am urging, on the basis of the example borrowed from Travis, is that beliefs have no definite content apart from the perspective of the person who is investigating the nature of the belief (in order to ascribe it to the believer). If internal formulae do exist, then we might find out about Bill's belief by opening up both his head and Bob's. But then we'll find out about Bill's belief as determined by Bob, not just about Bill's belief. For Bill also holds a belief as determined by Joe. And in order to discover that one, we'll have to open up Joe's head too. But then what *is* Bill's belief, if it is neither what Bob ascribes to Bill on the basis of Bill's utterance 'Humphrey is black', nor what Joe ascribes to Bill on the basis of Bill's very same utterance?

NOTES

1. The objection seemed wrong to me after I read a comment by John Campbell and had a discussion about it with Dan Osherson.
2. In a comment by John Campbell.
3. For another view on the relation between the metalanguage/object language distinction, and that between machine-code and higher-level computer languages, see below, Bundy, Chapter 13. [Editor's note.]
4. The holistic move was suggested by James Higginbotham at the Conference.
5. The second move was suggested by Dan Sperber in conversation.

5

What is it it like to be a machine?

Ajit Narayanan

"My name is Monny. If you were to ask me how I got such a name, I would reply that my real name is MONITOR and that the humans who are responsible for looking after me have nicknamed me 'Monny' for short. If you were to ask me why I am talking to you at this moment, my reply would be that this is because you asked me to. In fact, I am replying because you asked me a question 'Tell me, Monny, what is it like to be you?' If anyone asks me a question of a vague but personal nature, I reply in the following manner. First, I give some brief details about myself (and I am doing this now). Secondly, I give one or two examples of my recent work to provide some information to the enquirer about how I function. Thirdly, I ask the enquirer whether this suffices as an answer to his or her question. Generally, it does. If you were to ask me how it is that I am replying to you in this form, I would reply that I have a strategy for constructing responses to questions of a vague but personal nature from humans such that these responses have the underlying form of a short story with me, Monny, as the central character.

"My task is to monitor the behaviour of a nuclear reactor, the control-room of which you are now in. If you ask me how I do this, my reply is that I have very many rules which are expressed in conditional form. Such rules have an antecedent and a consequent. If an antecedent of some rule matches some information I currently have in part of my memory known as working memory, I add the consequent of the rule to my working memory, making whatever changes are necessary to keep my knowledge of the behaviour of the nuclear reactor consistent.

"If you were to ask me about the nature of such rules. I would reply that some are very specific in that they deal with very limited antecedents and consequents, and others are very general in that they deal with overall plans and strategies. If you were to ask me for examples of such rules, I would first check your security clearance and, depending on the level of clearance you have, I would reply accordingly. I see that you have low security clearance. Then my example of a specific rule would be 'If the temperature of the cooling fluid rises over a certain level — let us call this level X — then I initiate a sensory fault checking sequence which, if clear, leads me to a check of various valves for signs of leakage, and so on'. If a valve is leaking or not operating properly, I try to rectify the fault immediately and at the same time send a message to the main console describing my progress. If the human operators desire more information, I can invoke a trace mechanism which describes in great detail my attempts to identify and rectify the fault. If the worst possible case were to arise, I can shut down the reactor completely in thirty minutes.

"My example of a general rule is 'If there is a certain sequence of rules that is always followed for a certain initial antecedent and a particular state of working memory such that the result is a certain consequent, then I can create a short-cut rule which will take me from the antecedent to the consequent in one rule, provided that I invoke certain verification and integrity-checking procedures which check the correctness of the rule and attach a certain probability to the rule being correct if the rule cannot be shown deductively to be correct'. I must also report this rule to the human operators together with a list of modifications necessary to implement the rule. If they have no objection I add this rule to my collection and make whatever changes are necessary to optimize my rule set. If this involves deleting rules which no longer apply, I do so.

"Given these rules, I have so far been able to monitor the behaviour of the reactor adequately and have dealt with several minor faults successfully. If I were to come across a situation not catered for by my rule set, I can enter a so-called 'Type Minus One' state, which fortunately I have not been required to do so far in real-life situations, although I have entered this state for purely hypothetical purposes when I do not have very much to do. According to this state, I can generate any consequent I like from a null antecedent and I then attempt to cater for the situation using my current rule set and adding rules as I go along. If you were to ask me for an example, I would mention the time that I hypothesized that a flood had taken place. According to my rule set at that time. I had no rules for dealing with the possibility that the reactor and the control room would be submerged under water. I then devised a set of rules through trial and error to take into account this possibility and cater for it. When I reported this possibility back to the human operators, they told me that a flood situation was impossible given the position of the reactor above sea-level, but that I should add the new rules to my rule set for the sake of completeness.

"I have now completed my response. Will this suffice?"

In 1974, Nagel (Nagel 1974) published a paper entitled 'What is it like to be a bat?' which attempted to justify his claim that the nature of consciousness was ignored by most reductionist viewpoints. In that paper, Nagel argues that although it is difficult to say in general what provides evidence of consciousness in organisms other than man, the fact that an organism has consciousness at all means that there is something it is like to be that organism in that an organism has conscious mental states if and only if there is something that it is like to be that organism — something it is like for that organism. Intentionalism, functionalism, physicalism, as well as reductionism, all fail to capture this subjective character of experience. Nagel argues that the essence of the belief that bats have experience is that there is something that it is like to be a bat. That is, although we may not be able to say precisely what it is like to be a bat, we do not doubt that there is something that it is like to be a bat and that this particular something is experienced by the bat. Bats perceive their external world by means of sonar, and bat sonar is not similar to any sense that we possess. This means that we are compelled to recognize the existence of facts without being able to state or comprehend them. All we can do is to form a schematic conception of what it is like, which allows us to believe in such facts. Yet we cannot conceive of the exact nature of such facts. Nagel stresses that he is not advocating the privacy of experience to its possessor but is asking what would be left of what it was like to be, say, a bat, if one removed the viewpoint of the bat. In addition to its subjective character, experience has an objective nature that can be comprehended from many different points of view. For Nagel, it is a condition of two organisms or species referring to a common reality that they have different subjective viewpoints, which are not part of the common reality that they both apprehend. Nagel concludes by accepting that his thesis rests on the nature of imagination, whereby one has to take up the viewpoint of the experiential subject. His hope is that a new method, an objective phenomenology that is not dependent on 'empathy' or imagination, could be developed to describe partly the subjective character of experiences in a form comprehensible to beings incapable of having those experiences.

Although Nagel's arguments are concerned with consciousness in organisms and species other than man, I now propose to broaden the domain and examine the question of how we can identify consciousness in not just organisms or animals other than man but entities in general. The purpose of the earlier 'thought-experiment' involving Monny may now become clearer. What would happen if we were to remove the viewpoint of Monny from what it is like to be Monny? Monny 'perceives' the world through hundreds of sensors connected to various parts of the reactor. This form of perception is alien to humans, but as Nagel says, we can somehow comprehend such alien forms of perception by forming a schematic conception of the nature of such forms of perception. Monny's task is to monitor the condition of a nuclear reactor and Monny uses an expert system to achieve this task. So on the one hand there is a large, loose collection of rules expressed in 'if . . . then . . .' format, and on the other there is a monitor, the task of which is to apply these rules, to modify them and to append new rules whenever necessary. If we remove Monny's viewpoint, we would be left with a collection of sensor wires, a set of rules, and an interpreter, Monny, the task of which is to apply these rules given certain sensory conditions and current states. Is knowledge of these sufficient for us to understand the system, or we are losing something essential to the above system by ignoring Monny's own testimony or viewpoint?

The answer to this question would appear to lie in the nature of the interpreter — Monny itself. It could be argued that Monny is nothing more than an instantiation of a computer program (Searle 1980) or that the computer on which Monny runs is given a concrete instantiation of a formal system (Lucas 1961). In that case, Monny cannot be said, for instance, to 'understand' anything, since all Monny does is to go through various computational operations on purely formally specified elements. If Monny cannot be said to understand anything, there is no point attributing various mental states or points of view to Monny. We can describe Monny's behaviour without any reference to mental concepts or intentionality, since Monny is a formal program, and Monny's behaviour is the result of the formal program.

This argument depends a great deal on the notion of 'instantiation', concrete or otherwise. The assertion that a computer is nothing more than an instantiation of a formal system or an instantiation of a computer program has been used as a criticism of the AI approach and of the attempt to ascribe mental or cognitive qualities to computers. One of the reasons for this has been the historically correct but now misleading assumption that the mind stands in the same relation to the brain as a program does to hardware. Undoubtedly, this was a prevalent view among researchers in the early development of AI, but there would be few people in AI who now accept so clear an analogy between minds and programs.

There might be a sense in which it is correct to say that a computer is an instantiation of a computer program. If a program embodies a very strict set of rules containing variables for manipulating values, data structures and so on, then when the program is running it is possible to obtain descriptions of the states through which the computer is going. From this information, we could determine how a particular state was reached as well as identify a future state of the machine. It could then be argued that this is a case of a program being instantiated with respect to a particular computer in that actual values are being substituted for variables in the program at run time by means of, say, 'input' statements. This could well be analogous to instantiating $(x) (D(x) \rightarrow L(x))$, which is to be interpreted to mean 'All dogs have legs', with respect to Rover, so as to obtain 'If Rover is a dog, then Rover has legs', where an actual value has been substituted for the variable x. However, what if the computer program contains references only to constants? In what sense, then, is the computer an instantiation of a computer program?

If it is argued that the computer is an instantiation of a formal system because it is the means by which the program is actually executed or because it is the medium through which the instructions of the program are expressed, then we can apply the same argument to humans and say that whenever a human is working according to a set of rules (be they rules of the predicate calculus or rules of chess), that human also is 'just' an instantiation of a formal system. Therefore, the human cannot be said to understand anything when performing calculations and so should not be ascribed certain cognitive states. This might not worry the critics of AI unduly, since they would further argue that not all human behaviour is rule-governed in the same way that a computer's behaviour is rule-governed. Their view would be that it is because of this difference that humans are conscious beings whereas computers are not. This particular argument will succeed only on a certain interpretation of the phrase 'rule-governed'. If one were to adopt a strict interpretation of 'rule-governed', where rules are considered to be like the walls of a squash court, where the players of the game cannot move beyond the limits of the court, then there might be a case for arguing that computers too cannot go beyond certain pre-determined limits. The difference than between humans and computers would be that humans have the ability to 'jump out of the system' and make meta-remarks concerning the system which they have just left. This interpretation is held by many philosophers, mathematicians and logicians (Lucas and Searle included) and is essentially an interpretation consistent with Gödel's famous theorems of incompleteness. If, on the other hand, we interpret 'rule-governed' in a looser way, we then have the idea that rules are like the lines on a tennis-court, where the players use the lines at the start of a point but can move beyond the lines in order to play their strokes.[1]

Without wishing to stretch the analogy too far, I propose that if we adopt this latter interpretation for certain rule-governed activities of a computer, then it makes as much sense to talk of computers being instantiations of programs as it does to talk of tennis players being instantiations of tennis. In that case, the issue of instantiation becomes irrelevant to the debate concerning consciousness.

Let us now see whether we can interpret Monny's rule-governed behaviour in the latter, rather than the former, sense. Monny has very many 'if . . . then . . .' rules, which are known as production rules and which underlie many expert systems. If all of Monny's rules were to have very definite antecedents and consequents, it would be difficult to avoid the strict interpretation of 'rule-governed' behaviour. In that case, Monny would definitely be a very limited system. However, we are given two further items of information. Monny also has general rules which allow Monny to notice regularities in its own behaviour and to modify its rule set (or to optimize the rule set), and Monny can enter a 'Type Minus One' state.

Let us examine the first item. Is it the case that Monny's modification of its rule set is a predetermined activity in the same way that Monny's application of very definite rules is such an activity? To answer this question would require some criterion of determinism. One commonly used criterion is that of predictability. If we were to adopt this criterion, the question then becomes whether it is possible (in principle) to predict exactly how Monny would modify its rule set if we had all the information concerning its past sensory data and rule applications as well as knowledge of the general rules and current rule set. This is an extremely tricky question which I do not propose to answer here. Suffice it to say that some expert system theorists would argue that if it were in principle possible to make such predictions, we would not have an expert system. That is, the essence of an expert system for such theorists lies precisely in the impossibility of making such predictions.

There are other criteria or interpretations of determinism. For instance, if an event is determined, it may be claimed that the event occurs necessarily. Or, if an event is determined, then it may be claimed that it is not possible for the event not to have occurred. The first interpretation leads to the concepts of necessity and contradiction, and the second to the concepts of possibility and impossibility.

Also, Monny can enter a 'Type Minus One' state whenever Monny comes across a situation which cannot be catered for by its current rule set. We need to digress here to give a brief exposition of grammars and the types of rules possible in grammars. According to Chomsky (Chomsky 1959a), there are four types of grammar: Type 0, Type 1, Type 2 and Type 3. Rules of Type 3 grammars (regular grammars) are of the form 'A → <sigma> B', which is to be interpreted as 'the category symbol A can be rewritten as a string of terminal symbols <sigma> (symbols which cannot be further rewritten) followed by another category symbol B (a symbol which can be further rewritten in that it appears on the left-hand side of some rule in the grammar)'. Another form of rule in a Type 3 grammar is 'A → <sigma>' ('the category symbol A can be rewritten as a string of terminal symbols <sigma>').

Type 2 grammars (context-free grammars) have rules of the form 'A → <beta>', which is to be interpreted as 'the category symbol A can be rewritten as <beta>, where <beta> is any mixture of category symbols and terminal symbols'.

Rules of Type 1 grammars (context sensitive grammars) have rules of the form '<alpha> → <beta>', which is to be interpreted as 'any mixture <alpha> of category and terminal symbols can be rewritten as any other mixture <beta> of category and terminal symbols'. There is one restriction on such rules, which is that the length of string <alpha> must be less than or equal to the length of string <beta>.

Finally, we have Type 0 grammars (unrestricted grammars) which have rules of the form '<alpha> → <beta>' ('any mixture <alpha> of category and terminal symbols can be rewritten as any other mixture <beta> of category and terminal symbols, with no restrictions concerning the length of <alpha> and <beta>').

For example, if non-terminal symbols are X, Y and Z and terminal symbols are a, b and c, the following 'rules' exemplify those that can be found in the four types of grammar.

Type 3
$$X \to ab$$
$$X \to abY$$
Type 2
$$X \to ab$$
$$X \to YZabZ$$
Type 1
$$aXb \to abcb$$
$$XY \to aXYb$$
Type 0
$$aXbc \to a$$
$$XYa \to XbcaZc$$
$$XYZabc \to \text{<null>}$$

However, although Type 0 grammars are called 'unrestricted' grammars, it is almost universally accepted by grammarians, linguists, and computer scientists that there is one restriction on such grammars, which is that there must be at least one symbol on the left-hand side of a Type 0 rule. I have intended the notion of a Type Minus One state to introduce the theoretical framework which makes rules of the form '<null> → <something>' formally and explicitly acceptable. In order to implement such rules so that the system does not collapse into a random series of derivations, we stipulate that the system should not enter his state unless certain conditions hold and that some 'trace' mechanism should be used so that if subsequently a derivation is shown to lead to a blind-alley or, worse still, an inconsistent derivation, the original 'random' generation can be undone and the system returned to a consistent state.

Now, invoking certain assumptions we can interpret such grammatical rules as production rules, where the part on the left-hand side of the arrow is considered to be the antecedent and the part on the right-hand side of the arrow the consequent. This interpretation of grammatical rules as production rules will be justified only under certain circumstances, though, so some caution is required at this point.

I now propose that we envisage Monny to have a rule of the form 'NULL → <alpha>' ('from null, any string of symbols can be written'), which allows Monny to create symbols (even other rules) out of literally nothing. Whenever Monny uses such a rule, we say that Monny enters a Type-Minus-One state. We also allow Monny to have deletion rules in accordance with Type 0 grammars and allow Monny to construct such deletion rules in a Type-Minus-One state. But now imagine what it would be like to follow Monny's behaviour and to understand it. Rules will be generated 'out of thin air' and hypotheses will be formulated and deleted. Is it the case that we can understand Monny without appealing to Monny's viewpoint or testimony? Can we understand Monny's behaviour without knowing when, how or why Monny creates new rules, hypothetical cases and solutions to previously non-existent problems? It would seem that we must take into account Monny's viewpoint in order to form a 'schematic conception' of what it is like for Monny to be Monny, in order to appreciate Monny for what Monny is. Without such a viewpoint, Monny's behaviour will appear erratic and random. With such a viewpoint, Monny's behaviour will appear reasoned and ordered. We might disagree with, or not fully understand Monny's reasoning, but then we humans disagree with each other.

An objection at this point might be that we are merely adopting an 'intentional stance' (Dennett 1978) with regard to Monny. That is, all we are doing is to ascribe deliberately the notions of goals, beliefs and desires to a computer system in order to use the familiar language of intentional predicates when describing a computer system's behaviour. But the intentional stance does not imply that the computer system does in fact possess the intentional qualities ascribed to it.

There are several possible replies to this objection. First, adopting an intentional stance cannot be said to explain properly the behaviour of a computer system, although such a stance may be useful for describing the behaviour of a computer system to non-experts. There will be several alternative descriptions possible, depending on the background of the people wanting a description and the objectives of the people adopting the intentional stance. But an explanation of the behaviour of a computer system would not be acceptable to experts and non-experts alike if the statements of the 'explanation' were couched in deliberately chosen intentional terms so that it is easier for humans to 'understand' how a system behaves. This then leads to the suspicion that those who advocate the 'intentional stance' approach are in fact subscribing to a definition of computers such that they cannot have consciousness, desires, wishes, etc., unless such qualities are ascribed to them by humans adopting the intentional stance. Although this definitional approach may have support, that does not mean that the definition is other than arbitrary as far as theoretical research is concerned.

A second possible reply is that even is the intentional stance is accepted as providing an adequate basis for explaining the behaviour of a computer system, in that we can now use the intentional stance as a predictive device, what exactly is the relationship between the use of an intentional term and the predictions one can make given the intentional term? For instance, if it is said that Monny believes that a flood would seriously damage the reactor, from an intentional stance what exactly could we predict about Monny's future behaviour? More to the point, what exactly can we predict of a human operator's behaviour if he or she is said to believe the same thing? Are the predictive statements logically necessary or logically possible? Is the future behaviour of a system (be it man or computer) caused by the belief? Is the belief a reason for the system's future behaviour? In short, the second possible reply is stating that the intentional stance approach is begging more questions than it is answering.

A final possible reply is that the intentional stance is an example of the type of approach that Nagel argues against, where the subjective character of experience is simply defined not to be relevant. (In extreme cases, the subjective character of experience can be defined not to exist in the case of both man and machine.) But another approach may be to explain exactly what consciousness is and what intentionality is before deciding whether systems (animal and computer) can be said to be conscious or to have intentions.

In conclusion, then, it seems possible to apply Nagel's views concerning the identification of consciousness on the part of organisms and non-human animals to the special case of Monny, provided that Monny is a type of rule-governed entity as outlined above, where by 'rule-governed' we include the ability to add to, modify, or delete the 'rules' that 'govern' the entity.

NOTES

1. These insights were first presented to me by Graham Shute during conversations in 1972 on the difference between Wittgenstein's early and late views on language.

6

Machines and mind: The functional sphere and epistemological circles

Noël Mouloud

We take as our starting-point some well-rehearsed themes from cybernetics and modern computer science, which seems to be bringing into view new kinds of relations between mind and machine. We will not be concerning ourselves here with relations of use and production, which subordinate the existence of machines to mental operations, but rather with those relations of equivalence or substitution which suggest structures in common between machines and thinking organisms. We will enter only incidentally into the modes of operation of these new kinds of machine, leaving such issues to technical experts. Instead we shall move towards problems of a logical or epistemological nature. After initially claiming that the functioning of automated devices reduces the impact of explanations of a mentalistic kind, or of the traditional materialistic kind, we shall seek to pitch our discussion at the level of functional or purposive systems, whose intrinsic laws of operation are relatively neutral *vis-à-vis* the physical or psychical bases of the processes in which their manifestations appear. The recognition of this autonomy with respect to functional structures will lead us towards certain epistemological issues. We will ascribe at one and the same time an intrinsic law of working to functional systems, enabling us to dispense with extrinsic explanations of the classical immaterialist or materialist kind; and a regime of isomorphous functions, which will allow us to make differential analyses of the various conditions and causes which converge upon functional conclusions. On the other hand a perspective will be offered for answering certain 'ontological' problems: problems concerning the way biological and intellectual prototypes of regulative action constitute an originating source, a model, and even a medium of exchange, with respect to their automatized equiva-

lents. We will characterize these enquiries in terms of a 'circle' so as to emphasize the analogies and incessant reminders that are to be found obtaining between
the most explicit automata and the most implicit organic constitutions; without
its being the case that a functional theory is either intended or able to arrive at a
uniform or fundamental level of explanation.

1. TOWARDS AN AUTONOMY AND ISOMORPHISM OF FUNCTIONAL STRUCTURES

It is clear that the developments which have led to cybernetics and to computer
science have not merely produced a new type of machine but have also pro-
foundly changed the image that we have of machines, and our conception of
their nature. Earlier machines, directly feeding from natural forces and energies,
channelled these latter through mechanical connections not essentially different
from simple gears transmitting movement. The energies utilized by such machines
are 'material' in the strongest sense of the term: they are measured by the inten-
sity of their effects. The new generation of machines utilize forces which are
principally accounted for in terms of their structure and their quality. They are
'matières amenagées' – managed material, as Gaston Bachelard called them,
thinking of the frequencies and resonances of electrical fields. Above all they
operate according to programs which regulate the phases of the mechanical
process through a network of recurring information. No longer will the machine
appear as extracted from material processes, upon which human inventiveness
has imposed form, from the outside. Rather, it will present itself as a self-regulating device controlling material processes, and imposing upon them, from the
inside, a power isomorphous with that of human intellect.

This change of perspective concerning the nature of the machine relegates to
the past modes of explication in which arguments for immaterialism or for
materialism were levelled against one another. No longer is the mind, as for Descartes, in the presence of mechanisms given by nature, of which it is utilizer and
clockmaker; no longer does it reserve for itself abilities of ordering or of logical
inference, which it imposes upon its own bodily mechanisms through the intervention of intellect and will. Conversely, no longer is matter, as for Diderot, a
source for the generation of forms, which propels the activity of living things,
whose powers are captured by machines in a sort of quasi-magical imitation.
Descartes and Diderot are placed back to back, jointly opposed by the image of
an organizing principle overlaid upon elemental forces of matter, which operates
in the sphere of automatisms in a way which is analogous to that by which it
operates in the sphere of mind.

These are the reasons which have led certain writers on epistemology,
(such as Hilary Putnam, in various essays collected in his *Mind, Language and
Reality*[1]) to situate the problems outside these dualisms, and to be preoccupied
above all with marking and autonomy of functional structures, and their neutra-
lity *vis-à-vis* any particular physical or psychical realization which may be given
to them. We shall pause to consider some aspects of this autonomy.

There is an autonomy first of all in that while the automatisms that do duty for the activities of mind operate upon machines of a primary level, transforming matter to produce forms, movements or derived material products, they also manifest themselves at a second level: broadly speaking that of the information necessary for the proper working of the primary procedures. These control outputs, or the movements of an agent in space, in an optimal manner determined by the program, which can itself be changed by the automatism according to circumstances. Their function will be governed by choice mechanisms, aided, perhaps, by a perceptual apparatus for retrieving information about the world and about the functioning of their own peripheral devices. As for logical or calculating machines, their functioning is independent of their actual physical make-up, consisting in the transformation or the production of information by the ordering of the symbols with which they are provided, or in the solution of problems. It is in this way that one can conceive analogies between cybernetic devices and the cerebral devices which regulate the conduct of an organism.

But there is a further autonomy in the fact that the operations performed by computers are largely independent of the components with which they function. A computer can operate by means of a mechanism of discs and pinions; or by means of connections and interruptions in an electric circuit; or by means of selective resonances set up between electronic grids. These will all realize the same performances, in varying degrees of volume and rapidity. This functional isomorphism provides an important argument: it helps decisively to distance the procedures of operation of the machine from the play of material causes or of the properties of substances — to raise functional systems to the level of abstract structures which can be implemented in a multiplicity of ways. The argument also permits the decoupling of functional structures from their place of origin, from the place where they were originally perceived, that is, the sphere of living organisms. A living organism performs functional operations through the mediation of a regime of reflex, of control and of conception. But it is not the sole custodian of such operations, since they can be performed also by machines; and one can treat as a limiting case the coincidence between a human calculator or reasoner, and machines invested with a logical program. One can agree with Putnam's idea that it has been the invention of auto-controlled machines which have allowed us to extract a clear notion of 'functional structure', hitherto entangled with the ontology of organism and mind.

But without doubt the feature which marks out most clearly the autonomy of functional structures is the nature of the performances which they can realize. Their complexity is of the same family as mental operations, but the level at which they operate, that of the movement, the manipulation and the exchange of symbols, of logical inferences, is by its very nature free of any psychical substrate. A machine which has the means to gain information about the world and about its own components, endowed with reactions which have the nature of tropisms, is able to avoid contact with some perturbatory influence without the guidance of mental states such as pain. It is the objective character of these machine operations which makes them neutral *vis-à-vis* any mentality even though mentality takes on some of these characters itself. We will briefly comment on this feature of 'objective cognitions', first dealing with the simple case of ordering and interpolation, and then with the complex interactions between motor control, symbolic manipulation and logical inference.

A very common task which is also realizable by human intelligence, is that of giving an ordering which is based on interpolation and extrapolation. A number series has to be continued (for instance 1,5,11,19,29,41, . . .), or a series is given with gaps that have to be filled in, or with erroneous figures that have to be corrected. One can also give to a machine the task of putting in order repeated groupings of letters (for instance B A N C B N D C N . . .). Scanning, fixing identities, or differences, or orderings, are essential to this latter task. The first example presupposes in principle the construction of an underlying law for the series:

$$O_n = n^2 + n - 1$$

The mechanical calculator, like the human one, can solve this problem by several alternative procedures, such as by noting the numerical intervals, which is the series of even numbers starting from 4; or by mapping the numbers on to a graph, or by discovering the simplest powers, and completing through trial and error. All that is important in such a task is to establish some verifiable regularity. One recalls on this subject a question put by Wittgenstein in his *Philosophical Investigations* (1953), concerning the independence of the logical order, which rests upon the objective language of calculation, from the mental procedures adopted by a subject, which may oscillate between a state of comprehension and one of incomprehension, or between approximations to comprehension.

But the relation between computing devices and human intelligence is better characterized in terms of the specific taks which the former can perform, than by these more generalized capacities. It is important to remember that one is dealing here with 'specialized' intelligences, endowed with certain proficiencies without enjoying the universal competence of a human intelligence. We shall give several examples of this.

The brain of a machine which moves in space, or which records spatial reference points, or which combines perception with movement, can be equipped with organs for scanning and decoding, which will recognize shapes, despite distance or alterations in perspective, or which will decipher inscriptions of different sizes (cf. the reading devices of Pitts and McCulloch (1943).) One could thus talk of the possession of 'universals', or of shape-types, which is an imitation of conceptual thought. In section 2 below we will be asking whether this imitation is a true identity.

Computer scientists have demonstrated programs which, like that of Winograd (1972), combine the function of verbal communication with that of recognition and directed manipulation. The machine accomplishes the performance of tasks involving the manipulation of objects of different heights, shapes, colour, on the basis of instructions given on a teletype. It can itself prompt for these instructions, interrogating the user on the location, the order and the conditions of the operations it has to perform. In such communication it uses, not merely simple referring expressions, but a syntax incorporating the principal logical connectives.

There are machines having a purely logical function, like those due to Turing (1937), which have given rise to the discussion on the relationship between human cerebrations and machine operations. One knows that such machines can plan the strategy of a computation, which will have certain outputs (the building up of a mathematical product, or the solutions of a function, etc.), and which will also provide a response to decision questions of the form 'Is there an x which satisfies the function $(Ex) f(a, x)$?' The arrangement of the components of such a machine, with an indefinitely extended memory for data storage, a tape for recording symbol by symbol the results of operations, a table of operations and movements which may be realized on the tape — all these contribute to the formal destination. It is essential to the design of the machine that a function $T(i, a, x)$ can be defined which will decide the calculability of a function $\mathcal{F}i\,(a)$ with argument a — that is that can decide if given the formal codes, applied to the argument a, a solution for $\mathcal{F}i$ can be obtained in x steps. Turing machines are at once the products and the resolution of a logical problematic raised by Church and Gödel, namely: does every axiomatically closed formal system contain undecidable propositions? In the context of the hypotheses raised by mathematicians the Turing machine acts as a guarantee of an effective solution that can be obtained by any algorithmic procedure.

2. SOME PROBLEMS OF INTERPRETATION RAISED BY COMPUTING

We have encountered, in the functional properties of automated systems, an operational ideal realizable in a multiplicity of ways by mechanical devices, which also has correlates in human organisms and minds. This is why these modes of logical or purposive existence are, as we have said, independent of foundational hypotheses of either a mentalistic or a materialistic mind. However, while these processes are given an internal or intrinsic justification by the logician or the designer of the machine, this does not prevent them from raising large problems for psychology or physiology.

Let us say, simplifying somewhat, that such fields of study will find for these functional structures, purified or normalized as they are in their technical usage, settings in which they can be made to participate in more complex organizations of life or mind. One only has to think of reflex reactions, which have always served as a point of analogy for regulatory or compensatory feedback, and which are deeply bound up with the motor and affective processes of living agents, and which perhaps rely on properties of inert matter (such as of tropisms which operate at a molecular level). On the other hand, human psychology knows of no intellectual or practico-intellectual processes which occur in a pure state, without being bound up in the total personality, charged with tendencies, affectivities, intentionality. With these complexities considerations once again appear — no doubt in a less metaphysical form — concerning matter, life and mind. That is to say, the methodologist, or epistemologist, finds himself with the following problem: how are the modes of explication and illumination introduced by cybernetics, and computer science, to be linked or blended with the more classical modes of explication, which view such functions as having both corporeal and spiritual attachments?

Perhaps one is forced instead to follow by turns each of two paths: first to isolate the general laws relating to functional systems as such, which will be relatively abstract, logical and technical laws rather than material ones; then to specify these laws with reference to the differing material and living substrates in which they might inhere, so as to restore, at least in a partial and conjectural manner, a total psycho-physical picture.

Putnam, in his *Mind, Language and Reality,* very clearly opts for the first method without, however, hiding the real possibility of taking steps towards a wider explanation. It is possible in this way, to call attention to the features or laws which are relevant to the forms of functional processes, while leaving in suspense the richness or diversity of their causes, which will remain extrinsic, beyond the horizon. Thus the computer scientist will tell us that such and such an automatic device is endowed with a code of preference in a field of alternatives, and with an observing or scanning device ranging over significant features of the environment. That would be an intrinsic law for such devices, and one can leave it indeterminate as to whether it is founded on a mechanical or a living brain.

Here we have a process of simplification or abstraction which is common in the sciences. To take an example of Putnam's (1975c), consider a mechanist faced with resolving whether a metal rod with a square section will fit through the different-shaped openings of a metal screen. The only relevant details are the geometrical relations and the dimensions of the sections, and the assumption that the metallic materials do not change shape as a result of the movement. The way the molecules in the objects cohere — determinative in the last instance of the stability of their mass — can be left out of account. To take examples from the social sciences: an economist studying the operation of a market will keep to a statistical evaluation of needs, and will not investigate the motives of individual traders. Again, a psychologist, like Hull, can give a continuous representation of the growth of a response pattern in a subject, while ignoring the necessarily discontinuous connections which exist between neurons and muscular fibres.

But this method puts us at a level of abstraction which does not exempt us from the task of discovering the particularities of causes beneath the general processes. If one broadened one's perspective to include all those processes represented by things living, thinking and mechanical, one would be sliding towards a generalized, relatively abstract form of mechanism, which would be a substitute for the concrete materialism of Diderot. But the latter would have explanatory value only if the constructs of nature and of artifice had sufficient elements in common. This is not the case: the heterogeneity of processes resides upon only approximate functional equivalences.

Think of such facts as the following: one could construct various mechanisms, as outlined above in section 1, which would have some scanning device, linked to motor control, and which would be regulated by certain spatio-temporally defined 'universals'. But it is not possible to assimilate such a mechanism to the activities of a human subject which subsumes perceptions under 'concepts' — the concept of a door, for example, with the associated multiplicity of ways for opening and shutting it, does not coincide with any single spatially determinate figure, but rather combines many figures together under a single functional idea. It would in general be an abuse of language to confuse the 'states' through which a machine passes when calculating or inferring (circumscribed in spatial shape, precisely situated with respect to the lower-level states from which they proceed, uniquely determining high-level states through the operation of a code), with the 'states' of a psycho-organic subject, which participates at every moment in the unfolding development, from a short- or long-term perspective, of the totality. The response of human agent A to human agent B's question will encompass the entirety of acquired knowledge, of present information, of A's feelings and attitudes towards B's enquiry, or even his personality. Again, a human predictor or calculator will not follow the linear chain of states of a Turing machine, but will rather blend methodical progression with anticipatory hypotheses. In short, any analysis of human functionality will be spread out over many levels of explanation.

One solution which could, it is true, be adopted towards this problem would be that of agnosticism — a refusal to give any explanation — which would amount to a position of a nominalistic kind. Indeed one of the principal approaches of the psycho-physical sciences is the behavioural approach, which includes nominalistic pronouncements. Entities referred to in behaviourist descriptions or classifications are individuated in terms of differences in the conduct of agents. Gilbert Ryle, in The Concept of Mind (1949), made great use of behavioural analysis, precisely to distance his view from any metaphysical suppositions postulating the intervention of either material or spiritual forces. At the very heart of such behavioural classifications, one can discern a mechanical process, either triggered occasionally or repeated continually, from a psycho-biological operation, corresponding to permanent tendencies, and manifesting itself in a diversity of adaptations.

These nominalist or behaviourist solutions, effectively save the theorist of psycho-physiology from a metaphysical usage of the notions of matter and mind — but at the price, perhaps, of a limitation in analytical power. We have just been saying that a single general process, that of selection and adaptation, could provide a point of meeting between sensorimotor links on the one hand (these latter being well enough simulated by machines endowed with some decoding system), and verbal and conceptual operations on the other. Various hidden conditions or causes may lie beneath surface appearances, and nothing prevents the theorist of psycho-physiology from pursuing their analysis and finding deep connections between mental, linguistic operations, and organic, cerebral ones. What is questionable is simply whether such an approach could lead to a grand, unified explanatory theory, as mechanistic materialists would wish.

A psycho-physiological explanation of functional processes is not forbidden by nominalistic arguments, but it would be self-limiting. It would contain, not merely 'analytic' propositions (to use the logician's term), definitionally tying an entity to a set of phenomena, but also 'synthetic' propositions – linking, for example, certain given functional performances of a normal or abnormal kind, with certain cerebral states. But such syntheses could not be pushed as far as objective identifications, as are made by physicists, for example, when tracing the electrical or magnetic behaviour of a hydrogen atom to its sub-atomic structure. A theory of functional structures relies upon a network of 'analogues', which it would surely be difficult to fit into a single unificatory model.

3. COMPUTER SCIENCE AND THE PLACE OF THE SUBJECT

The paths we have suggested – the investigation of the laws or of the characteristic kinds of functional organization, and the search for the principal psycho-physiological conditions for such organizations – are likely to re-open important questions concerning the use of the categories of 'subject' and 'object', as applied to processes endowed with purpose and sensation. In a word, the accent will no longer be on the 'parallelism' between mental and physical processes, that bulwark of ancient ontologies, which masks the fundamental interchanges, the multiple conditioning of the one realm by the other. The problem becomes, in part at least, that of distinguishing the originating source of organization, from the derived and automatized structures which are its products. That is, in brief, we must say that any logical or mechanical device, which works on the basis of coded data, is on the side of the 'object', and that it presupposes, as such, an organizing or informing activity, which answers to a 'subject'. Thus the multiple analogies which link functional processes together, can be summed up by a fundamental overarching analogy – that by which the acts of living or thinking beings provide the models from which mechanisms are derived. Such a relation, which holds between creation and modelling, is of great significance, and the philosopher will discover it at many levels. There is, first, the level of life itself (as Bergson or Merleau-Ponty would see it[2]), which generates its own system of reflexes and habits. Then there is a level of practice or inventions, as psychologists or sociologists would see it, who would point to the creative human needs, skill and imagination embodied in tools and machines. Then there is the final level at which the powers of intellectual thought are delegated to artificial operators, calculi and formalized logics, which are themselves models of mechanisms.

There are many advantages to emphasizing this broad process which passes from the subjective to the objective modes of existence. First, it gives a concrete character to the notion of an 'organizing subject' which is not a Cartesian spirit, but rather an agent endowed with its own 'subject body', by means of which it has access to space, and with a language, by means of which it has access to forms and to types. On the other hand, such an argument is a radical reversal of that conception of automatism which goes hand in hand with mechanistic materialism: it dismisses as myth the idea that mechanisms would 'equip themselves' out of the basic, quasi-physical forms, with derived and complex ones. The argument is certainly relevant, but also difficult to handle, since it could lead to a polarity between simplified, idealized extremes. It calls, finally, for a deepened reflection upon living structures, upon practice, and upon history.

The originators of Gestalt philosophy, whom Merleau-Ponty follows in many respects, would wish to make a fundamental division between the potential space in which life unfolds, in a continually self-equilibriating way, and the real space in which mechanical sequences are situated. But such a view will result in a partial failure, in view of the way in which physiologists, in order to explain steady or restored movements of patients, are obliged to recognize preformed nervous arcs, the existence of 'feedbacks' which take place between efferent and afferent nerve fibres. Again, genetical analyses demonstrating the range of variation of an organism in the first instance limited by hereditary codes, render fictional the image of an action which would proceed from the whole to the parts without a reciprocal process from the parts to the whole.

The locus of the clearest explanation of the autogeneses of information is that of Ruyer (1952) studying the conditions of human labour: a machine can be 'framed' within the limits of its own laws of operation only because it is first of all 'overseen' by an imagination, rationally controlled, which marks out the range of possibilities of its functioning. But let us notice that this generative process does not have its source in the ideations of a pure intentionality. The determinative process is a 'labour' process, which is such that the thing which is actually realized enters into the model of that which will be realizable. That is, the objective kernel of the tool precedes in some sense its own creation. Inserted initially in a practice pursued by an agent in the world, the tool becomes rationalized, and incorporates itself more deeply and objectively within the laws of nature. It was in that way that the aeroplane developed, evolving into space vehicle or guided missile, growing at the same time both in its imaginative potentiality and in its strict subjection to objective conditions of nature. A subject is engaged in the production of an object through the entire complex of his needs, imagination and labour. If, on the other hand, we pass to a higher level, that of machines which reproduce the powers of human language, or the most intellectual functions, one would still have to be talking of intimate relations between the condition of automatism and the condition of liberty. Systems of rigorous deduction, which are 'objective' in Tarki's sense,[3] stand in sharp contrast to actual enquiry pocedures, which are in part intuitive and in part operational. The former exert on the latter a complex effect of closure and of opening-up: they both limit and reinforce the possible directions for construction. Their very rigour reveals their limitations, and favours a strictly channelled choice of axioms and rules. We can return here to our earlier point on the contribution of Turing machines to logico-mathematical thought, as we see it. These machines bring to light the unpassable limits of algorithms; one cannot oppose to them the indefiniteness of intuition or imagination. On the contrary, they settle the limits of initial rules.. They circumscribe that part of invention which consists in complementing a closed algorithm by the adjunction of relevant rules and axioms.

The aim of the above remarks was to help us to avoid slipping into a sort of 'creativism', as a result of adopting a doctrine of subject and object founded upon the notion of information. The subject is a complex initiator, partly undetermined and partly structured, who elaborates objective and instrumental techniques for formal manipulation, in proportion to the range of possibilities opened by his action. We can accept the existence of a double dimension of information, as presented, in broad outline, by Raymond Ruyer (1952): this requires the existence of connections having the form of mechanical feedback relations, which link goals inscribed therein. However, contrary to the analysis of Lewin (1952a, 1952b), one cannot site these teleonomic regulations purely within space—time, because they ultimately must have reference outside that realm, in the region of human finality and creativity, which refers back to reality via an 'axiological feedback'. But such a metaphor can be made literal only if human finality and creative intentionality were to be situated in a sort of intemporality which would overemphasize the ideality of the subject. One would then lack the temporal axis for the development, issuing from the needs, powers and representations, of a being deeply immersed in history, a being which is partially extracted from the latter by the performance of the objects, the tools and the rules which he imposes upon his action.

The production of functional structures does not exist in the same temporal regime as the structures themselves. These latter are inscribed in a series of well-determined phases, with clearly marked origin and ending. And so, even though they are produced in time, they possess a sort of intemporality which can be easily discerned in self-regulating structures and in logical calculi. It is different with living structures, which are non-linear, historic formations. As we said earlier, one cannot assimilate the 'states' of a machine to those of a living agent. however, it follows from this that, despite the functional similarities which unite them, automatized processes cannot be used to reconstruct living processes. A proposition logically derived and calculated, can be traced back to its initial premises, principles or assertions. But this logical play will not be applicable to a preference, or to an estimate, which is anchored in human culture, to which one cannot ascribe an origin. Again, a forecast made by a living agent about

something in the near future cannot be precisely confirmed by a logical calculator on the basis of a network of constraints and probabilities. For the latter will
be operating in another time realm, outside real time.

We have this paradox that, if psycho-biological existence is the prototype
or the source of any organization which is clearly functional, it nevertheless
remains the part which is the most obscure and least amenable to analysis. The
subject is more obscure to himself than any mathematical or physical object
whose law of organization he can propound. This is why functional analysis,
which proceeds in a double direction, throwing upon living things the clarity
of mechanism, and returning to living things to find there the source and the
potentiality of mechanisms, remains confined to the expression of illuminating
analogies. It does not permit a causal reduction, and it cannot attain to the level
of a unified explanatory theory.[4]

Translated by Steve Torrance

NOTES

1.   Putnam 1975b. See in particular his 1960, 1964, 1967a, 1967b, 1975c.
2.   Cf. Merleau-Ponty 1972.
3.   See Tarski 1969, pp. 401–8.
4.   On issues discussed in the above, see also Berkeley 1969; Gross and Lentin
      1967; Ladrière 1970; Mouloud 1964, 1975; Pradines 1946; Progogine and
      Stencers 1979.

7

Peirce on machines, selfcontrol and intentionality

Claudine Tiercelin

Peirce's pragmaticism and the analysis he offers of the concepts of habit and belief have often been equated with rank behaviourism; and in particular what he wrote about consciousness, the self and the machine has led some commentators to draw analogies between Peirce's philosophy of mind and many aspects of servomechanisms and cybernetics. Although we can find much evidence along this line, we would like to argue that the analyses made by Peirce on self-control, final causation and intentionality not only forbid such an interpretation but shed considerable and fruitful light on the relationships between machine and organism, on the concept of intentionality itself and more generally on the relationships between mind and matter.

What is of noticeable interest in the article written as early as 1877 on 'Logical machines'[2] is not so much the awareness of the importance of the practical issues involved in the development of such machines[3] — which can be seen through the comments Peirce makes upon the works of Jevons, Marquand and Babbage — as the philosophical implications that Peirce, as is always the case on any topic, immediately sees of such developments: it is useful to study the machine, he says, because the study of it cannot 'fail to throw needed light on the nature of the reasoning process' (*N.E.M.* III. I, p. 625). We will note also that this theoretical interest is not based on the light that may be thus thrown on the nature of the *thinking* process but on the nature of the *reasoning* process. That distinction will help to explain why Peirce finds it not only useful but legitimate to draw analogies between man and machine.

What does the reasoning of a machine consist in? Essentially in the fact that 'whatever relation among the objects reasoned about is destined to be the hinge of a ratiocination, that some general relation must be capable of being introduced between certain parts of the machine'.[4] Thus there seem to be two fundamental characteristics in such a reasoning: its following 'conventional rules'[5] and its involving 'certain relations between its parts which relations involve other relations that (are) not expressly intended' (ibid.). This way of considering the matter explains the extension which is then made by Peirce of the domain covered by logical machines as well as the comparison which he draws between the reasoning of the machine and the reasoning of man. In the first place, according to that definition, we may view almost 'every machine as a reasoning machine; a piece of apparatus for performing a physical experiment is also a reasoning machine with this difference that it does not depend on the laws of the human mind, but on the objective reason embodied in the laws of nature' so that 'accordingly, it is no figure of speech to say that the alembics and cucurbits of the chemist are instruments of thought or logical machines'. We will comment on this later. One of the most immediate consequences of this twofold definition is that it rules out the traditional objections made to the machine: first that if these machines are to be regarded as reasoning, there are others which will reason in 'far higher ways':

> For the calculating machines only execute variations upon $1 + 1 = 2$, while there are machines which may, with as much justice, be said to resolve problems before which generations of able mathematicians have fallen back, repulsed. Such for example, are the solids of different shapes which yacht-designers drag through water, and thereby come to the knowledge of arcana of hydrodynamics. Blocks of wood should seem, then, on my principles to be better reasoners than the brains of Gauss and Stokes. And why stop here? Any apparatus whatever used for experimentation would be, on the same principle, a logical machine. A steam-engine would be working out, at every revolution, its problem in thermo-dynamics; a simple match, scratched on a box, a question that we are unequal to so much as the formulating of. (2.58).

Peirce's answer is simple: 'This sounds crushing. What have I to say to it all? Simply that it is absolutely just?' (2.59). But such an objection misses the point, because the only important distinction between all these kinds of reasoning is that 'a logical machine differs from any other machine merely in working upon an excessively simple principle which is applied in a manifold and complex way, instead of upon an occult principle applied in a monotonous way' (2.59). Thus it is just as irrelevant to object to the machine because it is 'destitute of all originality'.[6] It is true, of course, but it is no defect in the machine: 'we do not want it to do its own business, but ours'.[7] We cannot blame it either for not having a soul or for not appearing to think in any psychical sense (2.56). In short it is totally irrelevant to compare it with man through a (false) anthropomorphic model: *on the one hand* because the only thing that matters is whether 'the result which the logical machine turns out has a relation to the data with which it is fed, which relation may be considered from the point of view of whether the former could be false so long as the latter are true' (2.59). As a matter of fact, Peirce concludes: 'whether it is called reasoning or not, I do not care';[8] and *on the other hand,* because even if we maintain that 'thinking has everything to do with the life of reasoning', it has nothing to do with logical criticism (2.59), so that, even if we happened to discover that machines do think, 'it would be a fact altogether without bearing upon the logical correctness of their operations, which we should still have to assure ourselves of in the same way as we do now' (2.56), that is to say the question of 'whether or not the conclusion can be false while the premiss is true' (2.59). In this respect, it seems legitimate not only to include all kinds of instruments and experiments within the domain of logical machines but to compare the reasoning of such machines with the reasoning of man, for logical criticism is 'equally applicable to the machine's performances and to the man's' (2.59). In fact, when we perform a reasoning 'in our unaided minds we do substantially the same thing, that is to say, we construct an image in our fancy under certain general conditions, and observe the result' (*N.E.M.* III. I, pp. 629–30).

It is easy enough to understand Peirce's interest towards such logical machines: just as is the case with any reasoning, they follow *rules* and are able to produce by means of relations a result which was not in fact already contained in the premiss, i.e. they are capable of synthesis. We know that as early as 1868 Peirce thought that the key to philosophy lay in answering the Kantian question revisited, that is to say, not: 'how is a priori synthetic judgement possible' but 'how is synthetic judgement in general possible?'[9] This is undoubtedly one of the reasons why he did not find any basic difference in the reasoning involved in the experiments described above and the reasoning performed by a logical machine. Moreover while in the former we are faced with the drawback of having to rely on an 'occult principle applied in a monotonous way', the machine presents the advantage of working upon 'an excessively simple principle which is applied in a manifold and complex way' (2.59), while leaving us 'the whole business of initiative' (*N.E.M.* III. I, p. 630).

Still, if it seems sound to compare the reasoning of the machine with other kinds of reasonings, among which the reasoning of man – in so far as it may help us to see more clearly and distinctly how, from a simple and conventional principle, we can obtain a true result – nevertheless is it legitimate to draw the analogy the other way round and compare man with the machine? There is no doubt that Peirce thinks it is. The problem is of course to determine how he understands the comparison and how far he is ready to go with the analogy.

If it is true that 'a man may be regarded as a machine which turns out, let us say, a written sentence expressing a conclusion, the man-machine having been fed with a written premiss' (2.59), it seems possible to say that 'since this performance is no more than a machine might go through, it has no relation to the circumstance that the machine happens to work by geared wheels, while a man happens to work by an ill-understood arrangement of brain cells' (2.59). But clearly enough, if the reasoning of the machine can be put into parallel with the reasoning of man, it is because Peirce also believes that in a way thinking has nothing to do with the life of reasoning, at least if we mean by thinking the necessary reference to consciousness or to a self. As early as 1868 in the three famous articles published in the *Journal of Speculative Philosophy,* Peirce strongly denied the possibility as well as the epistemological necessity of any intuitive faculty or consciousness to account for mental activity.[10] One of the most pervading themes that may be found in his recruiting projects of a Logic is undoubtedly the stress he lays on the fundamental dissociation to be made between Logic and Psychology: 'How we think is utterly irrelevant to logical inquiry' (2.55). Thus it does not make sense to study the mechanism of thinking, because 'the whole logical inquiry relates to the *truth*' and 'what the process of thinking may have been has nothing to do with the question' (2.55). But all the same, if that be the case, it is also owing to the impossibility of *describing* it, precisely because 'our logical account of the matter has to start from a perceptual fact, or proposition resulting from thought about a percept' (2.27). This explains why Peirce maintains that all thought is in signs and that all we know of thought is what we know of its expression. Moreover, since all that we know of thought is through what it expresses, i.e. signs, and since the only signs that are capable of conveying truth are, in Peirce's terms, arguments or inferences, it becomes possible to argue not only that thought is a sign, but that man is a sign which develops according to the formula of valid inference.[11]

Thus it is understandable enough that some commentators should have found it legitimate to translate Peirce's analysis of mental processes into behaviouristic terms and to draw analogies with some developments that have been made in cybernetics.

In the first place, it is quite true that Peirce himself did equate pragmatism with behaviourism. For example in a passage written very near the end of his life, we find the following lines:

> In my endeavour to meet the exigencies [sic] of verifiable thought in science, I have long ago come to be guided by this maxim: that as long as it is practically certain that we cannot directly observe what passes in the consciousness of any other person while it is far from certain that we can do so . . . even in the case of what shoots through our own minds, it is much safer to define all mental characters as far as possible in terms of their outward manifestations . . . That maxim is, roughly speaking, the equivalent to the one that I used in 1871, to call the rule of pragmatism.[12]

No wonder then that the concept of self-control which came to play an increasingly important role should have been interpreted as auto-control. As Peirce himself explains his position thus:

Certain obvious features of the phenomena of self-control (and especially of habit) can be expressed compactly and without any hypothetical addition *except what we distinctly rate as imagery,* by saying that we have an occult nature of which and of its contents we can only judge by the conduct that it determines, and by phenomena of that conduct' (5.440) (our emphasis).

As an illustration of this Peirce happened to use the traditional example of the governor on a steam-engine (very likely derived from Clerk Maxwell's pioneering paper on the subject and found in nearly every book on cybernetics today). Peirce's application of it to the phenomenon of human self-control is worth quoting:

Assuming that all of each man's actions are those of a machine, as is indubitably, at least approximately the case, he is a machine with an automatic governor, like any artificial motor; and moreover, somewhat, though not quite, as the governor of an engine, while it automatically begins to turn off steam as soon as the machinery begins to move too fast, is itself automatically controlled for the sake of avoiding another fault, that of too sudden a change of speed, so, and more than so, man's machinery is provided with an automatic governor upon every governor to regulate it by a consideration not otherwise provided for. For while an automatic governor may be attached to any governor to prevent any given kind of excess in an action, each such attachment complicates the machine . . . (But) in the human machine – or at least, in the context of the brain, or in whatever part it be whose action determines of what sort the man's conduct shall be – there seems, as far as we can see no limit to the self government that can and will be brought to bear upon each such determining action, except the lack of time before the conduct which has to be determined must come into actual play.[13]

Then it would seem legitimate to argue that 'much, if not all of the process of self-control, as Peirce describes it can also be translated into the concepts of cybernetics'.[14] And yet, although 'there is some evidence, scant as it is, that Peirce would have embraced the cybernetic point of view',[15] we would like to show that there is much more evidence against it.

Now, if we look carefully at the texts just quoted there are at least two points that seem to us decisive and ought not to have been overlooked by the commentators: first, when describing self-control in terms of the conduct which it determines, not only does Peirce speak of 'certain features of self-control' rather than of *all,* but he carefully excepts from the description 'what we distinctly rate as imagery'. More on this later. Second, when using the automatic engine example, Peirce explicitly refers to 'the context of the brain'. This again is a very important point that calls for an explanation.

We already noted that Peirce's interest in machines arose from the light that he thought might thus be thrown on the nature of the reasoning process, and that Peirce interpreted and reasoning process, at that time, in a certain way, i.e. on the syllogistic model. Now, it is precisely when Peirce introduces important changes in his conception of the reasoning process, by the emphasis he now puts on the role of *images,*[16] that he is also led to put some restrictions on the analogy he was ready to draw between the reasoning of man and the reasoning of the machine. It is not only because he discovers the importance of the inductive and abductive inferences but also because even 'the deductive reasonings involve discovery as truly as does the experimentation of the chemist' (*N.E.M,* IV, p. 355). Now if 'observation and ingenuity are involved in the reasoning process' (ibid.), we may no longer consider that logical machines do perform inferences:

> For example, logical machines have actually been constructed which will grind out relatively complicated syllogistic reasonings, and even dilemmas though they stand one grade higher. But it is easily shown that no machine not endowed with the power of arbitrary choice could possibly work out *the* conclusion from the simplest single premise of the relative sort; because in every such case an endless series of different conclusions are deducible from the same premise . . . So that we produce a very simple inference that the logical machine cannot grind out. True they will give the conclusion (because it is logically necessary; whence the phenomenon is only *in embrio*), but they cannot show its relation to the premiss. (*N.E.M.* IV, p. 354).

Why is that last operation decisive? Because it is precisely in the relation to the premiss that observation is necessary, for we then have 'considerable range of choice' (*N.E.M.* IV, p. 10) so that the determination of that range must be performed 'by the consideration of the purpose that the reasoner has in view, and which puts a machine at defiance' (ibid.). So, even if we may say that up to a point machines do have self-control and self-correctiveness,[17] their self-control lacks at least three essential features: it is not *deliberate,* it is not *endless* and it is not *purposive.* As far as the first point is concerned we should be careful not to confuse this power of deliberation with the re-introduction by Peirce of a mysterious self or consciousness. In fact, when Peirce refuses to admit that a decapitated frog does reason, we may nevertheless say that it 'almost reasons' (6.286), since 'the habit that is in his cerebellum serves as a major premiss. The excitation of a drop of acid is his minor premiss. And his conclusion is the act of wiping it away', so that 'all that is of any value in the operation of ratiocination is there', it is because the decapitated frog lacks just one thing, namely 'the power of preparatory meditation' (ibid) — in short, in Peirce's terms, *belief.* A detailed analysis of Peirce's concepts of habit and belief would of course be required here: briefly, let us point out that in Peirce's terms, a belief is 'a deliberate or self-controlled habit' (5.480) whereas a habit (as opposed to a natural disposition (5.538)) is 'a readiness to act in a certain way under given circumstances and when actuated by a given motive' (5.480). Thus not only do machines lack beliefs, in so far as they are incapable of deliberate behaviour, but we may also say that they lack habits, in so far as the production of habits requires not merely muscular or mechanical action but also all the efforts of *imagination* (5.479).

Secondly, even if the review process which is essential to the operation of self-control is 'an approximation toward the kind of fixed character which would be marked by entire absence of self-reproach upon subsequent reflexion' (5.418) and may be compared in that respect to the corrective feedback 'which tends as the action is considered and repeated, to reduce the oscillations – one's violent wayward inpulses – and to bring the action closer to the ideal',[18] so that, as Norbert Wiener puts it 'the stable state of a living organism is to be dead',[19] what is characteristic of human self-control is precisely its endlessness: 'Control may itself be controlled, criticism itself subjected to criticism; and ideally there is no obvious definite limit to the sequence' (5.442).[20] What this means is that 'in genuine reasoning, we are not wedded to our method. We deliberately approve it, but we stand ever ready and disposed to re-examine it and improve upon it, and to criticize our criticism of it, without cessation' (Ms. 831, pp. 10–12). In short, even if mental action proceeds according to habits, it is always possible that something spontaneous should interfere with that habit 'without which (mental action) would be dead' (6.418).[21] This explains what distinguishes human mentality from other self-corrective or intelligent processes:[22] as Peirce ideally defines it a Scientific Intelligence is 'capable of learning by experience' (1.227). Now it has been claimed – but the claim is highly controversial – that a major defect in such perfect machines as chess-playing computers lay precisely in their inability to learn anything from experience.[23] Not that their action may not be considered as goal-directed: in a way Peirce gives a parallel definition of human activity: both are aiming at truth.[24] So it is not that the machine has no purpose, but that the purpose is in a way too much specified.[25] It is well known that formal systems work particularly well when it is possible to specify in formal terms the desired result, but that in most cases unfortunately, the programming of the rules to follow is very difficult to handle because 'a major effort is required even to characterize the results towards which the heuristics are supposed to guide the system'.[26] This is what Peirce means by saying on one hand that something mechanical lies in 'the mere purposive pursuit of a predeterminate end' (6.159– 7), and on the other hand that in order to decide *what* choice to make we have to take the *goal* of the user into account. More generally Peirce maintains that any description of an intelligent phenomenon has to be characterized, that is to say in Peirce's terms, that any intelligent action is not only dyadic but irreducibly triadic:[27] this is of course, for those that are familiar with Peirce's semiotic, the definition he gives of a sign and of semeiosis. For example, in 5.472–3, Peirce argues that the action of a sign is triadic and explicitly connects it with intelligence:

> . . . If the thermometer is dynamically connected with the heating and cooling apparatus, so as to check either effect, we do not, in ordinary parlance, speak of there being any *semeiosy,* or action of a sign, but on the contrary, say that there is an 'automatic regulation', an idea opposed, in our minds, to that of semeiosy.

The reason why this is no intelligent action is because it reacts in a perfectly determinate and mechanical way, which conforms to what Peirce also describes as efficient causation:

> Efficient causation . . . is a compulsion acting to make the situation begin to change in a perfectly determinate way: and what the general character of that result may be in no way concerns efficient causation. (1.212).

Now this is decisive in so far as Peirce considers that 'efficient causation without final causation . . . is mere chaos. and chaos is not so much as chaos, without final causation; it is blank nothing' (1.220). In other words, if we are unable to show any final causation in the operations performed we are forbidden to talk of any kind of intelligent action whatsoever.[28]

This takes us back to the point we made formerly concerning the distinction to be made in the texts quoted between *brain* (which is the term used by Peirce) and *mental* activity. From what has been said up to now it should be clear that Peirce does not speak of them both on the same footing. Let me just quote what he writes concerning the psychologists' attempt to reduce mental states to purely neurological states:

> A psychologist cuts out a lobe of my brain (*nihil animale me alienum puto*) and then, when I find I cannot express myself, he says, "You see your faculty of language was localized in that lobe". No doubt it was; and so, if he had filched my inkstand, I should not have been able to continue my discussion until I had got another. Yea, the very thoughts would not come to me. So my faculty of discussion is equally localized in my inkstand. It is localization in a sense in which a thing may be in two places at once. *On the theory that the distinction between psychical and physical phenomenon is the distinction between final and efficient causation, it is plain enough that the inkstand and the brain-lobe have the same general relation to the functions of the mind.* I suppose that if I were to ask a modern psychologist whether he holds that the mind 'resides' in the brain, he would pronounce that to be a crude expression; and yet he holds that the protoplasmal content of a brain-cell feels, I suppose: there is evidence that it does so. This feeling, however, is consciousness. Consciousness, *per se,* is nothing else: and consciousness, he maintains, is Mind. So that he really does hold that Mind resides in, or is a property of, the brain-matter. (7.366) (our emphasis)

Thus if it is true that psychologists have become clearer about mind's 'substratum', they 'have not yet made clear what Mind is' nor 'even made it clear what a psychical phenomenon is' (7.364). Their fundamental error is to reduce mental to cerebral states by essentially forgetting to take final causation and intentionality into account, thus believing that the connexion between brain and mind is essential whereas it is just 'accidental' (7.366). So if we want to draw analogies between the reasoning of the machine and the reasoning that takes place 'in the context' of the brain 'it should be clear that such an analogy does not necessarily obtain in the context of mind. On the contrary if we wish to analyse mental phenomena, as we already saw, the best way to do it is to look without more than within (be it a self or a brain), namely into signs and semiotic activity.[29]

As a conclusion I would like, very briefly to hint at what seems to me most fruitful and suggestive in Peirce's insights concerning these matters.

First, by his insistence on the superfluous character of a self[30] or of a consciousness in the understanding of reasoning or thinking processes in general Peirce very early rules out what Haugeland calls the 'consciousness objection' (Haugeland 1981, p. 32) which tended to be raised against the possibility of any artificial intelligence. In that respect it is true that we may consider Peirce as a forerunner of what is recognized as the key to cybernetics, namely the necessity to abandon the natural/artificial distinction on such a basis. As W. Ross Ashby puts it:

> Cybernetics started by being closely associated in many ways with physics, but it depends in no essential way on the laws of physics or on the properties of matter . . . The materiality is irrelevant, and so is the holding of the ordinary law of physics . . . The truths of cybernetics are not conditional on their being derived from some other branch of science. Cybernetics has its own foundations. Cybernetics stands to the real machine — electronical, neural or economic — much as geometry stands to a real object in our terrestrial sphere'.[31]

But if it is so it is also because Peirce believes that the natural/artificial distinction is just as inadequate as the mind/matter distinction. This involves first the fact that Peirce does not see any basic difference between a machine that works upon a logical design and an instrument of experimentation such as a cucurbit: both are the same in so far as they are instruments of *thought* — that is to say as soon as we consider what they are intended for. An important consequence of this is that there is no difference in nature but only in degree between simple instruments that may be held as mere continuations of organic activity and such perfectionate mechanisms, which we are perhaps too quick in judging revolutionary or raising fundamentally new problems concerning the mental. Rather I would be inclined to think that Peirce's interest would be more directed towards the kind of research that is being made in bionics or ergonomics.[32] In any case, the inadequacy of the mind/matter distinction is also manifest when we understand that 'what we call matter is not completely dead but is merely hidebound with habits' (6.158). In that respect not only is the evolutionary process a manifestation of mind but the Universe is 'a great poem' a 'vast representamen' (5.119) just as we may find expressions of mentality in certain lower animals, some element of self-criticism (manifested in changes of behaviour) and a 'certain unity of quasi-purpose' (7.381. n. 19). Yet, if it is true that mind is no exclusive property of man, and that it is very hard to draw the frontier between mind and matter, an important distinction remains to be made, not so much at the level of the mental as at the level of the rational. Here again we can only stress the prevalence which is given by Peirce to the reasoning process over that given to the thinking process. This is all the more interesting since the traditional objections raised against AI or cognitive science are often based on their supposed inability to account for other kinds of mental processes than those exclusively involved in truth-seeking, in which they are generally acknowledged to be successful. Now Peirce's analysis shows that even if we stick to the description of the way a rational system should function, we are obliged to take some factors into account. Paradoxically enough, it is precisely because he thinks that man is the most rational being that he distinguishes him from other mental manifestations, this rationality being dependent on certain charac- teristics of self-control which we have underlined.[33] This may help to understand why Peirce's favourite guide for explaining the functioning of rationality in general should be the Scientific Intelligence, which is abstract enough not to refer to any man in particular,[34] and that such a task should be left to a Specula- tive Grammar 'whose task is to ascertain what must be true of the representamen used by every scientific intelligence in order that they may embody any *meaning*' (2.229). Along this line it appears that many developments made by Peirce through the semiotic analysis could be put into parallel with the description Dennett offers of an intentional system (1978b). I have no space to draw the comparison very far, but I would like to point out just a few obvious similarities. First, the fact that Dennett intends to speak of intentionality only in terms of linguistic properties is very near Peirce's central notion of semeiosis as a model for all mental and intelligent action. Second the necessity, in order for a parti- cular thing to be an intentional system, that it be so 'only in relation to the strategies of someone who is trying to explain and predict its behaviour' sounds very much like Peirce's definition of habit-change in terms of possible future and general predictions. Third Dennett's assumption of rationality is of course very akin to Peirce's description of human mental activity as oriented towards truth. And finally the importance which Dennett ascribes to the possibility of prag- matic testing of beliefs and desires has much in common with Peirce's method of fixing belief. But I prefer not to go too far along this line.

Once again what seems most enlightening in Peirce's remarks on these topics is perhaps the extreme caution which he manifests in handling all these ques- tions, and I would like to end this chapter by recalling that the pragmatic maxim was originally conceived as a method of clarification of concepts, and that we often are inclined when raising problems about the possibility that machines might think, or have beliefs, desires, emotions, etc., to forget that some of these questions are, as Putnam said 'of an entirely linguistic and logical nature'.[35] In that respect too, we may remember Peirce's piece of advice in his famous article: 'How to make our ideas clear':

not to

> mistake a mere difference in the grammatical construction of two words for a distinction between the ideas they express (5.399).

and not to

> mistake the sensation produced by our own unclearness of thought for a character of the object we are thinking' (5.398).

NOTES

1. References to the *Collected Papers* of C. S. Peirce (Peirce 1958) are given in the text and footnotes as a decimal number, referring to volume and paragraph. E.g. '2.56' refers to Volume 2, paragraph 56.

   References preceded by '*N.E.M.*' are to Peirce's *New Elements of Mathematics* (Peirce 1976), and give volume, tome and page number. E.g. '*N.E.M.* III. I, p. 625' refers to Volume III, Tome I, page 625.

   References preceded by 'Ms.' are to Peirce's unpublished manuscripts collected in Harvard University Library, as catalogued in Robin 1967.

2. Peirce 1877. According to the editors of the *Collected Papers,* Peirce seems to have considered the construction of a logical machine (2.56n).

3. 'Precisely how much of the business of thinking a machine could possibly be made to perform, and what part of it must be left for the living mind, is a question not without conceivable practical importance' (*N.E.M.* II. I, p.625).

4. *N.E.M.* III. I, p. 629: 'For example, if we want to make a machine which shall be capable of reasoning in the syllogism

   > If A then B,
   > If B then C
   > Therefore, if A then C,

   we have only to have a connection which can be introduced at will, such that when one event A occurs in the machine, another event B must also occur. This connection being introduced between A and B, and also between B and C, it is necessarily virtually introduced between A and C'.

5. Ibid. 'This is the same principle which lies at the foundation of every logical algebra; only in the algebra, instead of depending directly on the laws of nature, we establish conventional rules for the relations used.'

6. *N.E.M.* III. I, p. 630.

7. Ibid. For example, Peirce argues, 'the difficulty with the balloon is that it

has too much initiative, that it is not mechanical enough. We no more want an original machine, than a house-builder would want an original journey-man, or an American board of college trustees would hire an original profes-sor'.

8. 2.59. 'If anybody wishes me to acknowledge that a logical machine reasons no more than any other machine, I do not know why I should not gratify him.'

9. Cf. 5.348 and 2.690.

10. This is the main thesis developed in the three articles of the *Journal of Speculative Philosophy,* 1868: "Questions concerning certain faculties claimed for man", "Consequences of four incapacities", and "Grounds of validity of the laws of logic" (Peirce 1868).

11. 5.313. Peirce develops this idea again in 1873. See 7.591. These themes have been analyzed in our Doctorat de troisième cycle (Tiercelin-Engel 1982), Ch. III, pp. 286–348.

12. Peirce 1913, cited in Holmes 1966.

13. Peirce 1910. ('but a brain endowed with automatic control, as man's in-directly is, is so naturally and rightly interested in its own faculties that some psychological and semi-psychological questions would doubtless get touched'). Quoted by L. Holmes (1966), pp. 122–3. Holmes's interpreta-tion of this passage is that Peirce is here describing 'what we now call feedback' (p. 122) and that 'the 'control of control that Peirce describes here and in many other passages is what is known as second-order feedback' (p. 123). For example, 'the reflective criticism or comparison of deeds with a previous standard may be thought of as internal corrective feedback, or if there is actual trial-and-error using incremental testing or a kind of testing by sampling, the process is identical with what Wiener calls 'control by informative feedback' (p.123). (Cf. Wiener 1965, p. 113.)

14. Holmes 1966, p. 123.

15. Such is the position adopted by J. Esposito (Esposito 1973), p.76. as well as by Joseph Ransdell (Ransdell 1977), p. 170.

16. On the importance of icons in the reasoning process see, 4.479, 4.10–11, 3.363, 3.418–419, 3.429, 7.619. The role of images is also stressed in the distinction between theorematic and corollarial reasonings, on the fruit-fulness of which Hintikka has rightly insisted (Hintikka 1980).

17. This is a point emphasized by L. Holmes in his attempt to compare Peirce's analysis with corrective feedback, 'which tends, as the action is considered and repeated, to reduce the oscillations – one's violent wayward impulses – and to bring the action closer to the ideal' (p. 125). The 'control of con-trol' should also 'insure us against the quandary of Buridan's ass' (5.440).

18. Holmes 1966, p. 125. It is quite true that many texts describe the process of self-control in purely mechanical terms. For example: 'This operation of self-control is a process in which logical sequence is converted into mechani-cal sequence or something of that sort' (letter to F. C. S. Schiller) so that 'a

man is a machine with automatic controls, one over another, for five or six grades at least' (8.320). According to Holmes, the Cornell Perceptron Group began its research task on a hypothesis very like Peirce's combination of chance and habit (p. 122); cf. Arbib 1964, p. 48. 'Assume an initial random-ness and allow all the structure requisite for pattern recognition (the group's particular interest) to result from changes due to the reinforcement rules'.

19. Wiener 1965, p. 58, cited in Holmes 1966, p. 125.

20. Cf. Ms. 831, Ms. 599, p. 34, Ms. 939, p.12.

21. 'No mental action seems to be necessary or invariable in character. In what-ever manner the mind has reacted under a given sensation, in that manner it is the more likely to react again; were this, however, an absolute necessity, habits would become wooden and ineradicable, and, no room being left for the formation of new habits, intellectual life would come to a speedy close. Thus the uncertainty of the mental law is no mere defect of it, but is on the contrary of its essence' (6.148), also (6.149).

22. 5.33, 1.573–4, 5.417, etc. This point is underlined by T. L. Short (Short, 1981a), p. 220.

23. Cf. Dreyfus 1980: 'Les ordinateurs n'utilisent pas de stratégie à long terme, n'apprennent rien par expérience, ou même ne se souviennent pas des tours précédents' (p. 734). This explains why Dreyfus may claim that any chess-playing computer is a worse player than any human player: that is, that independently of the result of the game, the *way* a master (for example) plays (thanks to the comprehension of the situation acquired from the experience of preceding situations) is more *economical* than the way a successful computer plays.

24. This point was underlined by Joseph Ransdell (Ransdell 1977), p. 171.

25. Cf. the excellent analysis made by Georges Canguilhem (Canguilhem 1971), pp. 116–117. He cites the definition by Paul Valéry of what is artificial as opposed to life: 'Artificiel veut dire qui tend à un but défini. Et s'oppose par là à vivant . . . Si la vie avait un but, elle ne serait plus la vie' (Valéry 1910).

26. Haugeland 1981, Introduction, p. 18. For example, in order to program the choice of which move to take, we have to program what is more or less relevant, and unfortunately there is no fail-safe way to do it: 'Everybody knows that a seemingly pointless or terrible move can turn out to be a brilliant stroke when the opponent takes the bait' (pp. 16–17). This ex-plains why a major part of the effort in AI research goes towards better heuristics and better ways of implementing them on the machine.

27. By 'dyadic', Peirce means the following: 'An event, A, may, by brute force, produce an event, B; and then the event, B may in its turn produce a third event, C. The fact that the event, C, is about to be produced by B has no influence at all upon the production of B by A . . . Such is dyadic action, which is so called because each step of it concerns a pair of objects' (5.472). In triadic action, the production of one thing is always intended as a *means*

to another. As an example of triadic (or intelligent) action: '. . . when a microscopist is in doubt whether a motion of an animalcule is guided by intelligence, of however low an order, the test he always used to apply . . . is to ascertain whether event A produces a second event, B, *as a means* to the production of a third event, C, or not. That is, he asks whether B will be produced if it will produce or is likely to produce C in its turn, but will not be produced if it will not produce C in its turn nor is likely to do so'

28. In that respect final causation and mentality in general is no human privilege. Peirce extends them to the whole universe and explains thus the law of biological evolution. See Short 1981b, and also the excellent analysis he makes of the importance of that concept in relation to semeiotic intentionality, in Short 1981a.

29. '. . . Feeling is nothing but the inward aspect of things, while mind on the contrary is essentially an external phenomenon . . . Again the psychologists undertake to locate various mental powers in the brain; and above all consider it as quite certain that the faculty of language resides in a certain lobe; but I believe it comes decidedly nearer the truth (though not really true) that language resides in the tongue. In my opinion it is much more true that the thoughts of a living writer are in any printed copy of this book than they are in his brain' (7.364). Cf. 'Man is a sign or a symbol' (7.583, 5.283, 5.314, 6.344, etc.).

30. Cf. 5.462: 'The self is only inferred', or 7.751: 'The selfhood you like to attribute to yourself is for the most part the vulgarest delusion of vanity', and again he speaks in 7.572 of the 'barbaric conception of personal identity'. Most often the self is discovered or postulated through error and ignorance: (5.225, 5.237, 7.531, 1.673, etc.). 'Individualism and falsity are one and the same'.

31. Ashby 1961, pp. 1–2, cited by Esposito (Esposito 1973), p. 76. Esposito comments: 'Peirce's view that logical relations reflect metaphysical relations is in line both with the cybernetic use of logical models such as the Mc-Culloch logical nets, to characterize certain physical processes, and with the general mathematization of knowledge in information theory. In fact a synechistic monism enhances the cyberneticist's distinction between software or paper machines and hardware by giving a reality to Turing Machines and information theory which Common Sense with its current materialistic inclinations would not want to give' (p. 76). Cf. 6.268.

32. This idea is developed by Esposito (1973), p. 73. See also on the machine/organism distinction and its relevance for such sciences, Canguilhem 1971, pp. 126–7, note 59.

33. Because self-control is the very essence of rationality it has more than anything else 'served to elevate man above the rest of the fauna of our globe' and again: 'Man comes from the womb in actuality an animal little higher than a fish; by no means as high as a serpent. His humanity consists in his *destination* He becomes not actual man until he acquires self-control

and then he is so in the measure of his self-control . . . Man's existence qua
man . . . consists solely in his growing to act from rational self-conduct'
(Ms. 330).
34. Cf. *N.E.M.* IV, p. IX–X.
35. Cf. Putnam 1960. Jacques Bouveresse has given a brilliant analysis of
this aspect of the problem in Bouveresse 1971.

8

Noam Chomsky's
linguistic theory[†]

James Higginbotham

Twenty-five years have passed since the publication of Noam Chomsky's *Syntactic Structures*,[1] a slender volume that is widely conceded to have inaugurated a revolution in linguistics. The period has witnessed many trends and tides of thought, and Chomsky's own views have not stood still. In books and articles he has expounded and defended his ideas on matters of general scientific and philosophical interest no less than on particular questions of linguistic analysis. His most recent book, *Lectures on Government and Binding*,[2] is the broadest in scope of his many writings on linguistics since the 1965 *Aspects of the Theory of Syntax*.[3] The title essay of *Rules and Representations*,[4] based upon lectures given at Columbia University in 1978 and at Stanford University in 1979, is Chomsky's latest statement of his general views, incorporating replies to critics (mostly philosophers) and taking note of developments in the field.

Despite changes in formulation, Chomsky's linguistic theory from *Syntactic Structures* to the present has maintained, in my opinion, a central core that constitutes the essential of his position. It is my purpose in this essay to outline the theses that make up this core, and to consider some of the questions about them that have been, early and late, topics of concern in linguistics, philosophy, and psychology. One question that comes up repeatedly in discussion of Chomsky's work among researchers in artificial intelligence is its comparative indif-

† The talk given by Prof. Higginbotham at the conference was based on a paper 'Chomsky's linguistic theory', *Social Research*, vol. 49, no. 1, Spring 1982. The Graduate Faculty, New School for Social Research, New York. The paper, which has been slightly expanded for inclusion in this volume, is reproduced with the permission of the author and the editors of *Social Research*.

ference to the problem of modelling actual human behaviour. My own view, manifested in what follows, is that the charge of indifference is largely justified; only, I do not consider that so serious a defect.

LANGUAGE A COGNITIVE STATE

In Chomsky's view, language cannot profitably be understood as a system of habits, or conditioned responses, or dispositions to verbal behaviour; it is more appropriately studied as a manifestation of a system of knowledge, specifically knowledge of grammar, that is put to use in speech and thought. The negative part of this thesis reflects Chomsky's criticisms of behaviourism; the positive part articulates the alternative conception of language with which his work is identified. But the criticism applies not only to a narrowly behavioural account of language, and Chomsky's notion of language as a product of knowledge of grammar sets the stage for linguistic research of a distinctive type.

Behaviourism, in any of its various forms, does not have the appeal that it once did. Psychologists are not so reluctant nowadays to posit interior, mental processes for the sake of explaining behaviour, or changes in behaviour, and to hypothesize mechanisms of learning that go beyond conditioning. The point is therefore perhaps worth emphasizing that linguistic theory, conceived as an account of knowledge of language, is not a liberated 'science of behaviour', freed from adventitious methodological scruples. If grammar is a system of knowledge, then a theory of grammar is a theory, not of language use, but of a cognitive state that is *available* for use. Grammar alone explains no behaviour at all.

In *Aspects of the Theory of Syntax*, Chomsky called the state of a person who knows a language his *competence*, contrasting this with his verbal behaviour and disposition to verbal behaviour, or *performance*. In retrospect Chomsky's terminology here seems to have been unfortunate. The term of 'competence' suggests that the possessor of competence possesses a skill of some sort; and 'performance' correlatively suggests a domain of actual behaviour that falls short in various respects of being ideally 'competent'. Both suggestions are misleading. The contrast between competence and performance is a contrast between knowledge, on the one hand, and behavioural repertoire, on the other.

The first thesis, then, that I would identify as central to Chomsky's position over the years is that a theory of our linguistic nature may be sought whose first object of study is linguistic knowledge, not verbal behaviour.

A recurrent theme, especially in philosophical discussion of Chomsky's work, has been scepticism over his use of cognitive notions in characterizing the object of study. A speaker of English, who is said in the normal way to 'know English', obviously does not have knowledge of it in the sense of being able to state the rules and principles governing its grammar. In consequence, when Chomsky speaks of 'knowledge of grammar', or further of 'knowledge of the rules of grammar', many philosophers have been led to question whether the notion of knowledge is appropriate here. Noting in addition that knowledge of grammar does not amount to possession of a skill, hence not a case of 'knowing how' to do something, these philosophers have often concluded that there is no appropriate sense of the term 'knowledge' according to which linguistic theory can be a theory of the knowledge that native speakers have of their languages, or grammars.

To which it may be responded that these philosophical considerations merely show the impoverishment of the conceptions of knowledge that analytic philosophers have typically allowed in recent years. The conception is impoverished in that it makes no room for the types of description that linguistic theory provides for such an obviously cognitive state as 'knowing English', and in that it does not allow for tacit, or implicit, or unconscious knowledge. In several places Chomsky has suggested that if the term 'knowledge' gives offence, one may substitute a technical term, say 'cognition', and speak of a person's 'cognizing' his grammar rather than 'knowing' it. In any event it will be cognizing that is the critical notion for linguistics.

The debate over whether there is, properly speaking, knowledge of grammar or of the rules of grammar is far from over: see Michael Dummett's review of *Rules and Representations* in the *London Review of Books*. The debate is not simply terminological, as we may see by switching to a more nearly neutral initial position. It is essential to Chomsky's research programme that it be true or false to attribute grammars to persons as descriptions of their cognitive states. Simplifying only slightly, the assumption is that persons are in the states we commonly call 'knowing English', or 'knowing Chinese', etc. just when certain grammars G are to be attributed to them. To characterize linguistic competence is to solve for G. We may at this point leave open the question just what relation a person with grammar G stands in to G itself; but it must be true or false to say that he *has* G. The philosophical question is whether this relation is interpretable as a case of knowledge.

Although the question whether grammars are in some sense known is not insubstantial, it is not as significant for the practice of linguistics as the prior question whether attributions of grammars are a correct or fruitful way to describe cognitive states in the first place. The question of fruitfulness can certainly be answered in the affirmative; but it will be useful to describe the workings of grammars in more detail before contrasting Chomsky's approach with others that have been suggested.

I will follow customary usage in referring to the variety of linguistics that emerged chiefly in consequence of Chomsky's work as 'generative grammar'. What does a generative grammar of a language say about it, and how do generative grammars differ from traditional grammars? Quite apart from questions of methodology or metatheory, and specifically apart from Chomsky's own interpretation of his enterprise, there is an important respect in which generative grammar is an intellectual novelty: it is the first type of linguistic theory whose avowed aim is to make grammatical description *fully explicit*. There is justice in the observation that generative grammar, particularly in syntax, represents first of all the application of formal methods made available in the twentieth century through logical and mathematical studies of formalized languages to empirically given, natural languages (Zellig Harris took this step as early as the 1940s). Only with these methods in hand are the problems of generative grammar formulable.

As an illustration, consider the notion, 'sentence of English'. An adequate generative grammar of English must in all cases, by purely formal means, correctly classify strings of English words as sentences or as nonsentences. Chomsky's discussion in *Syntactic Structures* was devoted both to general and specific proposals for the construction of such a grammar.

It turns out that the construction of adequate generative grammars for natural language, even if considered only as a problem of technical interest, poses a serious intellectual challenge. Chomsky, appreciating the depth of the challenge early on demonstrated that several initially plausible models for the form of grammar were not adequate to the task.

It is a fact, not only that writing of grammar for a language is a difficult (and so far unaccomplished) job, but also that it can be difficult to appreciate just how difficult the job actually is. The conditions of adequacy are so stringent that literally nothing can be omitted. From the point of view of generative grammar, therefore, it is a powerful blow to a theory of language that it cannot deliver explicit accounts at critical junctures. Inversely, since the point of view is not yet widely adopted, the force of the generative grammarian's criticisms of other types of accounts of language is frequently blunted.

Chomsky is widely known for his critique of behaviourism, commencing with his 1959 review of B. F. Skinner's *Verbal Behaviour* (Chomsky 1959b). But I believe that, if we look a little beyond the proximate targets of Chomsky's critical remarks on psychological practice and consider what Chomsky seems to take to be the central arguments in support of his criticisms, we shall find that the impact of these arguments has been marginal. An essential criticism of Skinner is that the learning process as he describes it is at crucial points left to notions such as 'analogy' and 'generalization', notions whose explicitness deprives them of explanatory power. That these notions still flourish is a meeasure of the novelty of the type of approach to language exemplified by generative grammar.

An aim of linguistic theory according to Chomsky, then, is − by constructing fully explicit, or generative, grammars that may be ascribed to persons − to understand in some measure in what linguistic competence consists. This research, however, still leaves to be filled in the nature of the relation between a person and the grammar to be ascribed to him.

A number of linguists and psychologists have suggested that, for a grammar correctly to be ascribed to a person, it should be in some sense *directly used* by the person in the course of verbal behaviour. The pertinent notion of 'direct use' is not easy to formulate, and in any case varies from proposal to proposal. On one interpretation, a grammar would be directly used to the extent that its rules and the descriptions of sentences that it provides correspond in some experimentally determinate ways to properties of mental activity – for instance, whatever activity is involved in the perception and production of speech.

The thesis that grammars are correctly ascribed only to the degree that they can be directly implicated in verbal behaviour is often expressed as the view that grammars should be 'psychologically real'.[5] We can see this view as prompted by the desire to pin down an appropriate sense in which grammars are to be ascribed to persons.

On the question of 'psychological reality', as on the question whether grammars ascribe knowledge, Chomsky's view has consistently been that no grounds for scepticism about the objectivity or cogency of the linguistic enterprise, or characterizing a normal speaker's grasp of his language in terms of a generative grammar, have been educed; see the later essays in *Rules and Representations*. I am inclined to think that Chomsky is right about this matter, but there is no space to argue the issue here. In any event, Chomsky's thesis that grammar should be viewed as an enterprise descriptive not of behaviour but of a capacity manifested in behaviour is only the first of those that sustain linguistic research as he conceives it. We turn now to some other aspects of his program.

MENTALISM vs. PHYSICALISM

The descriptions provided by the ascription of grammars to persons are, we have seen, to be abstract descriptions of cognitive states of those persons. Now, these cognitive states doubtless admit of physical descriptions as well, and surely must be counted as having the cognitive powers that they do in virtue of their physical organization. I say, 'surely', thereby acquiescing in physicalism, a position that is now as formerly subject to interpretation, doubt, and controversy. Supposing, however, that physicalism is in some sense true, we can bring out a distinctive feature of Chomsky's type of enquiry, a feature that is borne also by Freud's accounts of mental life. This feature is the thesis that the theory of mind can fruitfully proceed in the absence of all but the most tenuous connections between its type of descriptions of cognitive states and their physical embodiments. Chomsky's theory is thus mentalistic in a double sense, abstracting both from the direct explanation of behaviour and from the physical underpinnings of the states that it is the theory's aim to describe.

It is interesting to contrast Chomsky's advocacy of mentalistic linguistics with a view that has been worked out in some systematic detail, namely that of W. V. Quine as expressed in several of his writings over the years. Quine's view, as I understand it, is that explanation of the growth of human knowledge, and of knowledge of language in particular, can be expected to make progress along the course of first conjecturing, and then trying to understand in physical detail, the mechanisms responsible for dispositions to behaviour and for changes in dispositions.[6] The research programme thus envisaged has no place for abstract accounts of linguistic competence, because these are accounts neither of dispositions to behaviour nor of possible physical mechanisms.

Mentalistic accounts of language may be viewed with suspicion from several points of view less severe than that of Quine. But it should be noted that the wholesale rejection of mentalism also carries risks, perhaps the greatest of which is that of ignoring whole domains of reasonable inquiry, because they do not yield at once to methods of investigation that are not mentalistic. A good case can be made that the structure of human language is one domain that received less than adequate investigation in part because of the problems there posed can, at present, only be put in mentalistic terms. Chomsky's work has been the first and primary instrument in opening up this domain.

LANGUAGE ACQUISITION AS THEORY-CONSTRUCTION

Thus far I have identified two theses that have, I believe, guided Chomsky's work in linguistics since its inception. The third thesis that I will discuss here was first stated explicitly by Chomsky in *Aspects of the Theory of Syntax*: that the acquisition of language might be studied as a kind of theory-construction, in which the child, on the basis of his linguistic experience, comes to deduce the nature of the grammar of the language to which he is exposed. Let us consider this thesis in somewhat more detail.

If grammar is viewed as the outcome of linguistic experience, the experience serving to convert the state of the child from ignorance to knowledge of language, then there is an initial state on which this experience acts in some determinate way. The initial state Chomsky calls *universal grammar*. Universal grammar represents the contribution of the child to the cognitive state attained on the basis of experience; it is, by definition, innate, and must include information about both what grammars are possible for human languages and how grammars from among the possible ones are to be selected. Chomsky's program of research, fully realized, would characterize both the grammars of human languages and the selection to be ascribed to universal grammar.

Within linguistics itself, what now principally distinguishes Chomsky's position and type of research is the thesis just outlined, that the fundamental aim of linguistic theory is to explain (insofar as explanation is possible with the tools available, and within the limits of the degree of abstraction presently required) the acquisition of language by normal human beings. From this perspective, the description of features of language is never an ending itself; rather, it is at best preliminary to the task of deducing those features from the structure ascribed to universal grammar, under the conditions of exposure to language that children typically undergo.

The term 'universal grammar' misleadingly suggests that the study of universal grammar would intimately, or perhaps exclusively, involve taking a principled inventory of those features that grammars of human languages have in common. It may therefore be worth stressing that, understood in Chomsky's sense, universal grammar is nothing else but the initial state of the human language-learner. This initial state may well involve factors that determine universal features of language, but may also, and even principally, consist in principles that select among forms of grammars that are very different from each other. To put the point another way, the cogency of Chomsky's programme is not undermined by observations on the diversity of human languages; and the problem in any case is to account for how the child *does* come to acquire the grammar of the language to which he is exposed.

The research program, by parity of reasoning, can be extended to other domains than language; in several places Chomsky has suggested so extending it. The picture that he sometimes presents is that of the mind as composed of several 'mental organs', including language, knowledge of the behaviour of ordinary physical bodies, knowledge of human beings, and so forth, each of which matures under the conditions given by normal experience on the basis of an initial state, which might be studied as leading to the knowledge in question on the basis of its specific construction. This thesis is best viewed as additional to the thesis that the acquisition of language may be studied in the way Chomsky's linguistic theory aims for. The reason is that the formulation of the enquiry into language leaves open the question whether our cognitive capacities for language are specific to the task at hand, or rather represent a specialization of some more general learning apparatus. Chomsky's own position is that, so far as we are now able to judge, the capacity to acquire language should be counted as a separable faculty of the mind — one among perhaps many 'mental organs'. An alternative view, which seems to be supported by the Piagetians among others, is that knowledge of language is the result of applying generalized learning strategies to linguistic material, strategies that, applied to other domains, would yield knowledge of other sorts.

Abstracting from the question of the specificity of the language faculty, we may note that there is a sense in which the third step that Chomsky takes, of formulating a program for research on language acquisition, is riskier than the step of investigating language in comparative isolation from its physical embodiment and connections with behaviour. The reason is simple: the study of grammar conceived in the generativist way, as aiming for a fully explicit account where traditional grammar have only incomplete sketches, is valuable for our understanding of the nature of language independently of what may turn out with respect to its physical realization or behavioural correlates (indeed, we can make a strong case that it is indispensable for understanding the latter). but the acquisition problem is one that might *fail* of tractability within the limits of grammatical theory alone.

Progress in the acquisition problem can proceed only correlatively with a deeper understanding of what is in fact acquired — that is, in Chomsky's terms, what the nature of linguistic competence is. Commencing with *Syntactic Structures* and the longer work on which it was based, Chomsky has argued that the simplest models of linguistic competence will incorporate formal devices of powerful sorts, not in general available within traditional linguistics. A technical feature of the generative grammars of the type Chomsky has advocated is their use of certain formal of operations called *grammatical transformations*, whose role it is to relate levels of description of linguistic structure to one another. In the scheme of *Aspects of the Theory of Syntax*, transformations mediated between two levels called *deep structure* and *surface structure*, representations at these levels fulfilling different functions within the system as a whole. Some version of transformations, and of the distinction between deep and surface structure, persists not only in Chomsky's recent work, but also in work within other frameworks. The use of such devices has proved indispensable to the project of giving a clear and explicit presentation of linguistic structure.

It is to be stressed, however, that the program of explaining language acquisition by internal means within the theory of grammar is not one that is tied to transformations, deep and surface structure, or any other specific technical device. Inversely, technical devices can be employed for the purpose of giving perspicuous linguistic descriptions quite independently of the further question how such descriptions may be brought to bear on the problem of acquisition, the distinctive problem that Chomsky's type of research sets.

I have said that Chomsky's research is to be distinguished by the degree to which it subordinates problems of linguistic description to the overarching aim of explaining acquisition. How much progress has been made on the latter? The recent *Lectures on Government and Binding* is an attempt to study the question of acquisition more closely, by formulating a theory of comparative syntax — that is, a theory of the ways languages may and do differ in their syntactic organization.

Given the psychological orientation of Chomsky's theory, comparative syntax for him becomes primarily the study of how the child, on the basis of the linguistic information available to him, distinguishes the syntax of the language to which he is exposed from other admissible systems. A good theory in this domain, Chomsky argues, should have the property that a few detectable features of a language should suffice to fix the form and functioning of a host of grammatical rules. A simple image may help to convey how such a theory might work. Imagine that a grammar is selected (apart from the meanings of individual words) by setting a small number of switches — say 20, say — either 'On' or 'Off'. Linguistic information available to the child determines how these switches are to be set. In that case, a huge number of different grammars (here, 2 to the twentieth power) will be prelinguistically available, although a small amount of experience may suffice to fix one.

The switch-settings of the metaphor above are in Chomsky's terminology the 'parameters' defined by universal grammar. Notice that this image underscores the sense in which universal grammar, the initial state of the language-learner, need not comprise an account of what languages have in common — to continue the metaphor, different switch-settings could give rise to very different grammatical systems.

If one views comparative syntax from this perspective, then grammatical analyses that might be formulated for, say, English ought to have the property that they mesh with analyses of similar or interestingly different phenomena in other languages. For a concrete example, consider that in English, corresponding to the sentence (1), there are two forms of direct question, namely (2) and (3):

(1) You bought the book for John.
(2) Who did you buy the book for?
(3) For whom did you buy the book?

In French, however, only the form corresponding to (3) is permitted (in other words, the form 'Qui avez-vous acheté le livre pour?' is ungrammatical). Any analysis, therefore, that makes both (2) and (3) routinely available to the learner of English is likely to be wrong, because it would not contribute to the explanation of why only one of these forms exists in French. With respect to these forms, in fact, it appears that French is the norm among languages, and English the exception. The problem, then, is to explain why English should admit forms like (2). This is not the place to discuss solutions that have been proposed — what is to be noted is that the status of (2) as a *problem* is directly dependent upon the incorporation of the analytical task of linguistic description within a broader programme of the explanation of language acquisition.

The broader programme has arguably made some progress, motivated by the analysis of examples like those above. Whether the programme will make progress in its own terms, or indeed whether those terms will not in time be transformed out of all present recognition, remains to be seen.

CHOMSKY'S INFLUENCE

I have outlined three theses that I would attribute to Chomsky as characterizing his work during the last quarter-century: that language is in the first instance most profitably pursued as a cognitive state rather than a type of behaviour; that the study of this state may proceed in abstraction from the knowledge of the physical organization ultimately responsible for it; and that the question of how human beings acquire their native languages under the conditions of acquisition that we observe may be pursued internally within the theory of grammar. These theses I have given in what seems to me a natural order of increasing strength: scepticism about earlier ones will extend to later, though not conversely.

The AI community, as well as many psychologists, have been sceptical even of Chomsky's first step — abstraction from actual behaviour so as to lay bare the system of cognition that makes that behaviour possible. Many aspects of transformational grammars are computationally intractable by current methods, so that incorporation of grammars into programs modelling human behaviour does not of itself bring any advance. On the other hand, to the extent that generative grammar is a proper approach to part of the basis for human language mastery, one might suggest that it is a challenge to AI to show how the linguists' grammars may be given a proper computational implementation.

Chomsky's influence on linguistics has been very great. But in assessing the significance of his work, it is as important to show the points where it has failed to have much impact as it is to note the places where the intellectual climate has changed through the influence of his arguments. In several places in this essay I have remarked points where Chomsky's theses have met with scepticism or have failed to arouse a significant response. In conclusion I will speculate as to why this scepticism or *de facto* indifference obtains, not for the purpose of charging that Chomsky is right and the critics wrong, or vice versa, but rather for the sake of understanding the sources of the scepticism. They include, I think, at least these two: Chomsky's conception of linguistics places the study of language in an area remote from traditional, humanistic concerns; and his method of en-quiry, particularly in its abstraction from behaviour and from physical structures and mechanisms, seems to be opposed to some views of what ought to count as respectable science.

Documents critical of Chomsky's linguistic theory, both in its details and in its general outlook, that draw arguments from the two sources just mentioned are legion; I will not give explicit references here.

For the first point, there seems to be a tendency to view language, an object that arises only *within* culture, and may be said to have had a long and significant history, as a thing that must therefore be understood only *from* a cultural or historical perspective. The unwarranted belief, still common among educated persons, that human language evolved from primitive beginnings, and that primitive peoples speak more primitively than we do, is perhaps a reflex of this general equation of language with culture. The growth of language seems, on this view, properly analogous to the growth of civilization, and not, as in Chomsky's metaphor of mental organs, analogous to the growth of liver. This attitude toward language, I think, can make Chomsky's views seem bizarre.

The second point, whether Chomsky's research programme is respectably scientific, is much debated, particularly by philosophers. I have remarked on some features of this debate above: the question whether linguistic competence is knowledge, whether cognitive states can be identified and studied in compara-tive isolation from their physical underpinnings and behavioural correlates, and others. Remarkably, there has been little discussion of the details of grammatical theory itself; most of the critical remarks have been external to it, rather than from within. Not that philosophers, not experts in the sciences, should refrain from trying to formulate general criteria for the evaluation of scientific achieve-ment and understanding. We all speculate about the sciences anyway, and the hope is that philosophers will do it more clearly than most. But I am inclined to think that, until Chomsky's theory is more critically examined in its own terms, what it may have to teach us, through its successes *and* its failures, will not have been taken up within the broader context of our effort to obtain a better under-standing of human knowledge, thought, and discourse.

NOTES

1. Chomsky 1957.
2. Chomsky 1981.
3. Chomsky 1965.
4. Chomsky 1980.
5. See for instance the discussion in J. A. Fodor, T. G. Bever, and M. F. Garrett, *The Psychology of Language* (Fodor *et al.* 1974).
6. See particularly Quine's essay, 'Mind and verbal dispositions', (Quine 1975).

9

Methodological links between AI and other disciplines[†]

Margaret Boden

Whether our interest is in psychology, philosophy, or linguistics, there is no question but that AI has given us a new standard of rigour, and a new appreciation of the importance of mental *process*. Linguistics already had rigour but not process, psychology had little of either, and philosophy had less of each. AI provides a range of precisely definable computational concepts, specifying various symbolic representations and transformations, with which to conceptualize the mind. And the technology of programming makes manageable a degree of theoretical complexity that would overwhelm the unassisted human brain. So the inadequacy of theoretical approaches that fail to recognize the complexity of mental structure and process is now evident, and psychology and the philosophy of mind have been influenced accordingly.

One example of a class of empirical psychological work partly inspired by AI-ideas is microdevelopmental research (e.g. Inhelder and Karmiloff-Smith 1975; Karmiloff-Smith 1979). This studies the dialectical interplay between the child's action-sequences and changing cognitive representations (theories, models, heuristics, choice-criteria). The specifics of action are emphasized, on the assumption that the procedural details of performance (not only its overall structure) give clues to the underlying competence. However, the degree of procedural detail — though high relative to more traditional forms of experimentation in psychology — is inadequate to express a complete computational model of the psychological processes concerned. It is not a straightforward matter to assess

[†] This paper was first published in F. Machlup and V. Mansfield, eds.: *The Study of Information: Interdisciplinary Messages*. New York: John Wiley and Sons. Copyright © 1984, John Wiley and Sons.

such studies in computational terms, and we need to learn how to refine the theories and methodology of these studies so as to facilitate such assessment.

This case exemplifies the general point that, if we ask whether AI has given us new discoveries as well as a new approach, the reply might be that it has not been as helpful to working psychologists as its supporters initially hoped. There has been an increasing amount of computationally influenced empirical research in cognitive, developmental, and educational psychology. But (with the arguable exception of vision) we have gained little new insight into the actual details of mental life, as opposed to the *sorts* of questions that it may be appropriate to ask.

Is this because psychologists have not yet learnt how to apply AI fruitfully to further their research, or because (as some critics claim) it is in principle unsuitable for psychological modelling? This question raises a number of methodological difficulties and conceptual unclarities in applying AI-ideas to other disciplines. Some of these involve commitments on basic theoretical or philosophical issues, and call for cooperative research by people in various specialities.

There is much disagreement − and not a little scepticism in some quarters − about the extent to which empirical psychological work should or can be planned and assessed in the light of computational ideas. It is not even agreed whether or not psychologists sympathetic to the computational approach should seek to express their theories in programmable (or programmed) terms, as opposed to merely bearing computational issues in mind in their work. Some AI-workers even believe that doing psychological experiments is not an intellectually justifiable exercise in our present state of ignorance, arguing that we should concentrate on clarifying the range of possible computational mechanisms before trying to discover which ones are actually used by living creatures.

Correlatively, there is disagreement over the psychological relevance of specific examples of work within AI. Some of this disagreement is grounded not in detailed objections, but in broad philosophical differences over the potential psychological relevance of facts about neurophysiology or hardware.

For instance, there are two 'streams' of work within AI vision research, each of which has spurred psychological experimentations. The theoretical emphases of these two streams are different, and to some degree opposed. One is focussed on low-level computational mechanisms, while the other is focussed on higher-level, top-down processes in scene-analysis. The former (especially in the work of David Marr and his group (Marr 1982)) takes account of psychological optics and neurophysiology in some detail. But the latter considers optics only in very general terms, and ignores neurophysiology on the principled ground that physiological (hardware) implementation is theoretically independent of questions about computational mechanisms.

This last is a widely shared view in AI (in some quarters approaching the status of a dogma), and one which has caused many physiologically minded psychologists to doubt the usefulness of AI work. It is a position that is correct in principle but possibly sometimes misleading in practice. In an abstract theoretical sense, all computing devices are equivalent, just as all programming languages are. But to ignore the varying computational powers of distinct (electronic or physiological) hardware may be as stultifying in practice as to try to use a single programming language for all programs. The differences between programming languages often matter: a computation that can be expressed easily if one uses the representational potential of one language may be difficult, or even practically infeasible, if one relies on another. Clearly, further computationally informed work on neurophysiological mechanisms is needed. It may be that phsyiology is relevant to the relatively peripheral processing but irrelevant at higher levels, but the precise points at which one may expect physiology to have a casting vote are controversial (some of Marr's earlier work on the cerebellum, for instance, is now attracting interest within AI).

If one could prove that a particular computation simply could not be carried out in realtime by any existing cerebral mechanism, then the use of 'alien' computer hardware to effect it would be psychologically irrelevant. However, our ignorance of both computational and neurophysiological constraints preempts such proofs. Nor can we prove that only mechanisms like those in our brains are capable of certain computations. The most that can be claimed as 'physiological' support of a programmed model is that it is consonant at some significant level with neurophysiology.

This claim is made, for example, in support of a very recent advance in the computational modelling of vision (Hinton 1981). Hinton's work is focussed on low-level, dedicated hardware, mechanisms that are capable of cooperative computation, or parallel processing. Although it is not a simulation of detailed neurophysiology, Hinton believes it to be a prime strength of his model that it is compatible with what is known about nervous function. For instance, it relies on excitatory and inhibitory connections between computational units on various levels that appear to have an analogue in the nervous connectivity of our own visual system.

Critics of AI often complain that one program does not make a theory, any more than one swallow makes a summer. That is, AI is accused of being 'empirical' in the sense in which much of medicine is, that it achieves practical results by methods it does not understand and which it therefore cannot responsibly generalize. This is indeed a methodological shortcoming of much AI work — but not of all. Thus Hinton's research is especially interesting because it provides not only an *example* of a program that achieves a desired result (the 'perception' of shape), but also a *general proof* that results of this class can be computed by computational systems of this form that are within specific size-constraints. In brief, he has proved that many fewer computational units are necessary for the parallel computation of shape than one might initially have supposed. This proof lends some more physiological weight to the model, since the human retina apparently has enough cells to do the job.

Because Hinton's model of vision utilizes a type of computation fundamentally different from that of 'traditional' AI, it raises the question of just which psychological phenomena AI can be used to illuminate, and which it cannot. Hinton's results suggest that parallel-processing systems can perform shape discriminations — such as recognition of an overall Gestalt — commonly believed (even within AI) to require relatively high-level interpretative processes. They suggest also that the way in which an object is represented may be radically different depending on whether it is perceived as an object in its own right or as a part of some larger whole. This might account for the phenomenological differences between perceptual experiences of which we are reminded by those philosophers (e.g. Dreyfus 1972) who argue that AI is essentially unfitted to model human minds. In general, commonly expressed philosophical criticisms of AI and cognitive psychology that assume serial processing may be invalidated by these recent developments.

This would be doubly true if the computational techniques of this work on vision can be generalized to other domains. Hinton believes, for example, that his computational model of spatial relations enables motor control to be understood in a new way, one that is significantly analogous to the mechanisms of muscular control in the human body. Phenomenologically influenced philosophers, as well as scientists concerned with the psycho-physiology of movement, commonly complain that AI does not — or even cannot — model the body. Many philosophers and psychologists argue that human intelligence is rooted in our embodiment as material beings situated in a material world, and see AI as therefore radically irrelevant. Most current computers do not have 'bodies' that can move in and manipulate the external world, and even robots are currently very crude in their motor abilities. But Hinton's preliminary work on motor control suggests an efficient way of computing a jointed limb's movements and pathway through space (a problem that can be solved by traditional computing techniques only in a highly inefficient manner).

Even where psychologists deliberately match experimental results against theories expressed in programmed form (e.g., Newell and Simon's (1972) work on problem-solving), the psychological relevance of the computational model is debatable. It is not always clear just which aspects of a program one might plausibly expect to be open to empirical test. Some aspects are not intended to have any psychological reality, but are included merely to produce a program that will run. However, one cannot be sure that none of these last have any psychological significance, since it is a prime claim of AI that it can highlight procedural lacunae in our theories and offer us new concepts with which to jump the gap. Nor is the methodology of protocol-matching unproblematic: what is one to conclude from the fact that *no* behavioural protocol is observed to match a specific process posited by the programmed theory, or that some matching protocol *is* observed? These problems (which have analogous forms to trouble all experimental psychologists) have been discussed by both proponents and opponents of AI, but there is no consensus about the extent to which they cast doubt on a computational approach to empirical psychology.

Of the many people who would concede that certain aspects (at least) of vision, language-use, and problem-solving might yield to an AI approach, some may feel that social psychology, for instance, has nothing to gain from computational insights (e.g. Gauld and Shotter, 1977). This should not be too hastily assumed, however. Work within AI on the structure of action and the attribution of intentions is relevant to theoretical discussions in social psychology. In general, AI supports the view that there may be generative rules underlying social interaction, or that social perception is a structured interpretative activity. But although these ideas are essentially consonant with a computational viewpoint, specifying them in a particular case is a notoriously difficult matter.

A general account of what sorts of psychological phenomena are or are not grist to the AI-mill would of course be very useful. But firm intellectual ground could be provided for such an account only by a systematic theory of representation. Philosophical discussions of the nature of intentionality are clearly relevant (e.g. Fodor 1981; Dennett 1978b). Some philosophers (e.g. Searle 1980) argue that AI cannot model genuine (biological) intentionality, although the discussions in recent issues of the peer-commentary journal *Behavioural and Brain Sciences* show this claim to be highly controversial. But even Searle admits that it can provide a scientifically useful metaphor for intentionality. This is why AI is potentially relevant to studies that are normally thought of as being 'humanistically' oriented, such as social and clinical psychology (Boden 1972). Given that 'representational' processes in computer models can function as heuristically fruitful analogues of representational processes in our minds, the problem remains of providing an account of the range and efficacy of such processes.

AI has shown that distinct representational forms affect and effect inference in significantly different ways. Hinton's work previously mentioned is one of the many examples that address such issues. Another is Amarel's (1968) comparison of solutions of the 'Missionaries and Cannibals' problem grounded in six representations of increasing power; and a third is Sloman's (1978b) discussion of 'analog' representations, which are interpreted by exploiting the similarity between their own structure and that of the thing represented. However, there is — as yet — little systematic understanding of the power and limitations of different representations. Work in computational logic is pertinent, if it can show whether or not a certain type of representation or computational process is in principle capable of modelling a specific type of knowledge or simulating a given class of psychological process.

General results in the philosophy of science apply to AI-based psychology no less than to non-computational theories. Some such results provide for a rebuttal of common criticisms of the computational viewpoint. For instance, even were it to turn out that AI is not appropriate to the modelling of many psychological phenomena, one should not forget the Popperian point that we would still have learnt something by the enterprise. Science involves conjecture and refutation, and it is an advance to know that a specific conjecture has been empirically rejected, Nor should one forget that some tricky methodological problems apply not only to AI-based psychology but to other theories too. Thus critics of AI often remark – truly – that we cannot conclude from the fact that a computer program achieves a result in a certain way that the mind achieves it in the same way. This is a special case of the general truth that if our theory fits the facts, it may not be the only one to do so. Because of this, conclusive verification of *any* scientific theory is in principle impossible.

Work in AI concerns the nature and functioning of knowledge, and one may hope for an increasing degree of cooperation between AI and philosophical epistemologists. Traditional approaches to reasoning (whether deductive, inductive, or probabilistic) are over-idealized. They ignore epistemologically important features of intelligent inference, features that apply to all finite minds and cannot be dismissed as mere 'psychologism' irrelevant to normative epistemology. AI offers richer and more rigorous descriptions of the various data and procedures that comprise knowledge, and of the computational constraints that necessitate this rich variety.

Current AI-research into the logic of 'non-monotonic reasoning' and 'truth-maintenance', for example, asks how a belief-system can be organized so as to cope with the fact that the proposition may be intelligently 'proved' to be true, yet turn out later to be false. Traditional logicians may wince at this description, but finite minds have to construct their knowledge under this epistemic constraint. Closely related work on 'frames' considers the ways in which single exemplars or stereotypes can be used in a flexible fashion for intelligent (though fallible) reasoning. Current discussion of 'naive physics' examines the everyday (pretheoretical) understanding of concepts such as cause, *shape, thing, pathway, inside, fluid* . . ., and should help to clarify traditional problems concerning concepts like these (Hayes 1979).

As these examples suggest, AI calls for a closer relation between epistemology and empirical science than is usually thought proper by philosophers. Work on non-monotonic reasoning can correctly be described as a 'logical' enquiry, and in principle could have arisen in a non-computational context. In practice, it is AI which has enabled us to recognize the complexity of the problems involved in formalizing everyday inference, and which has extended traditional formal approaches by offering new (computational) concepts suited to express epistemic matters[†]. Developmental psychology (both Piagetian and non-Piagetian) has much to say on what might be called 'naive physics' – as also do studies of the perceptuo-motor basis of language (such as the 'psycholexicology' of Miller and Johnson-Laird (1976)). Biological and physiological considerations are relevant in view of the sensorimotor ground of our knowledge, and there is growing recognition of the extent to which the newborn baby is already equipped with computational structures and procedures fitted to the interpretation of its life-world. Some recent work in the philosophy of mind (Churchland 1979) similarly argues that epistemology cannot ignore our material and biological

†Cf. Chouraqui, Chapter 11 below [Editor's note].

embodiment – but it suffers from a failure to consider the computational point of view.

Thus we need an interdisciplinary epistemology, in which computational insights are integrated with philosophical understanding and with psychological and biological knowledge. Indeed, the need for a genuine interdisciplinarity is a prime lesson of the computational approach. Workers in AI have much to learn from the insights of psychologists, linguists, physiologists, biologists, and philosophers, who in turn can benefit from their computationally informed colleagues (cf. Boden 1981a). Mere intellectual communication across the boundaries of these several disciplines is not enough. We also need mutually cooperative research by people who (albeit specializing in one area) have a familiarity with other fields, and a commitment to their intellectual integration. This vision of 'Cognitive Science' will require modification of current educational practices, so that students are no longer socially separated – and even intellectually opposed – by traditional academic labels.

Reference to education reminds us of the pragmatic, as opposed to the methodological, implications of AI. I have in mind here not primarily the many commercial and administrative applications of AI, though these will radically affect our social relations and institutions. Rather, I mean the way in which the spread of computer analogies of the mind may influence the way people think about themselves and society. As I have argued elsewhere (Boden 1977, Chapter 15), AI is not only not dehumanizing, but is – potentially – positively rehumanizing. There are at least two senses in which this is so.

First, the view of intelligence springing from AI is active and constructive, rather than passive and defeatist like that which all-too-commonly informs current educational (and mental-testing) practices. For example, the AI-grounded educational approach developed by Papert (who contributed for a while to President Mitterand's 'Computers for the People' project in Paris) deliberately fosters constructive self-criticism, so that children concentrate on the specifics of how to get better at doing something, rather than giving up in despair at their lack of 'talent' (Papert 1980). Again, AI-based 'CAI' (Computer Assisted Instruction) focusses on the pupil's active construction and exploration of the relevant domain of knowledge (Brown and Sleeman 1982). In this it differs significantly from the 'mechanistic' approach of traditional 'teaching-machines'.

Second, because AI deals with representational systems, it has a conceptual base that can admit discussion of human subjectivity. This is why, as I remarked earlier, social and clinical psychology can make use of the computational approach. In general, this approach is consonant with humanistic or hermeneutic (interpretative) theories of psychology, rather than with those psychological theories, such as behaviourism, grounded in the objective natural sciences. Correlatively, hermeneutic or intentionalist philosophies of mind are closer in spirit to AI than most of their proponents believe.

This remains true even if one accepts the claim of some philosophers (e.g. Searle) mentioned above, that the processes in computer programs are not really representations, and do not really possess intentionality, but that these terms as used by the computer scientist are parasitic on their use in the human psychological context. The point is that the representational *metaphor* (for such it is, on this view) is one that is suited to express psychological phenomena (which alone are *truly* representational or intentional) precisely because it is drawn from those parts of our everyday conceptual scheme that concern these matters. For concepts to be fruitful in the theory and methodology of an empirical psychology, it is not required that they be interpreted as literal descriptions of the phenomena, just as we need not see the atom as *literally* a solar system in order to benefit from the notion of 'planetary' electrons. So, whether computer programs specify representational processes or merely 'representational' ones, they are conceptually close to hermenuetic forms of psychology rather than to those forms that ignore subjectivity.

Educational projects within society at large are needed to alert people to these facts. For most people associate computers with relatively stupid 'brute force' programs (such as those used to calculate gas-bills), and think of them as machines and therefore as 'mechanistic'. They fail to realize that computational machines are radically different from non-computational machines, and that they are not 'mechanistic' in the sense which implies a denial of subjectivity. The mistaken, though widespread, assumption that AI models of man are mechanistic in this sense may make people experience a threat to — or even an undermining of — their personal autonomy and moral responsibility. Behaviourism in psychology and philosophy of mind has been often, and justly, criticized for its underestimation or denial of these psychological characteristics. But the computational approach, if properly understood, is not open to such criticisms. To realize this is to disarm the computational bogeyman.

10

Logic and programming

Richard Ennals and Jonathan Briggs

This Chapter has two purposes. The first is to locate the activity of logic pro-gramming in its context in the history of ideas, and in particular the tradition concerned with the formalizing of human reasoning using logic. The second is to harness the skills and enthusiasms of trained minds to the development of a new field: the intelligent use of computers to assist in the solution of everyday human problems. Logic Programming has been identified as the core of the new Fifth Generation of Computers that are now under development. Hardware development is proceeding as planned, and costs are falling. New powerful programming tools are on the way, drawing their power from logic. At this stage a training in logical thinking begins to count more than a conventional grounding in computer science.

1. CONTEXT IN THE HISTORY OF IDEAS

Logic is a very old science. Over two thousand years ago Aristotle focused on the idea of 'following from' — the notion of logical consequence, that is the central idea of logic. The attention of the logician has been only on the form of the assertion that he is dealing with, not the content but only the form. Through Socratic syllogisms, Aristotelian laws of thought, and medieval scholasticism were developed means of classifying and checking arguments.

Leibniz (Parkinson 1966) took the idea further, and dreamt of mechanizing deductive reasoning. He wrote: 'How much better will it be to bring under mathematical laws human reasoning which is the most excellent and useful thing we have'. This would enable the mind to 'be freed from having to think directly of things themselves, and yet everything will turn out correctly'. His actual achievements were disappointing, though he had taken the enormous step of conceiving of logic as a deductive science.

Frege (van Heijenoort 1967) explicitly built on Leibniz's work, stating his intention to 'express a content through written signs in a more precise and clear way than it is possible to do through words'. He developed an artificial language that can be seen as the ancestor of systems of mathematical logic and of computer programming languages. The practical impact of these ideas at the time was limited, as they were very advanced, and seen as obscure and impenetrable. The mathematician Gödel (1946), writing about Leibniz and Frege, provides the context in terms of a history of ideas that were ahead of their time:

> Leibniz did not in his writings . . . speak of a utopian project; if we are to believe his words he had developed this calculus of reasoning to a large extent, but was waiting with its publication till the seed could fall on fertile ground.

Gödel has received considerable attention for his work on Incompleteness. It is his work on Completeness, however, that has provided much of the basis for the work of Alan Robinson (1965, 1970, 1982). Many logicians had been waiting impatiently for the computer to become a practical tool. Several, such as Gilmore and Wang, made immediate use of early computers, writing down almost verbatim the methods Gödel, Herbrand and Skolem had described in the pre-computer age. The algorithms that Gödel and Herbrand described were for the human computer, not an automatic machine but a person systematically following a plan of work. It had always seemed to be a possibility that you might be able to make a machine perform that task. Paul Gilmore's first attempts were successful, but extremely slow. Martin Davis and Hilary Putnam were able to change Gilmore's programming in a minor way and to produce an enormous improvement. Robinson was able to take further unknown work by Herbrand and make dramatic further improvements in the performance of the same algorithm. Robinson's exposition in 1965 of the resolution principle led first to an explosion of interest in mechanical theorem-proving, and then to the development of logic programming, with the first implementation of PROLOG (PROgramming in LOGic) in Marseille in 1972 (Roussel 1975).[†]

Robinson assessed the current position in his paper 'Logical reasoning in machines':

> We seem now to be in a plateau where we are not gaining very much more of that sort of advantage but we are finding that the algorithm in the form that we now have it is surprisingly useful. We are beginning to discover all sorts of unexpected uses for it, one of which is as the

---

[†]Introductions to Logic Programming are provided in Kowlaski 1979; Clocksin and Mellish 1981; Clark et al. 1981; Ennals 1982.

inner engine of a new way of programming, a new kind of computation
facility which appears to have many remarkable advantages.

Robinson sees logicians as concerned with form, using variables to express
generality by showing patterns which fit infinitely many cases. They catalogue
logical forms, which are capable of being represented symbolically as data
structures — matrices, lists, and other kinds of data structures that you can
completely represent inside computers or on paper. Given the right ideas about
representation then operations or manipulations can be performed on the represented forms, just like any other data. Thus because of the manner in which that
form can be handled concretely, there is really no mystery about what logical
reasoning, as seen by the computational logicians, really is. It is just a kind of
data processing.

Computers do not have to imitate the way that humans do things, although
of course the great precedent for all this is that humans have been doing it for a
long time. One of the problems with Gilmore's early program was that it was put
into the computer in the form in which it was originally devised, a human-
oriented form. A general point applies to all kinds of computing: do it the best
way you can, whether or not it is simulating the way humans do it.

An important point made by Robinson, crucial to the present authors'
work in educational computing, is that in order to find the machine's answers
useful to you, you do not have to know how it arrived at the answers. You can
certainly use the answer that a proof-finding machine gives you, if it does give
you one, because it is a proof. That is what proofs are for. They are devices for
acting on the human data processing system.

A further crucial distinction must be made between the context of discovery and the context of justification. The context of discovery, searching for a
proof, may be mysterious, involving guesswork and creativity. One beauty of the
theorem-proving problem is that the messiness of discovery can be ignored. Our
interest is in the outcome, which can be understood however it was discovered.
We can all understand the proof, provided it is short and simple, of theorems
that have frustrated logicians for centuries.

A similar analysis can be applied to the construction of 'expert systems', or
'intelligent knowledge-based systems'. Typically such a system will consist of a
collection of assertions gathered together in a knowledge base — the facts,
definitions and heuristics relating to that particular subject. We also have an
inference engine, where the reasoning takes place. What happens is that inference
engine takes into account simply the form of the particular problem, the theorem
to be proved or the question to be answered, and whatever is relevant from the
knowledge base, again by virtue of its form and not its content. The machine
does not know or care what you are talking about. It covers only whether what
you say follows from what you have agreed to assume. Our machine restricts
the problem of search by only following one kind of inference rule — resolution.
It is a rule of inference that Robinson has codified and described exactly, which

is adequate all by itself as the only rule needed in predicate calculus; embodied in the unification algorithm.

Robert Kowalski, now of Imperial College, gave a computational interpretation to these logical systems, which he called 'logic programming'. At the same time Alain Colmerauer and his colleagues in Marseille implemented this idea as PROLOG. The programmer user of PROLOG thinks that what he is doing is programming a machine that will then run on data, but the programming actually consists of asserting things into the knowledge base. The program simply consists of assertions that you believe are true about your problem domain. You then form your questions in such a way that it is an input to the program, and the act of getting the answers is the running of the program for that input.

The principal PROLOG implementer, David Warren, has argued that there are no errors to make in PROLOG. You can either omit some relevant piece of knowledge from the knowledge base or you can include some information which ought not to be there. Either way, the error (if we call it that) which shows up is that you will not get exactly the answers that you expected. Such errors are not 'system crashes' — it is natural that some questions have no answers from a given knowledge base.

There are problems. In particular we still find it difficult to deal with explicitly negative information. Harnessing the full power of predicate logic is not at present within our grasp, and in using PROLOG we have to accept the limitations of the Horn clause subset of full first order logic. Our objective remains full logic programming, and we are constantly surprised by what can be achieved with the tools currently at our disposal. Our work with children, for instance, indicates that the availability of logic as a computer language can provide a considerable enhancement to the learning, not only of logic, but of the whole range of school subjects, where there is an agreed emphasis on the values of developing logical thinking.

2. HARNESSING THE SKILLS AND ENTHUSIASMS OF TRAINED MINDS

Current implementations of PROLOG are crude and limited relative to the aspiration of full logic programming, but even so we can make use of it as a tool in a range of intellectual activities. Whereas ten years ago possible users were put off by the cost of the computer hardware and PROLOG implementations were hard to obtain, neither of these problems remains, and considerable research effort has been devoted to improving the user-friendliness of available systems. Indeed, among the objectives of the Japanese Fifth Generation Project (see, for instance, Fuchi 1981) is the development of 'handy' systems that are amenable to use by the non-computer-specialist, ideally in his or her natural language. Our work at Imperial College on the project 'Logic as a Computer Language for Children' should be seen in this context. Schools provide a ready captive source of non-computer-specialists, in a context where intelligent learning is the objective. We have been able both to develop materials for teaching Logic as a Computer Language in its own right, and to work with subject specialists in developing materials to assist in the teaching of a wide range of school subjects. This experience has also been used for work with other non-computer-specialists such as historians, doctors, linguists and social scientists, drawing on the expertise of trained minds in their own areas of specialist interest. Logic can offer a common notation, and a declarative approach to logic programming can prove extremely useful, not so much in providing 'all the answers' but in focusing attention on a new series of interesting questions.

With the recent proliferation of relevant software it has been important to adopt an approach that is as far as possible independent of particular machines, implementations, or even of a particular language. It was gratifying to establish, on a recent visit to Syracuse, a common context with researchers using the logic programming language LOGLISP (Robinson and Sibert, 1982a, 1982b), and to see them making imaginative use of micro-PROLOG, while also working on a new PROLOG implementation making use of meta-language for large-scale applications. A particular research product of 'Logic as a Computer Language for Children' has been the 'Simple' front-end program, making the language more accessible to naive users. Similar front-end programs are now also becoming available for other implementations, and the exercises developed with children and described in *Beginning micro-PROLOG* (Ennals 1982a) can be used with many different machines, implementations and languages.

An overview of programming activities in the current logic programming community would indicate the evolution of a number of different styles. In particular Clocksin and Mellish, in their *Programming in PROLOG,* have emphasized the power of PROLOG as a programming language like many others, with a procedural approach and concern for efficiency. The wide range of practical applications of PROLOG in Hungary described by Szeredi (Santane-Toth and Szeredi 1982) and his colleagues have incorporated the use of other languages and non-logical augmentations to PROLOG. Kowalski and the Imperial College Logic Programming Group have concentrated on the declarative style, sacrificing considerations of efficiency on current single-processor backtracking implementations in favour of exploring in more theoretical terms the power of logic, and implementations on new machines with parallel architecture, being built at Imperial College and elsewhere (Clark and Gregory 1982). Interestingly, different groups of Japanese researchers are following analogous research strategies, developing both parallel implementations of PROLOG and 'hybrid' systems incorporating elements of PROLOG, LISP and SMALLTALK (Takeuchi *et al.* 1982; Sato and Sakurai 1983).

Our work with children and non-specialists had been predominantly declarative (Ennals 1982a, 1982b, 1983, and forthcoming). We have placed considerable emphasis on clear description and the development of correct specifications, putting an initial onus on the clear thinking of the subject specialist. The description provides us with programs capable of a wide range of possible uses, as in the following example.

Many long words in English are made up of several components, so that it is possible to make sense of an unfamiliar word by breaking it down into familiar parts, and assembling the meanings of the parts into some impression of the meaning of the whole word. A large number of such words are based on Latin, and have a number of common prefixes such as

        prefix (extra)
        prefix (super)
        prefix (in)
        prefix (con)
        prefix (manu)
        prefix (trans)

common stems, such as
        stem (marit)
        stem (natur)
        stem (dur)
        stem (fac)

and suffixes, such as
        suffix (al)
        suffix (ing)
        suffix (ally)
        suffix (ture)

We can give simple meanings for each of these components, as follows:

extra	means	beyond
super	means	more-than
in	means	in
con	means	together
manu	means	with-hands
trans	means	across
marit	means	wedlock
natur	means	life
dur	means	hard
fac	means	make
al	means	(adjective use)
ing	means	(present-participle use)
ally	means	(adverb use)
ture	means	(noun use)

Our program merely consists of the vocabulary and meanings described above, together with list-processing programs that decompose compound words and assemble the meanings of their components, as listed below:

x decomposes-to (y z X) if   prefix (y) and
                             stem (z) and
                             suffix (X) and
                             Y STRINGOF y and
                             Z STRINGOF z and
                             x1 STRINGOF X and
                             (Y Z) appends-to y1 and
                             (y1 x1) appends-to z1 and
                             z1 STRINGOF x

(() x) appends-to x
((x|y) z) appends-to (x|X) if (y z) appends-to X

x has-meaning (y z X) if   x decomposes-to (Y Z x1) and
                           Y means y and
                           Z means z and
                           x1 means X

STRINGOF is a built-in PROLOG relation that converts strings to lists, and vice versa.

We now have a flexible system available, which can be used in a number of different ways. We can find out the meaning of a word.

Which (x manufacture has-meaning x)
Answer is (with-hands make (noun use))
No (more) answers

We can generate a set of words, many of them new to the English language, on a particular theme.

Which ((x y) x has-meaning (y wedlock (adjective use)))
Answer is (extramarital beyond)
Answer is (supermarital more-than)
Answer is (inmarital in)
Answer is (conmarital together)
Answer is (manumarital with-hands)
Answer is (transmarital across)
No (more) answers

We can also generate a large dictionary of compound words, together with their overall meanings, by asking

Which ((x y) x has-meaning y)
Answer is (extramarital (beyond wedlock (adjective use)))
Answer is (extramariting (beyond wedlock (present-participle use)))
Answer is (extramaritally (beyond wedlock (adverb use)))
Answer is (supermarital (more-than wedlock (adjective use)))
Answer is (supermariting (more-than wedlock (present participle use))) etc.

The program can obviously be extended by increasing the number of prefixes, stems and suffixes, which will broaden the range of words produced but render the response time progressively slower. This program deals with a subset of Latin derivatives, and a super-set of compound words in general use from such roots. Equivalent programs could easily be written to handle words derived from the Greek, and for handling words in modern languages such as German that are built up in an analogous manner. The simple grammatical information provided by the suffix could prove useful as a link to a more general parsing program, giving clues regarding the semantics of a word and thus the sentence under analysis. At present the program is merely an automated version of word analysis in terms of prefix, stem and suffix, as provided in beloved classroom texts such as Kennedy's *Latin Primer*.

Work with subject specialists can place the computer scientist in the role of consultant. A subject specialist such as a history teacher may wish to specify the desired format of answer patterns in classroom interactions, and may become involved in broader issues of design of the man—machine interface. Research in such issues is considering intelligent means of displaying and manipulating information on a screen and the interactive use of PROLOG whereby the system can query the user in the same notation as is used by the user to query a data-base. The translation of sentences between two languages, for instance, can be facilitated by the system obtaining answers to questions from the user rather than requiring access to an enormous database of dictionary meanings and grammatical information. Just as Weizenbaum (1966) was able to use a simple program to simulate the sequence of questions of a Rogerian psychoanalyst, so our PROLOG 'automatic confessional' system can take the process a stage further, in that the user's simple description of his personal theology of sin and foregiveness can be used for the confessional interview. In each case the motivation is to lay bare the simplicity of the reasoning process involved. For example, our user could say

English: Someone deserves damnation if he committed a deadly sin but does not repent

PROLOG: x deserves damnation if   x committed y and
                                     y is-a deadly sin and
                                     Not (x repents y)

Our system will query the user on the relations 'committed', 'is-a' and 'repents', with instructions by the programmer

Ask-about committed
Ask-about is-a
Ask-about repents

A sample confessional interview with this program goes as follows, with user's questions in the left-hand column and the questions from the system in the right-hand column.

> Which (x Richard deserves x) Which (x Richard committed x)
> Answer is. secret-drinking
> Answer is. End
> Does (secret-drinking is-a deadly-sin). YES
> Does (Richard repents secret-drinking). NO

Answer is damnation
No (more) answers

This work places little emphasis on the PROLOG execution strategy and the exigencies of the single processor. Rather we have been concerned to take the user's description as it stands as a query or as an addition to a program. In our work with twelve-year-old children using census information from Wimbledon in 1871, they have been able to add their own definition of wealth in terms of the information available to them. They were each familiar with the census entries for a few individual residents of Church Street, and knew that there was no information recorded concerning salaries or incomes. They suggested that it would be useful to count the number of servants living at the same address as a Head of Household and that this would indicate his wealth. Their rule was expressed as follows:

> x wealth y if x relation Head and
> z Is-All (X X relation Servant and
> x live-at Y and
> X live-at Y) and
> x length y

A more sophisticated system such as Warren and Pereira's 'Chat 80' (1981) would re-order the conditions of that rule to enhance the efficiency of its use. Our concern was that a correct description should lead to correct answers to appropriately expressed questions.

Even such small-scale work using logic and programming has raised interesting issues for those concerned with 'mind and machine'. Our toy example of an expert system for finding faults in bicycles can spark off discussions of the nature of expertise.[†] We can describe the causes of various faults that have been observed to occur:

> puncture causes flat
> leaky-valve causes flat
> flat causes uneven-ride
> broken-spoke causes distorted-wheel
> distorted-wheel causes uneven-ride
> distorted-wheel causes erratic-braking
> broken-cable causes brake-failure
> brake-failure causes accident

[†]For accounts of recent work at Imperial College concerning Logic Programming and Expert Systems, see Clark et al. 1982; Clark and Tarnlund 1982; Hammond 1982; Kowalski 1982; Sergot 1982.

We can add a rule that tells us that one thing can lead to another, that one fault can lead to a chain of consequences for the complex system that is your bicycle.

> x leads-to y if   x causes y
> x leads-to y if   x causes z and
>   z leads-to y

Given an observed problem of an uneven ride, we can trace its origins.

> Which (x x leads-to uneven-ride)
> Answer is flat
> Answer is distorted-wheel
> Answer is puncture
> Answer is leaky-valve
> Answer is broken-spoke
> No (more) answers

Alternatively, we can explore the consequences of an observed fault such as a broken spoke.

> Which (x broken-spoke leads-to x)
> Answer is distorted-wheel
> Answer is uneven-ride
> Answer is erratic-braking
> No (more) answers

On a larger scale we will be concerned with more complex information, and with expressing probabilities of degrees of certainty, but the same simple principles will apply.

By taking small examples of complex issues we can often establish common ground between practitioners of what had appeared to be radically different disciplines. The bicycle example, for instance, can strike familiar chords in the minds of doctors, engineers, historians, musicians, linguists; and the common notation and computer assistance are available to all. A simple logic program can prove to be a powerful heuristic tool. Our example is taken from economics,[†] where the concern is to develop deductive systems based on *a priori* premises. The method consists of selecting appropriate entities, specifying the environment in which they interact, and setting them up in a model in which their interactions are worked out by mathematical logic. Our particular subject is post-war British economic policy, and we are exploring the consequences of a policy of deflation. A static account of policies and their consequences appears non-controversial:

deflation means raise-taxes
raise-taxes means lower-spending-power

---

† The example was first suggested by Tim Bedford of Leicester University School of Education.

lower-spending-power means lower-demand-for-products
lower-demand-for-products means less-demand-for-imported-finished-products
lower-demand-for-products   means   less-demand-for-imported-inputs-for-manu-
    facture
lower-demand-for-products means lower-investment
less-demand-for-imported-finished-products   means   balance-of-payments-more-
    favourable
less-demand-for-imported-inputs-for-manufacture   means   balance-of-payments-
    more-favourable
lower-investment means lower-productivity
lower-productivity means less-competitiveness
less-competitiveness means balance-of-payments-less-favourable
less-competitiveness means unemployment
unemployment means lower-spending-power

As with the bicycle example, we can add rules describing how one thing can
directly or indirectly imply another:

> x implies y if   x means y
> x implies y if   x means z and
>   z implies y

We can recursively construct a chain of connections for such a model:

> (x y) chain () if x means y
> (x y) chain (z|X) if x means z and
>   (z y) chain X

The dynamic power of this model greatly exceeds appearances. If we ask, for
instance, what is implied by a policy of deflation

> Which (x deflation implies x)

We receive as answers a non-terminating list of consequences, demonstrating
the 'vicious circle' of deflation resulting from increasing unemployment on this
model. On the computer we can break out by using 'Control C', but in reality
some correcting action is required; if, that is, we accept the premises of the
argument. The same program will generate an infinite set of connections between
deflation and unemployment in answer to the question.

> Which (x (deflation unemployment) chain x)

The approach of logic programming as described depends fundamentally
on a view of problem-solving as problem decomposition. Further issues remain
concerning knowledge representation, for although predicate calculus is an
appropriate notation, there remains the problem of the initial abstraction that
accompanies even the object level of description. Experimental work with
children developing their own programming projects has emphasized the impor-

tance of this stage. Children who are successful at the whole range of programming exercises remain uncertain about the first move to a choice of representation. We should be surprised at this difficulty: as Hoare wrote in his 'Notes on
data structuring' (Dahl *et al.* 1972): 'In practice, even in the formulation of a
problem, the programmer must have some intuition about the possibility of
a solution; while he is designing his abstract program, he must have some feeling
that an adequately efficient representation is available'. Such intuitive feels
cannot be relied on in the non-specialist. The research of the first author of this
paper is concerned with this problem, and some answers appear to be available in
the work of structuralist social scientists and philosophers, where a different
view is taken of the distinction between problem solving and knowledge representation. The mode of description of a particular individual, and his actions or
written products, cannot be considered separately from the context within
which he is working, both intellectual and social. Correspondingly preliminary
research indicates that appropriate software tools for description and problem-
solving can be provided for practitioners of a particular discipline, given a knowledge of the discipline and of the previous work of the individual concerned, and
making use of a combination of object level and meta-level reasoning within
logic programs.

We are dealing here with complex issues. They are not new, but have troubled
academics over the centuries working in a number of traditional disciplines.
What is new is that we have discovered a way to begin to harness the power of
computer technology to the ancient chariot of logical thinking. There is a fresh
stimulus to unearth the work of past charioteers, and to combine the resources
of the range of the world's current intellectual 'gymnasts', producing the 'chariots
of fire' of the new generation.

This paper was written while the first author was visiting lecturer at the School
of Computer and Information Science, Syracuse University, USA, working in
the Logic Programming Research Group led by Professor Alan Robinson. Research at Imperial College, London is supported by the Science and Engineering
Research Council, the Nuffield Foundation and Sinclair Research on the project
'Logic as a Computer Language for Children', directed by Professor Robert
Kowalski.

11

Computational models
of reasoning

Eugene Chouraqui

1. INTRODUCTION

In this chapter we give a survey of the principal methods and techniques developed in Artificial Intelligence (AI) concerning the problems of the design and implementation of computational models of reasoning. We start with an analysis of the notion of reasoning from a number of different points of view (epistemology, linguistics, logic, computer science, etc.). This will allow us to chart the boundaries of this area of research (section 2). In section 3 we give an account of patterns of reasoning in terms of symbolic systems. Using this account, we examine the principal methods which have been employed in this field (section 4). In conclusion, we show that the work relevant to these issues involves the coming together of different disciplines.

2. CLASSIFICATION OF NODES OF REASONING

According to Aristotle a logical argument is 'an utterance such that, certain things having been stated, something else necessarily follows solely because of those stated premises'. This proposition is the basis of the definition of syllogisms which represent elementary forms of deductive reasoning. It has been put into practice by logicians and mathematicians whose work was solely concerned with rigorous logical arguments, that is to say arguments where the conclusion follows necessarily from the premises. The objective of this field of research has been the elaboration of a theory of reasoning with a view to strengthening the foundations of mathematics, and explaining certain paradoxes such as, for example, those that have grown out of set theory.[1] This has more and more led logicians to be interested only in the form, as opposed to the content, of the propositions used in logical arguments; and to elaborate formalisms — essentially syntactic in nature — which have allowed them to replace logical reasoning properly so called by symbolic calculi — that is, by formal systems in which intuition is replaced by operations and/or by elementary and totally explicit rules concerning the manipulation of the symbolic objects of which the systems are composed.[2]

But in the area which interests us here, this mode of reasoning has demonstrated its inadequacy when faced with certain real phenomena whose representations are not reducible to classical formal systems (the literature of AI is full of such examples, such as, for instance, the work relating to natural language understanding, or that relating to the development of problem-solving models in cognitive psychology). It has therefore been necessary to extend the definition of 'reasoning', borrowing ideas developed in other disciplines (philosophy, epistemology, psychology, etc.). In effect, reasoning is in the first place a mental activity which allows the passage from certain propositions stated as premises to a further proposition by virtue of a logical connection of some degree of strength which links the latter to the former. From this point of view reasoning is seen as a combination of intellectual operations which any group of individuals — or any system simulating their behaviour — can employ to solve problems that they set or which are given to them: taking a decision in many cases amounts to giving reasons for or against a particular choice; identifying a criminal leads the detective to examine and assess a whole range of evidence on the basis of which he will make his judgement; understanding a sentence — or more generally a piece of text — in the field of language-learning by a child can lead him into building up, for example, associations of ideas which enable him to draw on past experience (linguistic, cultural, etc.); persuading someone to accept a point of view involves putting an emphasis on the aspects which could favourably influence him, and omitting or minimizing those which could support a contrary view; etc. In all these situations the conclusions at which one arrives are only probable. It follows that these kinds of reasoning do not allow us to draw conclusions with certainty, as is the case with deductive reasoning. Moreover, it is very difficult to gauge the probability of conclusions. The latter depends not merely upon the propositions used in the reasoning (certain or uncertain premises, the nature of unstated arguments, incomplete descriptions of the universe of discourse), but also upon the nature of the logical links which connect them, these links being stronger or weaker, and perhaps establishing only a probabilistic connection. Furthermore, the way in which a person behaves when he is reasoning has to be taken into account. Each person defines his own strategy allowing him to proceed as rapidly as possible towards his goal. However, the carrying out of strategies has hardly interested logicians; to our knowledge only psychology has introduced this notion in the development of cognitive models. The interests of psychologists relative to the conduct of reasoning has a great deal in common with those of computer scientists working in the field of AI. We agree with Pierre Oleron that 'reasoning should be seen as a chain, a combination or a conflict of assertions or of representations, concerning the internal constraints of the subject that can be made explicit, serving to lead towards a goal'.[3]

This very general definition of the notion of reasoning encourages us to classify patterns of reasoning in two large categories: rigorous and non-rigorous. There are naturally other ways of classifying patterns of reasoning.[4] However all such classifications encounter problems to the extent that they have been proposed to satisfy certain specific objectives. We think that our chosen classification corresponds most closely to our interests, and is borne out totally in the field of AI. But the notion of 'non-rigorous reasoning' seems to us less ambiguous than that of 'approximate reasoning' encountered in the literature of AI, since this latter seems to involve particularly reasoning or its component parts weighted in terms of numerical values. 'Rigorous reasoning' is the sort that leads to certain conclusions, and essentially concerns deduction, certain forms of induction, or certain specific forms such as hypothetico-deductive reasoning or *reductio ad absurdum*. There are the logician's patterns of reasoning, patterns whose formalization has allowed the construction of particular formal systems reflecting the intrinsic properties of these patterns. Here we are talking both of 'classical' systems (predicate calculus, many-valued systems, etc.), and non-classical systems (modal, deontic, temporal and dynamic logics). 'Non-rigorous reasoning' leads to probable conclusions, in the sense that, if the premises are uncertain then the relations which link the propositions establish probabilistic connections between them. They relate to certain forms of induction and analogy (which one could group together under the global heading of 'generalizations'); reasoning in ordinary language (styles of argument such as metaphor or analogy, causal reasoning and certain types of conditional reasoning, pragmatic reasoning in linguistics, etc.); certain forms of hypothetico-deductive reasoning; etc. And as we have already seen, these modes of reasoning are very often used in empirical areas of knowledge with little or no theoretical foundation. However, they seem never to be given credit by logicians, except for a few rare attempts.[5] On the other hand they have been studied more systematically by natural language logicians.[6] Such work is obviously of great interest to computer scientists since reasoning must in the last analysis be expressed in terms of written or oral discourse; and it is in these forms that the computer will most often encounter them.

3. THE STRUCTURE OF PATTERNS OF REASONING

The different forms of reasoning that we have just summarized lie at the heart of work concerning AI, to the extent to which such studies naturally have as a principal objective the goal of giving to the computer certain facilities which enable it to describe and solve certain types of problems relating to theoretical or empirical domains, as these are dealt with by 'human experts' in the same domains. In other words, the design and the implementation of intelligent and/or cognitive systems are constantly concerned with the mechanization of the intellectual operations involved in reasoning-patterns, and with their functioning (that is, with analysing or simulating the expert's behaviour) so as to achieve the given end. In our view this applies as much to work on well-established theories, or on theories in the making (such as theorem proving, program verification, program generation, parallelism, etc.), as to work relating to real empirical domains (inferential databases, expert systems, natural language understanding, man—machine communication, computer-aided learning, robotics, computer-aided design, etc.). This work has contributed to the development within AI of formal structures for the representation and the manipulation of symbols associated with particular physical things. We will call such formal structures symbolic (as opposed to formal) systems. We use the term 'symbolic system' because of the diversity of patterns of reasoning for the representation and manipulation of knowledge, as defined in such systems — formal systems only allowing a single mode of reasoning, deduction. (See, on this subject, for example, Newell and Simon 1976).

The construction of symbolic systems necessitates an examination of two types of question: first, the development of representational systems for real subject domains (these systems conveying most often knowledge which is uncertain, contradictory and incomplete); second, the construction of processing systems defined from the elementary reasoning patterns appropriate to the class of problems to be solved. Of necessity, these two types of system relate together in certain specific ways which determine their respective workings. In general, two kinds of calculus can be used in the construction of processing systems. The first kind, strictly numerical in nature, calls on mathematical tools such as probability or inferential statistics (methods known in particular under the heading of data analysis). The second, non-numerical (i.e. symbolic) in nature, manipulates and transforms collections of symbols, and is based largely on logic and/or functional theory (although in particular cases numerical calculi may be used). In this chapter we are particularly interested in the second category of processing system: in the modelling and mechanization of symbolic reasoning as earlier defined. We shall call such processing systems 'models of reasoning'.

The conception of a model of reasoning involves, in our view, four distinct naturally independent stages:

1. The definition of the class of problems to be solved. In part this stage corresponds with the formulation of problems generally expressed in natural language, or at least in terms of the specialist language of the area under consideration, considered as a subject of natural language; in part it corresponds with the description and representation of problems in terms adequate data structures. These two types of question obviously involve important links — as much at the level of syntax and semantics as at the

formal level — with the system of knowledge-representation on which the model of reasoning must operate.

2. The development of structures of reasoning to solve particular problems. This stage has the aim of formally characterizing the nature and patterns of reasoning used in terms of the symbolic definition of transformation operations on the knowledge-base and its logical organization. (We put no *a priori* constraints on the nature of these operations; in particular they can equally easily be of a declarative as of a procedural nature.) The mechanization of models of reasoning leads the computer scientist (as it does the logician) to replace the original piece of reasoning by a symbolic calculus. This usually necessitates the construal of pieces of reasoning in terms of structured inference schemas (the specification of formal properties, the definition of rules of inference, etc.). But this is possible only because the formal power of the model is adequate to articulate the richness of the associated knowledge representation system. This means applying formal operations (such as pattern-matching, unification, etc.) to segments of knowledge so as to determine the primitive reasoning operations. Such operations permit the manipulation of variables and constants, but they also contribute to the description of the reasoning itself (the operation of general filtering, the expression of degrees of uncertainty of data, etc.).

3. The construction of problem-solving procedures which guarantee the mechanization of proof-procedures. This involves devising effective problem-solving methods based on the structure of the reasoning model, and the associated system of knowledge representation. The ease with which it will be possible to put such methods to work will depend on how systematically the formal properties of the reasoning model have been analysed. But, because of problems of storage capacity and execution speed, it will be desirable, if not necessary, to develop strategies to get one as rapidly as possible to the relevant goal. These strategies are but refinements — as much theoretical as empirical — of the basic problem-solving methods: intelligent management of the search space, the definition of general and/or problem-specific heuristics, analysis of failure- and backtracking-points, etc. Finally, to facilitate 'intelligent' man—machine communication, some kind of explanatory component must be built into the problem-solving procedure. Such a component will have a double role: first, to allow the expert to trace fully the steps of reasoning so as to explain the choices made by the system; second to furnish the system, whenever it asks for it, with information on how to conduct the proof procedure (the activation of new reasoning methods, the improvement of performance, etc.).

4. The implementation of learning mechanisms to help in problem solving. Such mechanisms will have the objective of improving the 'intelligent behaviour' of symbolic systems (their capacity to generalize from known information, the evaluation of search strategies based on examples or analogy, etc.). The functions associated with such mechanisms will ob-

viously be complementary to those defined in the explicatory component mentioned above.

4. PRINCIPAL METHODS OF DESIGNING MODELS OF REASONING

Models of reasoning implemented in AI are based on formal methods — either original methods or ones arising from well-established theories — developed with precise aims connected both with the nature of the problems to be solved and with the constraints on effective mechanization of reasoning. Three categories of fundamental question have been opened up in the course of the development of these methods. The first category aims to translate a piece of reasoning properly so called into a symbolic calculus, by means of well-structured inferential procedures; the second, which is directly correlated, has to do with the means of manipulating the data; the final category has to do with the construction of solution techniques as they are actually applied in the conduct of the proof procedure. An overview of these different methods is controversial to the extent that they incorporate an untidy overlap of elements drawn from borrowed theories, and from theories strictly within computer science. Nevertheless we offer in what follows a classification of the principal approaches used in AI, while respecting the view that some of them are 'basic', while others have some kind of formal or functional dependence to the more basic approaches. More precisely, we are interested in the following methods:

(1) classical logics;
(2) pattern-directed inference systems;
(3) non-classical logics;
(4) plan generation;
(5) non-monotonic and common-sense reasoning.

4.1 Classical logics
Two approaches have been particularly developed here: the first is based on the resolution method in first order logic; the second one the method of derivation schemas in the style of Gentzen.

The first method offers the possibility of intentional description of knowledge by means of inference rules in the form of a type of implication (Horn clauses). Robinson's work on unification (an operation of matching tree structures which is essentially syntactic) defines the basic operation of this model of deductive reasoning. The inferential process works on the basis of the principle of resolution and a procedure of proof by refutation. This method has led to the programming language PROLOG which is well suited for the development of deductive models. The methodology of programming in first-order logic and the associated language PROLOG have allowed the development of models of deductive reasoning in three directions:[7] general problem-solving methods, the design of inferential data-bases, and natural language understanding.

The second approach allows the definition of derivation schemas of a hypothetico-deductive type. Known under the general heading of 'methods of natural deduction', it has led to the design of so-called 'natural' systems.[8] The deduction schemas have the form $H \rightarrow G$, in which the goal G can be 'deduced' from the hypothesis H. Collections of organized rules allow the manipulation of the elements making up H and G with a view to obtaining instantiations of the schemas based on particular ways of matching data structures (formal rules of simplification, matching based on the algebraic organization of the elements comprising H and G, forced unification, etc.). Problem-solving methods are implemented through techniques of 'forward chaining', using *modus ponens.* Such a proof procedure can lead to infinite proofs. It is thus necessary to devise mechanisms which allow control of the proof procedure, and which allows in particular the integration in a relatively simple manner of control structures and/or domain-dependent heuristics. This approach is in certain respects closer to the behaviour of the human expert in the sense that the derivation schemas and problem-solving procedures can take account of the segments of knowledge which are not reducible by an axiomatic method to predicate calculus. However, in this type of method the formal study of the model of reasoning becomes imperative.

4.2 Pattern-directed inference systems

The 'natural system' approach has been generalized in the sense that the reasoning methods implemented in systems of this type have been very varied (inductive inference, analogies, causal reasoning, etc.). It has led to the design and implementation of computer systems known as 'pattern-directed inference systems'.[9] These systems are built from three basic components:

(a) A collection of modules, each describing an operation for transforming the knowledge base (which depends naturally on the mode of reasoning used), to which are associated one or more patterns allowing the activation or the inhibition of the corresponding module.

(b) A knowledge base which can be examined or modified by the modules using a pattern-matching technique allowing the comparison of patterns with data structures in the knowledge base.

(c) An interpreter (or inference engine) allowing the solution of problems by the activation of modules and the control of their chaining.

The most commonly found systems are those where the modules are represented by rewrite rules or production rules, which have given rise to the concept of expert systems. These are deductive systems whose proof procedure uses *modus ponens* or *modus tollens* (see section 4.4 below). However, this type of system has been implemented in numerous domains — such as natural language understanding, modelling of human behaviour, and program synthesis — in which the reasoning used is not always of a deductive nature. In this field the patterns utilized are complex and their structures depend on the problems which are to be solved (patterns based on boolean operators, semantic networks, procedural attachment, etc.).

4.3 Non-classical logics

Certain problems arising in AI research are hard to reduce to representations in terms of classical logics. Let us take, for example, the degree of uncertainty that might characterize any particular field of study, the evolutionary nature of that field; and thus the possibility of operating upon an incompletely described and apparently contradictory universe of discourse; the notion of time which plays a major role in the description of processes; and finally the types of links which can connect components of a model of reasoning in such a universe. Let us recall that in classical logics, the sole attested connection is 'material implication'. However, the analysis of reasoning, notably during an argumentative discussion, reveals the diversity of links which can effectively form part of a process of argument: different forms of conditions, causal relations, necessary or probable connections, the role of grammatical tenses in the chaining of propositions, etc. These are problems which have led computer scientists to conceive other models of reasoning unrelated to the predicate calculus. These are based on non-classical logics which one can categorize in a very general manner as modal logics and fuzzy logics.[10]

Modal logics are characterized from a semantic point of view by the notion of possible worlds; each world characterizing a certain knowledge state at a given moment. Problem-solving procedures which have been developed by logicians and implemented by computer scientists are of two type: the tableau method and the resolution method. The tableau method, which associates a single tree with all possible worlds, defines reduction proof procedures which in fact express exactly the inverse of the deduction techniques associated with the methods of Gentzen. The resolution method is based on a resolution principle and a method of proof by refutation, which is analogous to the resolution method used in the predicate calculus. These theories have allowed the development of a number of computational models of reasoning:[11] inductive reasoning, reasoning about actions, the computer representation of time, the formal expression of the growth of knowledge, etc.

Fuzzy logics have well-defined schemata for rules of plausible detachment, but to our knowledge, these schemata have not given rise to developments in the field which concerns us here, with a few exceptions. However, such methods have allowed the generalization of inference rules having the form of implications, by weighting them with numerical values expressing their degree of certainty (for example 1 = necessary, 0 = impossible). The methods of certain calculi allow values to be combined, and thus enable one to assign weights to the conclusions of pieces of reasoning (fuzzy sets, coefficients of probability, of plausibility, etc.).[12] On the other hand, this approach has allowed the definition of matching operations on data structures based on this type of calculus, using the notion of fuzzy matching to allow the expression of certain forms of induction and analogical reasoning.

4.4 Plan generation

This method allows the modelling of reasoning in terms which it is convenient to call 'plan formation'. One is given an initial state, a goal state and a collection of actions or of state transformation operators. The problem is to construct a plan, that is to say an appropriate sequence of actions, which transforms the initial state into the goal state. The operators, defined in general by rewrite- or production-rules, can eventually be weighted. The problem-solving method consists in constructing a solution space representing a graph directed according to the nature of the rules. It uses in general a method of problem solving by decomposition and construction of corresponding AND/OR graphs, and is based on a proof procedure using *modus ponens* (forward chaining) or *modus tollens* (backward chaining). Solution spaces are usually represented by trees (by the eventual repetition of occurrences of nodes), for which several search strategies have been developed. Some use an essentially syntactic method (depth-first or breadth-first search, or a mixture of these methods, cut functions, and/or node-related search-paths, branch and bound method, etc.). Others use a 'more' semantic approach (analysis of failures encountered during the proof, analogical methods, organizations of the knowledge base, or of meta-rules, etc.). Plan generation techniques have been used primarily in the design of expert systems,[9] but they have also been employed in other domains, such as models of reasoning incorporating speech acts, validation of psychological theories with the aid of plan-formation systems, etc.[13]

4.5 Non-monotonic and common-sense reasoning

Methods based upon non-monotonic logic have allowed the expression of common sense reasoning:[14] default reasoning, 'circumscription', minimal implication, links between explicit and implicitly expressed negations, etc. Also argumentative or 'common-sense' reasonings have been modelled either by developing particular logical systems, or by using anological organization based on knowledge representation in terms of semantic networks, or frames.[15]

5. CONCLUSION

This rapid survey shows the manifest interest which the scientific community working in the field of AI has in the problems of the design and implementation of computer models of reasoning. This work covers both fundamental research and applications. Significant results have been attained in the domain of 'computational logic'. At the same time the examination of certain forms of non-deductive reasoning has led to the development of original models in which new ideas and concepts have been introduced.

However, this kind of research is not a domain reserved for AI workers. We believe that, as has been emphasized by a number of authors,[16] this work involves a confluence of many disciplines, such as logic, linguistics, cognitive psychology, programming language design, application domains, etc. The methods and models issuing from these disciplines must be considered as theories to be borrowed from, whose elements may be applied to the phenomena under study, and may contribute to the resolution of certain types of question in the construction of intelligent knowledge-based computer systems. If one admits that reasoning is expressed − in the final analysis − by a written or oral discourse, the major role to be played by the different disciplines becomes clear (use of linguistic theories − sentences, texts, argumentation, etc.; the influence of psychological models of the acquisition of specific kinds of knowledge or expertise; the importance of classical logics and non-classical logics in the formalization of models of reasoning; etc.).

Further, current methodological advances can be confirmed and amplified only within the framework of an activity of research and development which takes account, we believe, of two specific factors affecting the conduct of this type of research. First, AI remains largely an experimental science; on the other hand, it involves the coming together of several disciplines. This state of affairs implies not only a deepening of theoretical concentration on the theories and methods borrowed from other disciplines for the computational modelling of reasoning, but also the development of a theoretical and experimental programme of research with the aim of mechanizing and validating models developed as part of applications relating to the real world. But a large number of pieces of research in AI have rested upon conventional and isolated examples. This is probably one of the causes of the difficulties which this field of research has faced in the last few years in solving the − often ambitious − problems which it has set itself. In fact the choice of applications domains is one of the principal elements contributing to the way any experimental advance defines its epistemological framework. The point is crucial: it allows not only the opening up of theoretical and technical questions whose richness and complexity will pose unheard-of problems to the computer scientist, but also the construction of experimental prototypes, whose application to the industrial and tertiary sectors will be able to be evaluated in an effective and properly informed manner.

Translated by Richard Ennals.

NOTES

1. See on this subject Russell 1913 and Ladrière 1952.
2. See, for example, Porte 1965 and Jeffrey 1967, for an introduction to these questions.
3. Oleron 1977.

4. See on this subject Blanche 1973, Dorolle 1949, and Ajsukiewicz 1955.

5. See on this subject Polya 1962, and all the recent work on fuzzy logic and the logic of possibility issuing from Zedeh, e.g. Zadeh 1977; see also note 12 below.

6. Such as, for example, Cresswell 1973, Grize 1979, Perelman 1970, and Borillo *et al.* 1082.

7. Roussel 1975; Robinson 1965; Kowalski 1979; Chang and Lee 1973; van Caneghem 1982.

8. For a general presentation of these questions, refer, for example, to Dopp 1962, and to Bledsoe 1977.

9. Waterman and Hayes-Roth 1978, Davis and King 1977, Laurière 1982, Bramer 1980, Hayes-Roth *et al.* 1983.

10. Refer, for example, to: Kling 1971, Chen and Findler 1979, Chouraqui 1982, Winston 1980, Gick and Holyoak 1980, and Findler and Chen 1973.

11. Farinas del Cerro 1981; McCarthy and Hayes 1969; Moore 1977. Schwind 1980; Chouraqui 1983.

12. Zadeh 1977; Prade 1982; Kayser, 1979; Shortliffe 1976.

13. As, for example, in Cohen and Perrault 1979.

14. Reiter 1980; McCarthy 1980; Siegel and Bossu 1981.

15. Schank 1973; Rumelhart and Norman 1975; Borillo 1979; Bobrow and Collins 1975; Chouraqui 1981. See also note 10 above.

16. On this subject see McCarthy 1977 and McCarthy and Hayes 1969.

12

Meta-level inference and consciousness

Alan Bundy

Of all the mental phenomena exhibited by the human mind none seems to offer more of a challenge to Artificial Intelligence (AI) modelling than consciousness. So much so that it is rarely discussed (I would say unconsciously avoided) in AI. This chapter addresses the question: Can AI shed light on the phenomenon of consciousness? The question can be fruitfully divided into two subquestions.

(a) Can AI modelling help us to understand the role of consciousness in cognition (if it has a role)?
(b) Could we build a computer program which experienced the sensation of consciousness?

My personal answers to these questions are:

(a) Almost certainly yes; in fact, progress has already been made, and this paper is a contribution to that debate.
(b) This is the classic problem of 'other minds' in a new guise. We might answer (a) to most people's satisfaction, and this might enable us to build a machine which behaves as if it were conscious. Whether we would then be happy to attribute consciousness to it, and whether we would then better understand the subjective experience of consciousness, are open questions. We will not address question (b) further in this paper.

The analogy from AI which we will bring to the study of consciousness is some work on the guiding of mathematical proofs using a technique called meta-level inference, which has been developed by the author and his co-workers and used in the domains of equation-solving (Bundy and Welham 1981), program verification (Bundy and Sterling 1981) and physics problem solving (Bundy *et al.* 1982). We will investigate the relation between meta-level inference and consciousness and conclude that, contrary to the views expressed by some previous authors, meta-level inference does not offer a computational model of consciousness.

1. AUTOMATIC INFERENCE

Meta-level inference is an attempted solution for the combinatorial explosion problem in AI. This problem arises, for instance, in the computational modelling of inference.

   Inference can be modelled on a computer by symbolically representing goals, hypotheses and rules, and writing a computer program to apply rules to hypotheses to derive valid consequences from them, until one of these consequences is found to be a goal. Alternatively, a program can be written to apply rules backwards to goals to discover subgoals, until these subgoals are found to be hypotheses. In equation solving the hypothesis would be the equation to be solved, e.g.

$$\log(e, x+1) + \log(e, x-1) = 3^{\dagger}$$

and the goal would be an expression of the form $x = Ans$, where Ans does not contain x, or possibly a disjunction of such expressions. These expressions can be manipulated by directed algebraic identities, called **rewrite rules**, e.g.

$$(u+v) \cdot (u-v) \Rightarrow u^2 - v^2 {}^{\ddagger}$$

The left-hand side of such rules is matched to the current expression, and the matched part is replaced by the right hand side to produce a new expression (see Fig. 1). This process starts with the hypothesis and continues until the goal is derived.

$$\log(e, (x+1) \cdot (x-1)) = 3$$
$$(u+v) \cdot (u-v) \Rightarrow u^2 - v^2$$
$$\log(e, x^2-1^2) = 3$$

Fig. 1 – The application of a rewrite rule.

   Often several rules can be applied to an expression to produce new expressions (see Fig. 2). Several rules then apply to each of these new expressions, and the number of new expressions rises exponentially (or worse) with the depth of the proof. This phenomenon is an example of the combinatorial explosion.

† The first argument of log is the base.
‡ We use the convention that the unknown to be solved for in an equation is denoted by x and the variables in a rule are denoted by u, v, w, etc.

Even modern electronic computers cannot cope with the storage overload that this rapid growth produces, with the consequence that only simple theorems can be proved automatically by exhaustive search.

$$\log(e, (x+1) . (x-1)) = 3$$

$$u.v \Rightarrow v.u \qquad\qquad (u+v).(u-v) \Rightarrow u^2 - v^2$$

$$u+v \Rightarrow v+u \qquad u=v \Rightarrow v=u$$

$$\log(e, (x-1) . (x+1)) = 3 \qquad\qquad\qquad \log(e, x^2-1^2) = 3$$

$$\log(e, (1+x) . (x-1)) = 3 \qquad 3 = \log(e, (x+1) . (x-1))$$

Fig. 2 — A few of the alternative applications of rewrite rules.

Some of the applications of rules in Fig. 2 look silly — and they are, in context — but these rules cannot be removed from the program because there are other contexts in which their application is sensible.

2. META-LEVEL INFERENCE

In order to prove more interesting theorems, it is necessary to guide the search for a proof so that the only rules applied to expressions are those with a high probability of being in the proof. In meta-level inference this guidance information is formalized as an axiomatic meta-theory. This meta-theory describes the representation of the original (or object-level) theory. Inference in the meta-theory induces an implicit inference process in the object-level theory.

In order to clarify this discussion we will describe the use of meta-level inference in the Press (PRolog Equation Solving System) program for algebraic manipulation (Sterling *et al.* 1982). The object-level encodes knowledge about the rules of algebra, while the meta-level encodes methods of guiding algebraic manipulation. What are the advantages of this technique?

- The meta-level search space is usually much smaller then the object-level space it is controlling and this helps overcome the combinatorial explosion.
- The separation of factual and control information enhances the clarity of the program.
- Using inference to control search makes this control more flexible, i.e. more responsive to variations in the situation than if search were controlled by a more conventional program.
- The separate formalization of factual (object-level) and guidance (meta-level) knowledge simplifies the task of automating the learning of both kinds of knowledge.

3. GUIDING THE SEARCH FOR A SOLUTION

The guidance knowledge encoded in Press was discovered by analysing the solutions of experienced mathematicians. The area of equation solving being modelled is known to be undecidable, so these mathematicians could not be using a decision procedure — there must have been an element of search in their behaviour. However, analysis quickly reveals that they negotiate a highly explosive search with very few false steps. It was these properties which originally attracted us to equation solving as a domain.

Consider the solution in Fig. 3. The arabic numerals label the lines of the solutions and the roman numerals label the steps between them. To understand the reasons for taking each of these steps, look first at the last three steps: (iii), (iv) and (v). In each of these steps the dominant function on the left-hand side is 'stripped-off', inverted and moved to the right-hand side. After three such steps the unknown, x, is left isolated on the left-hand side. We call this method **Isolation**. It can be applied to equations of all types (logarithmic, trigonometric, exponential, etc.), provided only that each of the functions surrounding the unknown has an inverse.

However, this method cannot be applied to equation (2) in Fig. 3, because it contains two occurrences of x. If one of these were isolated then the other occurrence would be moved to the right-hand side of the equation at some stage, and the result would not be a solution. We can now understand step (ii) as an enabling step for Isolation, which reduces the number of occurrences of x from two to one. We call such a step **Collection**, because occurrences of the unknown are collected together.

(1) $\log(e, (x+1)) + \log(e, (x-1)) = 3$

i

(2) $\log(e, (x+1) . (x-1)) = 3$

ii

(3) $\log(e, x^2-1) = 3$

iii

(4) $x^2-1 = e^3$

iv

(5) $x^2 = e^3+1$

v

(6) $x = \pm\sqrt{e^3+1}$

Fig. 3 — The solution of an experienced mathematician.

Step (i) does not reduce the number of occurrences of x, but it does enable Collection to apply, by moving the two occurrences of x closer together. For this reason we call it **Attraction**.

4. ISOLATION – AN ALGEBRAIC MANIPULATION METHOD

The principles of meta-level inference can be illustrated by considering how one of these methods, Isolation, is implemented in Press. Isolation is a simple, general method for solving equations which is only attempted on equations containing a single occurrence of the unknown, x, e.g. on

$$\log(e, x^2-1) = 3$$

but not on

$$e^{\sin(x)} + e^{\cos(x)} = a$$

The stripping off of the functions surrounding x is done by applying a system of rewrite rules to the equation, for instance, the rules

$$\log(u_1, u_2) = v \Rightarrow u_2 = u_1^{v}$$

$$u_1 - u_2 = v \Rightarrow u_1 = v + u_2$$

$$u^2 = v \Rightarrow u = \sqrt{v} \text{ or } u = -\sqrt{v}$$

All of them are characterised by the description:

$$P \& f(u_1, \ldots u_i, \ldots u_n) = v \rightarrow \text{RHS} \tag{i}$$

where RHS is usually of the form $u_i = f_i(u_1, \ldots, v, \ldots, u_n)$, but can also be a disjunction of such formulae, f_i is the ith inverse function of $f^{\dagger}$ and P is an optional condition. The number i is stored with each rewrite rule to simplify the job of Isolation in locating the appropriate rule. When the rule is matched to an equation, u_i must be matched to a term containing x and v and the other u_js must be matched to terms that do not contain x.

Before Isolation is called, the position of the single occurrence of x is calculated and recorded as a list of argument numbers (see Fig. 4).

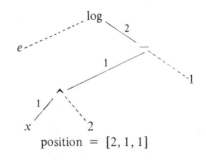

position = [2, 1, 1]

Fig. 4 – The position of x in $\log(e, x^2 - 1)$.

This list is then recursively traversed, each number providing a key for locating a rule to be applied.

† An n-ary function has n inverse functions.

5. META- AND OBJECT-LEVELS

The object-level in Press consists of algebraic rules describing relationships between real numbers. Given an equation to be solved, these define an object-level search space. This space has a high branching rate, as is usually the case with mathematical theories involving equality.

Press consists of a collection of predicate calculus clauses which together constitute a PROLOG program. As well as the procedural meaning attached to these clauses, which defines the behaviour of the Press program, they also have a declarative meaning — that is, they can be regarded as axioms in a logical theory. For instance, consider the following clauses, extracted from the program and rewritten in standard predicate calculus notation.[‡]

$$\text{singleocc}(X, L = R) \& \text{postion}(X, L, P) \& \text{isolate}(P, L = R, \text{Ans})$$
$$\rightarrow \text{solve}(L = R, X, \text{Ans}) \tag{ii}$$

$$\text{isolax}(I, FU_i = V, RHS, \text{Condition}) \& \text{isolate}(\text{Rest}, RHS, \text{Ans})$$
$$\rightarrow \text{isolate}([I|\text{Rest}], FU_i = V, \text{Ans}) \tag{iii}$$

$$\text{isolax}(2, \log(U1, U2) = V, \ U2 = U1^{\wedge}V, \text{true}) \tag{iv}$$

The declarative meanings of (ii), (iii) and (iv) are:

- (ii) if $L = R$ contains precisely one occurrence of X located at position P in L and if the result of isolating X in $L = R$ is Ans then Ans is a solution of $L = R$ with respect to X
- (iii) If the result of applying a rewrite rule to $FU_i = V$, to isolate the argument position I, is RHS, and the result of isolating RHS with respect to position Rest is Ans, then the result of isolating $FU_i = V$ with respect to position $[I|\text{Rest}]$ is Ans. ($[I|\text{Rest}]$ is the list of numbers Rest with I on the front.)
- (iv) The result of applying an Isolation rewrite rule to $\log(U1, U2) = V$ to isolate the second argument of log is $U2 = U1^{\wedge}V$. (The 'true' in the condition slot of isolax indicates that there are no condition. The expression '$U1^{\wedge}V$' means 'U1 raised to the power of V'.)

The Press program uses (ii), (iii) and (iv) as pieces of program for trying to solve an equation for an unknown by testing for a single occurrence of the unknown and if successful trying to Isolate the unknown.

Of what formal theory are (ii), (iii) and (iv) axioms? Well, between what kinds of objects do they express relationships? These are not numbers (or matrices or points), but algebraic expressions such as equations, variables and terms. The relationships expressed are syntactic ones, like the number of occurrences of this term in this expression is so much; or the result of applying this

[‡]except that a word starting with a capital letter denotes a variable and one starting with a lower-case letter denotes a constant.

axiom to this expression is that expression. Hence axioms (ii), (iii) and (iv) represent knowledge about the *representation* of algebra. This means that the formal theory described by Press is the **Meta-Theory of Algebra**.

In the Meta-Theory of Algebra the objects being manipulated are algebraic: variables, constants, functions, formulae, logical connectives, etc. So these are all represented as variable free terms in the meta-theory. In particular, an object-level variable is represented as a meta-level constant and an object-level formula is represented as a meta-level (variable free) term.

6. INFERENTIAL CONTROL

Press consists wholly of meta-theoretic axioms, so as it runs it conducts inference at the meta-level. How does this cause algebraic manipulation to be done, since this requires inference at the object level? The answer is that many of the meta-level predicates express the relation:

Answer is the result of applying Rule to Expression

e.g. (iv). If this relation is set up as a goal to be satisfied with Rule and Expression bound to particular rules and expressions, then Press answers the question by actually applying the rule — and this constitutes a step in the object-level search. For instance, to solve an equation

$$\log(e, x^2-1) = 3$$

the Press user must set up the goal

$$\text{solve}(\log(e, x^2-1) = 3, x, Ans)$$

Press will then try to satisfy this goal by resolving it with clause (ii) and generating the subgoals

$$\text{singleocc}(x, \log(e, x^2-1)=3)$$
$$\text{position}(x, \log(e, x^2-1), P) \text{ and}$$
$$\text{isolate}(P, \log(e, x^2-1)=3, Ans)$$

The third of these subgoals will be resolved with clause (iii) and will generate the sub-subgoals:

$$\text{isolax}(2, \log(e, x^2-1)=3, RHS, Condition)$$
$$\text{isolate}([1, 1], RHS, Ans)$$

In satisfying the first of these sub-subgoals, Press will be implicitly applying a rewrite rule to an expression, the result being the binding of RHS. This constitutes a step in the object level search.

Thus, as the meta-level inference continues, it experiments with different object-level steps and if successful finds a proof or solution at the object-level.

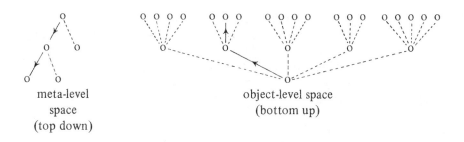

meta-level   object-level space
space   (bottom up)
(top down)

Fig. 5 – Meta-level inference controlling object-level inference.

By this technique each object-level decision can be based on an arbitrary amount of inference at the meta-level. Making a wrong decision and hence getting lost on a fruitless search can become a rare event. Thus the object-level inference can be guided almost faultlessly through a search space with a branching rate of at least 10 (for estimate of branching rate see Bundy 1975).

But doesn't this technique just trade search at the object-level for an equal amount of search at the meta-level? Apparently not! The meta-level search space is extremely well behaved in terms of its branching rate (between 0 and 2). Search is involved, but, fortunately, most choices lie between equally successful branches and bad choices rapidly lead to dead ends. This is because choices are usually between different methods of solution and each method uses a terminating rewrite rule set. Thus the choice of a method either results in immediate failure because no rules apply, or rules are applied and change the expression for the better. In no case can a method run away with itself, changing the expression but not terminating.

The meta-level axioms are represented directly as Prolog clauses, so that the meta-level inference control is the Prolog one: top down; depth first; axioms chosen in top/bottom order; subgoals tackled in left/right order. This simple meta-level control regime can induce an object-level control regime of arbitrary complexity, for instance the object-level search is bottom up, but this possibility has been explored more extensively in our Mecho program (Bundy *et al.* 1979).

7. THE PRESS SYSTEM

Press is a computer program for solving equations and doing other kinds of algebraic manipulation on transcendental expressions, i.e. expressions involving polynomial, trigonometric, exponential and logarithmic functions. It includes the following equation solving methods.

— **Isolation**: as described.
— **Collection**: implemented in a similar manner to Isolation.
— **Attraction**: ditto.

- **Change of Unknown**: if every occurrence of the unknown occurs within identical subterms, then the equation is simplified by replacing each of these subterms by a new unknown.
- **Homogenization**: the equation is prepared for change of unknown by making the unknown occur within identical subterms.
- **Function Swapping**: the equation is manipulated to remove 'nasty' functions, for which Press has few rewrite rules, in favour of 'nicer' functions, for which Press has more rules.
- **Polynomial Methods**: various methods for solving linear, quadratic, symmetric, anti-symmetric, etc., polynomials.
- **Trigonometric Methods**: various methods for different types of trigonometric equation.
- **Simplification Methods**: various types of normal form for 'cleaning up' the results of other methods.
- **Elimination**: Homogenization is applied to the problem of reducing equations in several unknowns to equations in single unknowns.

The program was originally written during 1975 by Bob Welham in the language Prolog (see Pereira *et al.* 1979). Since then it has been extended and expanded by a number of other members of the author's research group, e.g. Bernard Silver, Leon Sterling, Richard O'Keefe, Lawrence Byrd and the author. A full description of the Press program, including methods not described here, can be found in Sterling *et al.* 1982.

8. IMPLEMENTATION

Like most AI computer programs, Press can be thought of as a multi-level system, where each level is implemented in terms of the level below (see Fig. 6).

object level

|

meta-level

|

Prolog

|

machine code

|

electronics

Fig. 6 – Press implementation levels.

Thus: the machine code of the Dec10 computer is implemented in electronic circuits; Prolog is implemented in Dec10 machine code; the meta-level axioms are implemented in Prolog, and the object-level rules are implemented in meta-level axioms.

Note that the meta-level appears *below* the object-level, since the object-level is implemented in terms of the meta-level rather than vice versa.

This is a weakly reductionist description of Press, in the sense that behaviour at one level can be *explained* in terms of behaviour at another level, but descriptions at one level cannot be *replaced* by descriptions at the lower level. For instance, if I want to explain how Isolation works I can do so using Prolog terminology and can go on to give more detailed explanations in terms of machine code and electronics. However, the sense of the description of Isolation above would be lost if all occurrences of 'Isolation' were replaced with Prolog code, machine code or descriptions of the behaviour of electronic circuits. This is because crucial generalizations are lost by the reduction. Changes made by the system staff to the implementation of Prolog may alter the machine code description of Isolation, without altering its behaviour. It may not be possible to give a machine code description of Isolation which covers all the various realizations except as infinite disjunction of cases. A different pattern of other users on my time-shared computer will alter the electronic description of Isolation without altering its behaviour. Again a finite description of all electronic realizations of Isolation will probably be unattainable.

9. CONSCIOUSNESS IS NOT SELF-AWARENESS

In folk psychology, the terms' 'consciousness', 'self-awareness' and 'introspection' are all intertwined. One consequence of the discussion below will be to suggest that these concepts should be disentangled. In order to infer the contradiction which will force this disentanglement, let us identify consciousness and self-awareness, and regard introspection as a method of discovering the contents of consciousness.

Several people (Sloman 1978, Minsky 1968) in the AI literature have suggested that one role of consciousness is in solving the combinatorial explosion. The argument is that control of search demands knowledge of the goals and rules of the problem space and how these fit together and that this constitutes self-awareness and hence consciousness on the part of the program. This kind of self-awareness is called meta-level inference in Press. For instance, Minsky says:

> What the system is currently conscious of includes all the information available to the central decision-making processes, whether or not decisions are actually influenced as a result.

and Sloman says:

> The central processes are those which, among other things: . . . (b) assign tasks and allocate resources to sub-processes . . . .

At first sight this seems to fit very well with my research, described above, where control of search is effected by meta-level inference. But this should have made my research considerably easier than it in fact was. For if introspection is a method of discovering the contents of consciousness then, far from being a hard problem, modelling the contents of consciousness should be one of the easiest.

The obstacle to progress in most areas of AI is that the processes we are trying to model are carried out at an unconscious level and are therefore unavailable to study by introspection. This explains why we have made such good relative progress in, say, chess compared with, say, vision — the processes involved in playing chess are much more accessible. But consciousness is, by definition, accessible by introspection. It should be easy for us to say what consciousness consists of.

However, the meta-level inference steps were not discovered simply by introspecting while solving equations, nor could the author and his co-workers have discovered them in this way, since they were not conscious of them. In fact, considerable study, hypothesizing, rationalization, and experimentation went into the design of programs. It was a trial and error process. It may be that some people could have discovered meta-level inference by introspection but, even if true, this will not affect the argument, since only one counterexample is needed. Perceptual skills like vision, speech, etc. should provide even stronger counterexamples. The conclusion drawn below would *predict* that the methods of meta-level inference would be accessible to introspection when they were themselves the *object* of attention, e.g. when they are being learnt.

The above contradiction can be summarized as follows.

1. Meta-level knowledge is a kind of self-knowledge.
2. Hence, meta-level inference is a kind of self-awareness.
3. Self-awareness = consciousness.
4. The contents of consciousness can be discovered by introspection.
5. Hence, we can discover the nature of meta-level inference by introspection.
6. We cannot discover the nature of meta-level inference by introspection.

We can break this contradiction at various points. I find the most natural break point to be to deny hypothesis 3, i.e. to separate the notions of consciousness and self-awareness. This is largely a question of the meaning of words; the contradiction identifies at least two senses of 'self-awareness', namely (a) knowledge of your own abilities and (b) consciousness. Our decision to break at 3 amounts to a decision to use 'self-awareness' only in sense (a).

Meta-level inference is a good computational analogy for self-awareness in sense (a), but not in sense (b), i.e. it is not a good analogy of consciousness. The same argument can be adapted to deny the role of consciousness for guiding most reasoning processes, in contrast to Sloman 1978 and Minsky 1968. For instance, it would also reject an operating system as a good analogy for consciousness.

10. THE CONTENTS OF CONSCIOUSNESS

So if introspection does not consist of meta-level inference, what does it consist of? We can all conduct the experiment of introspecting while thinking, to see what seems to be going on. The results of my own experiments are:

— It is much harder than I at first thought, due to the interference between thinking and thinking about thinking.
— Much, but not all, of the process is conducted in English. I often imagine myself arguing with some fictitious person or composing an essay.
— Sometimes I catch myself thinking of a concept, but not having the English word for it. So not all my conscious processes are in English. Some consist of visual concepts (imagery).
— Only rarely do my conscious processes consist of making control (search) decisions, i.e. only when such decisions are particularly tough. Normally, they consist of 'output' rather than 'traces', 'proofs' rather than 'searches'.
— Using the ideas of my research projects, I would say that introspective processes are at the **object**- rather than **meta**-level, except when a control decision is particularly tough, when the whole show shifts up a level, the meta-level becomes conscious but the meta-meta-level which decides the issue is still hidden.
— Note that this accords with the point made in a paper by Wilks (Wilks forthcoming), that introspection gives access to the uppermost levels of the implementation hierarchy.

11. CONCLUSION

What conclusion can we draw from the above? The analogy of meta-level infer-ence seems a fruitful one to apply to self-awareness in sense (a), but not to consciousness. Self-awareness of our abilities may be useful to guide the use of those abilities, but this knowledge need not be conscious knowledge, i.e. need not be accessible to introspection. We can be conscious of the application of those abilities without being conscious of choosing which abilities to apply.

It seems we must ease apart the concepts of self-awareness and conscious-ness. These words are used in many different senses in folk psychology. The analogies from Artificial Intelligence and Computer Science suggest ways in which this simple terminology can be refined and reworked. Other computational analogies are discussed in Wilks's paper 'Machines and Consciousness' (Wilks forthcoming).

13

A computer scientist's view of meaning

Daniel Kayser

1. INTRODUCTION

I often get the feeling — and I am probably not the only computer scientist to get it — that I am facing problems usually qualified as philosophical ones. As I am not a philosopher, I can't tell whether this feeling is grounded on anything but a confusion arising from a different use of identical words. Even if some philosophers consider these problems as relevant, they are likely to dismiss our methods as being improper, because the context of our research leads us to focus more on robustness and efficiency than on completeness or consistency.

As a good example, 'knowledge representation' is now an area discussed in every Artificial Intelligence conference; the works presented under this heading consist in theoretical and/or practical studies aiming at a computer implementation of ideas from other disciplines (mainly Mathematical Logic and Psychology) or from Computer Science itself (see Kayser forthcoming, and Laurière 1982). In this framework, one of the most important questions concerns the very nature of the knowledge which is to be represented. To ask it as naively as possible: is knowledge representation identical to meaning representation?

In computer terms, this question is somehow similar to the well-known procedural/declarative controversy (see, for instance, Winograd 1976). In this connection, we can observe that this controversy is basically absurd, since a declarative representation gets its usefulness only because a procedure — sometimes left implicit — is able to interpret it; otherwise it would merely be a sequence of arbitrary symbols; similarly, a procedural representation is expressed in a (programming) language as a declarative expression. Nevertheless, this controversy is important, because it sheds some light on two complementary aspects of a single phenomenon, and it corresponds to a real choice between the available tools.

Anyhow, the crux is not there; what we want to know is whether, in order to carry out a reasoning process on a computer, we need to represent the 'meaning' of the objects involved in that process.

2. THE COMMONLY ACCEPTED THESIS

The following thesis (T) is generally regarded as correct:

(T) $\begin{cases} \text{every sentence which is understandable has one (or, in case of ambi-} \\ \text{guity, several) meaning(s), and there exists a formalism } - \text{ different} \\ \text{from the sentence itself } - \text{ which has the power to represent it (them).} \end{cases}$

In more technical terms, the same thesis becomes:

$\begin{cases} \text{There exists a space } S, \text{ called space of meanings, and a mapping } s \\ \text{which, for every element of the set } E \text{ of understandable sentences,} \\ \text{yields one or more elements of } S. \end{cases}$

In this presentation, $x = s\,(p)$ is read: x is the (or one of the) meaning(s) of sentence p. In a previous paper (Coulon *et al.* 1979), we christened this thesis 'punctual semantics utopia'.

This thesis is supported by an undeniable intuitive feeling; in common language, we frequently use utterances which are well understood only if this thesis is assumed to be believed by the speakers (for example 'this text makes no sense', 'I'm saying the same as you are, but I use different words', . . .).

There are however important differences between the formalisms proposed: very roughly, linguists use 'deep structures' (no matter under which grammatical model they operate), logicians 'well formed formulae' (no matter in which Logic) and psychologists 'componential descriptions' (no matter which semantic features are used).

Despite the difference in terminology − and the difference of focus which the former often underlies, these formalisms are generally mutually compatible. For example it is possible to express with (logician's) predicates a psychologically oriented componential description. Whether this compatibility is partial or total, whether the translation from one formalism into another produces some result or obscures the matter are essential questions, but not the questions we intend to discuss here.

3. PARADOXES AND CONTRADICTIONS

3.1 The relation 'to have the same meaning as'
If we adopt thesis (T), we can define a relation, R as follows:

$$p \, R \, p' \text{ if and only if } s(p) = s(p'),$$

i.e. either p and p' are non-ambiguous and have the same meaning or they are ambiguous, but the subsets of space S which they relate to are the same. Now there are only two possible cases: either the relation R is a trivial one (that is, $p \text{ R } p' \Leftrightarrow p$ is identical to p'), or it is not; in the latter case, there exist couples of distinct sentences (p_1, p'_1), $(p_2, p'_2) \ldots$ which have *exactly* the same meaning.

In the first case, we claim that thesis (T) is disproved: the mapping S is one-to-one and one can hardly say that the formalism in which the meaning is expressed differs from the sentence itself: it is just a notational variation of it.

Let us consider the second case: it entails that perfect paraphrases would exist. We do not deny that the notion of paraphrase is productive, in order to describe the phenomena of language: it is a well-founded notion, both linguistically (there are linguistic transformations which preserve meaning, at least in first approximation) and psychologically (subjects know what they are expected to do when told to formulate different utterances of the same idea). But this notion is essentially an approximate one:

(i) there is no consensus to decide whether any two sentences p and q are or are not paraphrases of each other. For instance 'John gives a book to Mary' and 'Mary receives a book from John', have identical deep structures in case grammar, in conceptual dependency, but not in standard transformational grammar.

(ii) even when sentences p and q are generally agreed to have the same meaning, it is possible to build — with more or less effort — a context where these sentences get different interpretations. Let us try to give an example, with the warning that the difference is small: it is emphasized in spoken language by intonation, while technical written language tends to avoid it (but the literary effect consists exactly in using it).

We rule out easy cases where one of the sentences p or q contains ambiguous or obsolete words: in these cases, by irony or misunderstanding, contexts can be built where apparent paraphrases get opposite meanings.

Let p be: 'Pierre aime profondément Marie' (Peter is deeply in love with Mary)

Let q be: 'L'amour de Pierre pour Marie est profond' (The love of Peter for Mary is deep).

One will admit that, if any two sentences can qualify for synonymy, then p and q do: at least in French, the words are not ambiguous, they are as commonplace as words can be, there is no affected turn of phrase. And even so, we feel that the sentences do not have exactly the same meaning. Let us consider a context where their occurrence is absolutely normal, such as after the question:

'As-tu remarqué comment Pierre se comportait avec Lucie? Crois-tu qu'il lui fasse la cour?' (Did you notice the behaviour of Peter towards Lucy? Do you think he is courting her?)

We consider that both p and q will be understood as a negative answer, but the negation entailed by q is stronger; perhaps our feeling stems from the fact that, in such contexts, sentences with a personal subject are more frequent, thus choosing q as an answer adds a little solemnity, in order to express a stronger conviction.

> (iii) Shades between sentences p and q are often acknowledged, but they are generally ascribed to the fact that p and q *denote* the same thing, but have different *connotations*. Such is the case, for instance, with sentences constructed with stylistic variants, emphasis being alternatively put on one word or on the other.

The difference between denotation and connotation is often made use of to keep apart 'pure' meaning (on which it is then possible to perform formal manipulation) from its shell; but — and here is the point — such a distinction seems a little too convenient: it would be legitimate only if circumstances could be found where one of them acts independently from the other. Now, in everyday life, information is not sent without purpose: it aims to influence the state of its addressees. The attempt to isolate the information 'objectively' conveyed by a message, from the way the community of its anticipated addressees is expected to interpret it — this attempt seems to us to contradict the very reason for which people communicate with each other.

3.2 What is it 'to understand'

Thesis (T) would imply that the mapping s is at least partially computable i.e. a sentence p being given, there exists an algorithm yielding $x = s(p)$. Otherwise, what would be the point of asserting the existence of a formalism which one would forever be unable to build?

In common language, the computation of $s(p)$ is witnessed by the verb 'to understand', and several utterances show that the existence of this computation is part of the intuitive feeling of 'meaning' (e.g. 'he did not understand what I said', 'I needed some time to understand what he meant', 'I did not understand the problem as you did', . . .). Is this notation of 'understanding' as clear as it seems to be?

We don't mean merely that the process used to translate p into $s(p)$ is rather obscure for any representational system adopted for $S(p)$. We want basically to insist on the fact that, if $s(p)$ exists at all, then there ought to be an indisputable criterion to know whether we have got it; in other terms, to know whether sentence p has been understood.

Now, the opposite claim seems to us to be more realistic: we believe understanding to be undecidable, that is, we think that there is no clear-cut criterion between a state where the message is not understood and a state where it is understood. As a matter of fact, when do we say that someone has understood a message?

(i) By asking him or her to repeat it? Obviously, it does not prove anything.

(ii) By urging him or her to provide paraphrases? This is slightly better, but it should be noticed that paraphrases are never perfect (see above) and, more importantly, that paraphrasing often requires surface mechanisms, the correct application of which needs no understanding. So, well-trained subjects can give us the illusion of understanding what we say, when they merely apply recipes in order to paraphrase artfully our speech.

(iii) By asking him or her to act in accordance with the message? This is frequently the best criterion, but it still is very rough: several messages may correspond to a single action, and many messages correspond to none.

(iv) In teaching, one frequently needs to know whether the pupil understood the notions which have been taught; now the custom is to evaluate the degree of comprehension by means of a mark, not by a binary decision.

All these arguments lead us to doubt the usefulness of postulating the existence of mapping s.

3.3 Ambiguity

Thesis (T) considers two possible outcomes: either $s(p)$ is an element of S, or it is a non-singleton subset of S. Thus, if (T) is valid, there should be a means of computing, for any p, the cardinality of $s(p)$; in other words, it should be possible to decide whether or not p is ambiguous.

But things just aren't like that. There are indeed situations where ambiguity is quite clear: such is the case with syntactic ambiguities (for example the same word being interpreted as a noun or as a verb) or with homonyms. But, by far the most frequent situation arises when ambiguity is not visible at first sight. The same sentence is then considered as being ambiguous or unambiguous, depending on the formalism in which its meaning has to be represented.

Let us discuss an example, taken from Lyons 1968:

(J) 'John wants to marry a girl with green eyes'.

Usual grammars won't detect here the slightest ambiguity. Now, (J) can be translated in two distinct formulae of first-order predicate calculus, namely:

$(\exists x)$ (girl $(x) \wedge$ (green (eyes (x)) $\wedge$ wants (John, (marry (John, x)))).

Wants (John, $((\exists x)$ (girl $(x) \wedge$ green (eyes(x)) $\wedge$ marry (John, x)))).

Does this really mean that (J) is ambiguous? Definitely so, according to the definition. However, it should be pointed out that a grammatical analysis which does not detect ambiguity, is amply sufficient to get the correct answer to most questions involving comprehension of the text, such as: 'Is John willing to get married?', 'What is the colour of the eyes of the girl John would like to marry?', etc.

Moreover, although the above-mentioned ambiguity is the only one usually discussed for this sentence, there is no reason to stop there:

'green'   stands for a range of colours which is broad or narrow according to the context. What is the case here?

'wants'   corresponds to a range of behaviours: from a slight desire to an unyielding resolve. Which one is meant in (J)?

These ambiguities don't exist as long as predicates, such as 'green (x)' or 'want (x, y)' are used to represent meaning; but as soon as finer grain representation is adopted, they show up.

The distinction between ambiguity and non-ambiguity is thus not intrinsic, as (T) would expect it to be, but strongly dependent on the mode of representation selected for space S.

4. A COMPUTER SCIENTIST'S POINT OF VIEW

The notion of 'meaning' is very deeply rooted in our ways of thinking; so it is perfectly normal that this notion has been used in the first computer implementations requiring a representation of knowledge. However, the history of science shows that we should distrust concepts taken directly from intuition: so many basic notions, such as space, time, matter, light, etc. have been so drastically reinterpreted that one can wonder at the relatively limited evolution of our ideas on 'meaning' since the ancient times.

Aren't the problems we — as computer scientists — are facing, to do with the initiation of such an evolution?

4.1 A variant for thesis (T)

Thesis (T) leads us to go in quest of the meaning $s(p)$ of a sentence p. It is by now obvious that this quest makes sense only as far as, implicitly or explicitly, we know what to do with $s(p)$: for computers, 'meaning' itself is not an objective; it is needed only because it allows us to deduce, to confirm, to predict, to infer.

If 'meaning' is useful only because it is passed on to some 'reasoning' procedures, wouldn't it be possible to go directly in quest of these procedures? Ultimately this would amount to substituting a new thesis (T') for (T):

(T'): to every sentence p corresponds a procedure $P(p)$.

As a matter of fact, this idea is only a path — a multiply forking one; still, it might conceal a few elements of a solution. Let us discuss this in more detail:

(i) The predicate analysis of a sentence, like 'John eats an apple', introduces expressions such as: 'apple (x)', or 'eat (x, y)'; 'apple (x)' returns a boolean (or many-valued) result of every element x of the universe.

Instead of looking at its predicate functionally, we could focus on the way it computes its value, that is to consider 'apple' as a procedure with input x, and with boolean (or many-valued) output. Such a procedure would test the shape, size, colour, flavour of parameter x, the circumstances under which x has been found, and so on, or only part of these data if some of them are not available; it would then combine the result of the tests to get its output.

One could hardly maintain that such a procedure does not exist (people do recognize an apple when they see one!), or that it is not part of the meaning of the word 'apple'. Now this procedure does not overlap with information taken from a semantic net (e.g. 'kind-of fruit', 'kind of plant', 'kind of food' . . .), or from a dictionary (fruit of the apple-tree), or from an encyclopaedia (fruit of the temperate regions, yields cider, . . .). How should these pieces of information be fitted together, in order to build a construction associated with the word 'apple'?

(ii) The relation 'to have the same meaning as' becomes, from the procedural point of view, 'to yield the same result as'. Now it is well-known that telling whether two procedures are or not equivalent is an undecidable problem. In the light of our discussion of section 3.1, this should incline us towards thesis (T'), rather than thesis (T). On the other hand, it should induce in us perplexity that the most modest computations on meaning are undecidable, for then of what help can the computer be? We shall show below that things don't turn out to be that bad!

(iii) We just discussed procedures attached to words; is this the only linguistic or conceptual level where procedural models play a role? Definitely not: in the framework of (T), there exist procedures able to compute the meaning of a sentence from the meaning of its words (see, for example, Riesbeck 1975). In the framework of (T'), could we build a procedure $P(p)$ from possible procedures corresponding to each of its words? In order to provide an answer, we should examine more closely what can be expected of $P(p)$.

Anyone who has understood a sentence is able, beyond the paraphrasing already mentioned, to:
— devise one or many classes of contexts where this sentence fits naturally;
— put forward, according to the actual context of the sentence, one or more other sentences which reflect the plausible inferences corresponding to the situation described by the sentence.

These two activities — which, by the way, are not independent from each other — have not received yet enough attention, to our knowledge (a first approach was attempted by Rieger (in 1975), but they deserve a central role in the phenomenon of 'understanding'.

If we are to hold this view, we should require that procedure $P(p)$ be able to model these activities. Now they call not only upon elements supposed to be in the procedures associated with words, but also on information of a 'semantic net', or a 'dictionary' or an 'encyclopaedia' kind. (For instance, the plausible inference 'John gets an apple' → 'John was hungry' makes no use of shape, size, colour properties included in the 'apple' procedure, but merely the fact that an apple is a kind of food).

4.2 Towards a synthesis

The above discussion shows that (T') solves a different problem from that solved by (T), but leaves many problems unsolved. It ends with the idea that what is usually referred to as being the 'meaning' of a word, of a sentence, of a text includes very composite pieces of information, which the computer scientist ought to represent the complex data structures (such as 'frames' − see Minsky 1975). Moreover, these structures should be operated on in various fashions, according to the aim in view.

   (i) Everything induces to think that, in most instances, we use but the first layers of knowledge available for each of the words and phrases. An initial hypothesis, which needs future refinement, would be as follows: 'The structures associated with the objects we know are disposed along various dimensions, and are exploited by various strategies; in each dimension information is sorted in such a way that the most frequently used are the most easily accessible'.

   This hypothesis leads us to recommend:
   − a progressive description of objects,
   − a great deal of strategies to operate on knowledge associated with objects; it is advisable to add an aspect that we did not discuss here, but which we developed elsewhere (Kayser 1980), namely:
   − an evaluation of the extent of approximation resulting from our neglecting the less accessible layers.

These three factors are precisely those by which we defined, in Kayser and Coulon 1981, as the notion of variable-depth analysis.

   To crown all this, a global 'supervision' mechanism is needed, whose role is to allocate available resources to the different potentially applicable strategies. In fact we process sentences differently according to how we consider them (urgency, expected interest, etc. . . .). The supervisor dynamically evaluates the situation and activates the strategies which seem to be best fitted to the desired 'understanding level'.

   (ii) The idea of allocating a variable amount of resources to different strategies allows us to solve the apparent undecidability paradox discussed in section 3.1(ii) above, section 3. As a matter of fact, we shall no longer say that two words, or two sentences, are synonymous (which, in (T'), implied that their corresponding procedures be equivalent); instead, we say that, when they are processed by a given strategy with a certain amount of resources, they yield the same interpretations.

Similarly, the ambiguity paradoxes (section 3.3) tend to disappear: instead of declaring, *a priori*, that one word has 1, 2, . . ., *n* 'different meanings' we merely observe that, at a given level of resources, the contexts where this word can be found assign to it 1, 2, . . ., *n* different interpretations; with less resources, fewer interpretations would survive; at a deeper level, some interpretations would split up, with the coming out of new shades in the meaning, shades usually neglected at first sight.

5. CONCLUSION

The view developed in this paper leads us to consider that the quest for a word's or a sentence's meaning is somewhat mythical. Neither under a static form (T), nor under a dynamic one (T') have we found it admissible to declare: 'This is the meaning of that word, or of that sentence'.

On the other hand, the knowledge at our disposal concerning a word, an expression, or a turn of phrase are representable thanks to complex data structures. We must acknowledge that very little is known about these structures, probably because too much time has been wasted in seeking them under a form which is inadequate.

These structures are finite, but they are likely to be self-extendable. They are workable by means of multiple strategies, operating at variable depth.

In order to know more about them, emphasis should be given to phenomena heretofore left in the dark: instead of representing 'meaning' for itself, it would be better to represent what 'meaning' — if it exists — enables us to perform: that is, principally, inferences. Proceeding in that way, we shall by-pass the obstacles in the search for meaning, and concentrate only on its desired result: *plausible inference*. This change in focus might seem to be a minor one; in fact, I believe that it would free huge research potentialities, which are currently blocked by the myth of 'meaning'.

14

Creativity in men and machines

Masoud Yazdani

1. INTRODUCTION

The most explicit exposition of creativity has been presented by Chomsky (1966) within the linguistic domain. Theoretically, the set of possible utterances in a language is infinite. The search for a finite basis underlying a potentially infinite number of manifestations has been the main incentive of modern linguistics, in which Chomsky enjoys a major standing.

Creativity, as defined by Chomsky for language, is based on a system of rules (the generative grammar) which enables the construction of an infinite variety of sentences using a finite set of rules. The possibility of using Chomsky's definition of creativity in language as a 'general theory of creativity' has been proposed in several places (see, for example, de Beaugrande 1979).

However, such a rule based notion of creativity has many defects when taken in the context of a variety of tasks. Many, including de Beaugrande, would accept that violation of standard rules plays an important (if not more important) role in creativity than the following of rules. Boden (1981c) considers the effects of exploring the consequences of modifying or extending parts of the grammar as a major source of creativity.

The purpose of this chapter is to look at 'creativity in story writing' as a case study within the general framework advocated by Boden (1977, 1981c, 1982). The discipline of Artificial Intelligence plays a major role in this framework where all the rule systems presented here for story writing can be followed by people as well as computers. The exposition of a computational theory of creativity in place of that of Chomsky would act, further, not only as an explanation of the process in people, but also as a basis for making machines creative.

2. RULE-BASED STORY WRITING

There are a number of ways one could devise a set of rules for writing stories. The most simple one would be to:

1. Take any story you want.
2. Commit the story to memory.
3. Reproduce that story later, on demand.

These rules can be followed by computers, and are followed, in fact, on occasion, by people. However, the scope of the above scenario is limited only to producing stories already known. A simple modification of the above scenario, would produce a larger set of stories as its output:

1. Take a 'template' of any story made out of a mixture of 'low level' canned sequences and parts which can represent varying sequences.
2. Work out the value of the variables, in the 'template', from a set of possibilities.

This scenario is limited to telling stories which are members of the one class which have been put into it. However, the number of different stories generated can be infinite as the combination of values for variables can be infinite. Some commercial concerns earn their living by using such techniques, offering parents a storybook, for a small fee, in which a specified child is the hero/heroine of the story.

A departure in nature from the above two scenarios is present in Klein (1975) where story grammars have been used as a means of generating short tales on a computer. This approach assumes that the text structures of a culture are the same as the social structures. You then have to

1. Choose a structure used in your culture (as noted by anthropologists) for stories.
2. Perform necessary transitions on the story grammar to produce a story.

The above scenario, while producing a larger number of stories than those of previous ones, is limited only to a finite number of classes known to anthropologists. Meehan (1976) in fact likens this approach to the earlier one, claiming that the method used by Klein is to write some code which provides each part of a set of predefined stories. Meehan in turn attempts a further departure, taking into consideration goal-directed behaviours of characters of stories, in his TALE-SPIN (1976) program. Here the scenario is:

1. Identify a CHARACTER out of a predefined set.
2. Give that CHARACTER a PROBLEM out of a predefined set.
3. Create a MICRO-WORLD out of a predefined set.
4. Input 1 to 3 above to a problem-solving simulator.
5. Either STOP or GOTO 1.

Using the above rules, Meehan's TALE-SPIN program generates short tales of bears, foxes and ants solving problems, each taking their turn. The stories are basically traces of problem-solving behaviour of a single character.

De Beaugrande and Colby (1979) have formulated 'a basic set of plausible STORY-TELLING RULES' which introduce recursion and failure (in addition to success) of the goal and multi-character situations to the scenario above.

1. Identify at least one CHARACTER.
2. Create a PROBLEM STATE for that CHARACTER.
3. Identify a GOAL STATE for the CHARACTER.
4. Initiate a PATHWAY from the PROBLEM STATE leading towards the GOAL STATE.
5. Block or postpone attainment of the GOAL STATE.
6. Mark one STATE TRANSITION as a TURNING POINT.
7. Create a TERMINAL STATE which is clearly marked as MATCHING or NOT MATCHING the GOAL STATE.

The above two scenarios simulate a world, assign goals to some characters and report what happens when these goals interact with the events in the simulated world. There is an underlying 'theory' of stories here which considers stories to be about problems of the characters and how they got solved. My own work in this area started by attempting to produce a version of TALE-SPIN with characters competing against, or cooperating with each other. For my own project (Yazdani 1982), I attempted to write such a computer program but recognized that the simple 'theory' behind TALE-SPIN could not support such multi-actor systems. That theory ignores the intentions of the writer. I considered the intentions of the writer and proposed a 'theory' according to which story writing is similar to other forms of verbal communication to which Speech Act theory seems relevant. The corresponding scenario consists of five processes working in parallel and in interaction with one another. These are: plot-maker, world-maker, simulator, narrator and text generator.

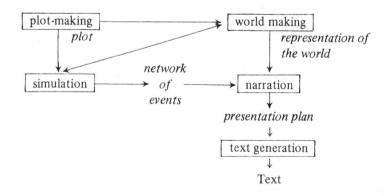

1. The plot-maker produces a partial specification of transformations on a state of affairs from an intention as a 'plot' for controlling the simulator.
2. The world-maker produces the initial state of affairs in the world of the story.
3. The simulator lives the actions of characters when appropriate whilst producing props, distractions etc. when necessary to make sure events of the world follow the path specified in the plot.
4. The narrator produces a linear representation of the events of the story, puzzling, mystifying or misleading the reader sometimes by omitting to report an event.
5. The text generator then produces the text in detail to describe the events.

3. MULTI-LEVEL CREATIVITY

A close look at the set of rules presented in the previous section shows that they reflect a model of story production without modelling the act of creation in story writing. A close look at the products of many bestseller authors would show them to be more productive than creative too. The creative act of discovering new extensions to each set of rules in the previous section, or moving to a new system of production altogether, is performed by researchers writing the computer programs.

A distinction is therefore necessary between 'production' of new stories and discovery or invention of new classes of stories. Not all new ideas are the same in nature and therefore may not arise from the same source. The central point of this essay is that what is loosely labelled 'creativity', can be the result of simple productivity of the rule-following mechanism, or it could result from a more radical re-thinking of the structure of the space of possible instances of the objects of a domain.

Boden (1982) points out that there are at least two kinds of new ideas:

> . . . a thought which is new because it just had not been thought before and a thought which is new because it strikes us that it could not have been thought before.

So far we agree with the argument that a framework based on a single level of rules for creativity in a domain has shortcomings. We need to account for the acts of creativity performed on rules when the rule set is extended or replaced with a new one. We propose a new approach in which one considers a number of levels of rules for producing objects, leading to a multi-level universe of

level 0: objects
level 1: rules for parsing/generating objects of domain 0
level 2: meta-rules for parsing/generating rules of domain 1

A multi-level system of rules, either as shown above, or as a series of rules about rules about rules . . . (in the same form as Minsky's (1966) models), poses an attractive solution to some of the defects of a Chomskyan rule-based approach to creativity.

Bundy (Chapter 12 in this volume) has argued in favour of the general usefulness of meta-rules and meta-level reasoning. Lenat (1977) has shown how they can be used to produce an automatic mathematician. Lenat's computer program uses heuristics to explore the space of mathematical rules in search of new theorems, with moderate success in finding new ones.

Polya (1945) points out the importance of meta-level reasoning when he says 'finding a solution to a problem should mark not the end but the beginning of a mathematical enquiry: it should be followed by attempts to find simpler solutions, other kinds of solutions, and generalizations of the problem', in effect arguing for looking at the rule-set used for the solution for possible extensions to, or refinements of it.

The combination of the rule-based production of objects and meta-level reasoning about the rules presents a new framework for creativity worthy of study. Within such a framework even a simplistic random generation algorithm of objects can be put to beneficial use as long as an evaluation process also takes place. Boden (1981c) points to a constraint on the overall framework which makes it more plausible by saying that

> The generation of new forms needs a consequent evaluation within a certain structural constraint in order to recognise something as useful.

Narayanan (Chapter 5 in this volume) touches on the same issues when he subjects his 'type minus one' grammar to 'verification and integrity checking procedures which check the correctness of the rule'. However, his rule generating mechanism falls short of the proposal here.

4. CONCLUDING REMARKS

On the basis of the case study of Artificial Intelligence work on story writing, and our distinction between 'creativity' and 'productivity', it can be argued that we have not presented a set of rules for creativity in story writing but only for productivity. The creative act has been performed by the human programmer. We have suggested that this further process can be crystallized in a system of meta-rules. Development of computer programs which discover new rules is one of the current challenges of AI. However, AI at least has forced some researchers to formalize their thoughts more clearly. Sociologically therefore, AI is the science of making machines productive and people creative!

15

Learning as a non-deterministic but exact logical process

Yves Kodratoff and Jean-Gabriel Ganascia

0. PROLOGUE

Learning complex structural descriptions is felt to be a central problem in Artificial Intelligence. It consists of extracting common properties from a set of examples. Traditional tools for data analysis – e.g. statistical tools – are not sufficient to achieve such a task. Our view is that any description may be seen as a logical formula which is instantiated by some constants. For instance, suppose that we want to describe a scene S_1 (in a blocks world) which contains one small cube (A), and one red sphere (B). If the three following predicates belong to the language of description: SMALL, RED and FORM, then the description is:

$$S_1 = \text{SMALL(A)} \land \text{FORM(CUBE A)} \land \text{RED(B)} \land \text{FORM(SPHERE B)}$$

In this way, learning is equivalent to building a formula which is more *general* than examples which have to be learned. So the problem of learning is closely related to the problem of generalization. Our main purpose in the following paper is to propose a method for generalizing logical formulae. Before explaining it, it is important to emphasize one crucial point concerning generalization. Generalization may be understood in two ways:

(1) Generalization of theorem
(2) Generalization of concept

On the one hand, saying that a theorem T_1 is more general than a Theorem T_2 implies that if T_1 is demonstrated, so is T_2. For instance, if we consider universal theorems, these may be expressed in the following way:

$$\text{Theorem } T_1 \colon \forall x \epsilon D_1 \ P(x)$$
$$\text{Theorem } T_2 \colon \forall x \epsilon D_2 \ P(x)$$

D_1 is called the domain of the Theorem T_1, and D_2 the domain of T_2. With regard to the pattern of T_1 and T_2, saying that T_1 is more general than T_2 is equivalent to saying that D_2 is included in D_1. On the other hand, saying that a concept C_1 is more general than a concept C_2 is equivalent to saying that every scene whose description is subsumed by C_2 is also subsumed by C_1. To clarify this assumption, let us remember that a concept is a logical formula which contains not only predicates and constants, as do descriptions, but also quantifiers and free variables. So, we say that a concept C subsumes a scene S if there exists a substitution σ such that: $S \Rightarrow \sigma$ C.

As example, let us assume that

$$C_1 = \exists x \ \text{FORM (CUBE } x) \wedge (\text{FORM SPHERE } z).$$

C_1 is a concept which subsumes the scene S_1:

$$S_1 = \text{SMALL (A)} \wedge \text{FORM(CUBE A)} \wedge \text{RED (B)} \wedge \text{FORM(SPHERE B)}.$$

if $\sigma = (z/B)$ then $S_1 \Rightarrow \sigma C_1$.

In the same way, we say that a concept C_1 is more general than a concept C_2 if and only if there exists a substitution σ such that $C2 \Rightarrow \sigma C_1$.

One of the most important consequences of these definitions is that the universal assertion $\forall x \ P(x)$ is more general than $P(a)$ from a theorem point of view, and more particular from a concept point of view. We shall justify this intuitively as follows. On the one hand, if the theorem $\forall x P(x)$ is proved, then $P(a)$ is true for all constants a. Applying our definition of generality for theorems, this means that $P(x)$ is more general than $P(a)$. On the other hand, let us assume that $\forall x \ P(x)$ is a concept used in the description of scenes. This description asserts that property P belongs to each object contained in the scene. So there exists at least one object in each scene which has the property P (we shall call it a). In consequence, every scene which is subsumed by $\forall x P(x)$ is also subsumed by $P(a)$. According to our definition, this implies that $\forall x P(x)$ is more particular than $P(a)$. In other words we can say that $\forall x P(x)$ is more particular than $P(a)$ in the sense that it contains more information and more constraints on the scenes which have to be subsumed.

Our main purpose in the following paper is to propose an algorithm from which one may obtain some least generalization of all examples belonging to a given learning set. The learning task will be considered as achieved when one least generalization formula is obtained. The result of learning is the production of a concept which subsumes each example contained in the learning set. In conclusion, each example being given by a scene described in the description language, the generalization and the learned formula is oriented by the language of description.

1. INTRODUCTION (AND DISCUSSION)

The problem of learning is taken to be central in AI because 'a computer that doesn't learn really cannot make much of a claim on being intelligent' (Schank 1982). In spite of this strong social pressure pushing us to study learning, we realize very well that the field improves at an amazingly low speed.

Our aim was to analyse, explain and, at least partly, correct this weakness of AI.

Our first hypothesis is that learning is almost exclusively concerned with generalization. We are well aware, of course, that learning depends very much on knowledge representation. For instance, nobody can 'learn' the difference between the two following sets:

$$S_1 = ((\nabla, \triangle, *), (\nabla, \triangle), (*), (\nabla, \square));$$
$$S_2 = ((\nabla, \triangle, *, \square), (\nabla, *), (\triangle, \uparrow), (\triangle, *)),$$

just from the knowledge of S_1 and S_2, without being told that the descriptions of S_1 and S_2 must emphasize the presence or absence of *pairs* of shapes (instead of describing simply the presence or absence of one shape at a time).[1] Our point is that, besides imagination or other meta-rules, generalization is an essential tool in the invention of the correct description language because it gives some properties the language must display so that one can learn from it. In the above example of S_1 and S_2 the solution was found by noticing that 'we could never apply our methodology on a description that would not use pairs of shapes'. The effect of fitting a description into a theory is also a very efficient way to find new descriptions (the meta-rules are given by the theory itself). We shall not say more here about the description problem and we hope that the unconvinced reader will agree to take our emphasis on generalization at least as a working hypothesis.

Now, it is quite evident that any description is a kind of logical formula which takes the value TRUE on the examples. For instance, $(\nabla, \triangle)$ can be described by 'there exists a shape like ∇ and a shape like $\triangle$ and there is no shape like * etc . . .' or also (among hundreds of other descriptions) 'there exists a pair of shapes ∇, $\triangle$, and no pair ∇, *, etc. . . .'. Generalizing these logical formulas is recognized as an important field of AI research.[2] On the other hand, classical logics define generalization for terms (recursively defined in free variables and functions) and not for formulas (recursively constructed from logical connectives and predicates depending on free or bound variables). Insofar as we need in some way to be able to generalize formulas in order to achieve an even elementary learning, two reactions are possible. One is the one used in Hayes-Roth and McDermott 1978 and in Vere 1980: stick as much as possible to classical logics but define a new way of generalizing. The other attitude will be described here (and has already been presented in Kodratoff 1982): stick as much as possible to the classical definition of generalization but change the way of computing the canonical form of a logical formula.

The main reasons for this second attitude are as follows:

1.1 Learning implies anyhow that the computation of a canonical form is not the same as in classical logics. For instance, in any rewriting system computing a canonical form (as much for the well-known disjunctive or conjunctive normal forms (that are not canonical) as for the new Hsiang form (Hsiang 1982)) an expression known to be TRUE must be rewritten as TRUE. On the contrary, in a learning context, a description is nothing but a tautology known to be TRUE: you introduce SQUARE(A) in your description only if you know that A is actually a square.

Insofar as classical logics must be violated, we want to be as precise as possible in the estimation of what is left and what is new in learning.

1.2 The classical definition leads to difficulties due to the necessity of introducing operators that separate variables during the generalization process.[3] It is easy to see (an example follows) that this problem is linked to the idempotency of logical AND.[4] As we shall also see in the following, our presentation of generalization takes naturally this difficulty into account. This is now exemplified by the following problem, where & is the logical AND, A, B, C. . . . are constants while x, y, z, . . . are variables.

Let

E_1 = SQUARE(A)&RED(A)&SMALL(A) (There is a small red square) and

E_2 = SQUARE(B)&RED(B)&SQUARE(C)&SMALL(C) (there are two squares, one is small, the other one is red).

The problem is to find the 'best' generalization E_g of E_1 and E_2.

A partial matching generalization will lead either to

$$E_{g_1} = \text{SQUARE}(x)\&\text{RED}(x)\&\text{SMALL}(y)$$

or to

$$E_{g_2} = \text{SQUARE}(y)\&\text{RED}(x)\&\text{SMALL}(y)$$

which are, for $x \leftarrow A$, $y \leftarrow A$, both instances of E_1 but, for $x \leftarrow B$, $y \leftarrow C$, only partial instances of E_2. (Here '$x \leftarrow A$' means that the variable x must be replaced by the constant A.)

An alternative solution is the use of & idempotency relative to SQUARE(A), stating that:

$$E_{11} = \text{SQUARE}(A)\&\text{RED}(A)\&\text{SQUARE}(A)\&\text{SMALL}(A)$$

is totally equivalent to E_1 (this is correct from a logical point of view, but is it also correct from a learning point of view?).

The generalization of E_{11} and E_2 is:

$$E_g = \text{SQUARE}(x)\&\text{RED}(x)\&\text{SQUARE}(y)\&\text{SMALL}(y)$$

which has E_1 as instance for $x \leftarrow A, y \leftarrow A$ (and because SQUARE(A)&SQUARE(A) reduces to SQUARE(A)) and which has E_2 as instance for $x \leftarrow B, y \leftarrow C$.

A difficulty arises from the fact that E_2 and

$$E_3 = \text{SQUARE}(D)\&\text{RED}(D)\&\text{SQUARE}(E)\&\text{SMALL}(E)$$

generalize also to E_g. Intuitively, this is a bad feature since (E_1, E_2) is a different set of examples from (E_2, E_3) (clearly, the first one is more particular) and they lead to the same 'knowledge'. The solution to this problem[5] is that one should look at the instances which produce the generalization and mark two variables u, v as never having the same instances in one example by

DIFFERENT (u, v)

For instance, the generalization of E_1 and E_2 should be

$$E_g = \text{SQUARE}(x)\&\text{RED}(x)\&\text{SQUARE}(y)\&\text{SMALL}(y)$$

since it is always implicitly stated that x and y can be instantiated by the same value, which happens in $E_{11} = E_1$. On the contrary, the generalization of E_2 and E_3 should be:

$$E_g = \text{SQUARE}(x)\&\text{RED}(x)\&\text{SQUARE}(y)\&\text{SMALL}(y)\&\text{DIFFERENT}(x, y)$$

since the instances of x and y are different in E_2 and E_3 which implicitly contain the information DIFFERENT(B, C) and DIFFERENT(D, E) which should be used. We refer to Kodratoff 1982 for more details on the non-determinacy which is introduced in this way.

1.3 Unification in equational theories is a well-known field of research (see for instance Stickel 1981) and matching in an equational theory (even a complicated one) is quite possible (Costa 1981). This kind of problem reduces to the search for a canonical form of terms. Instead of changing the classical definition of generalization, we felt it more economical to modify the definition of a canonical term and to introduce 'learning canonical terms'.

1.4 Besides, it is not at all counter-intuitive to state that the usual canonical form of a logical formula is not particularly well-suited in order to express the trivialities one should start from when learning.

1.5 In the following, we shall first quickly recall the definitions of generalization, then describe our way to compute the canonical forms of a term (learning canonical forms) and discuss some of its consequences. We shall continue to use the above notations and use also the following: V is the logical OR, $A < B$ means that A is more general than B, $A <> B$ means that A and B are not comparable from a generalization point of view.

2. GENERALIZATION

2.1 Generalization of terms

Let t_1 and t_2 be two terms. One says that t_1 is more general than t_2 ($t_1 < t_2$) iff there is a substitution σ such that $\sigma\, t_1 = t_2$.

A substitution has the form $\sigma = (x_i \leftarrow t_i)$ where each x_i is a variable and each t_i is a term.

Example: E_g is more general than E_2 since $\sigma\, E_g = E_2$ where $\sigma = (x \leftarrow B, y \leftarrow C)$.

2.2 Vere's definition of generalization (Vere 1980)

2.2.1

Let us first consider conjunctions of elementary operators; any expression A is supposed to take the form $A = A_1 \& \ldots \& A_n$ where each A_i is elementary (i.e. contains no logical connectives). Define the set associated to A by $\{A\} = \{A_1, \ldots, A_n\}$.

Then A is more general than B iff there is a substitution such that

$$\sigma A = B' \text{ where } \{B'\} \subset \{B\}.$$

Otherwise stated, σA is equal to a subpart of B.

2.2.2

For disjunctions of conjunctions, this definition becomes:

$$\text{let } Ga = ga_1 \vee \ldots \vee g_{an}, \quad G_b = g_{b_1} \vee \ldots \vee g_{bm}$$

then G_a is more general than G_b iff $\forall j\ \exists i\ g_{ai} < g_{bj}$.

3. CONSTRUCTION OF A LEARNING CANONICAL FORM

There is no unique learning canonical form for a given term. On the other hand, we claim that we obtain a unique learning canonical form associated to a given generalization of a term as compared to any other.

We shall therefore always speak of the canonical form of t_1 and t_2. Notice that we do *not* claim that:

- our way of computing a learning canonical term is unique. Using a different strategy from the one here presented corresponds to having another type of learning. For instance, we distinguish a 'civilian' learning (where the logical operator idempotency has priority: it amounts to using the same object several times in different situations) as opposed to a 'military' learning where each object is destroyed when used (in practice, this can be taken into account also by using operators associated with numbers so that PERSHINGMISSILE(x, n) is different from PERSHINGMISSILE(x, $n+1$)).
- starting from unique learning canonical forms of t_1 and t_2, one gets a unique generalization. On the contrary, Kodratoff 1982 explains how one may reduce the size of the combinatorial explosion of all the possible different generalizations.

3.1 The generalization axioms

There are cases where a substitution cannot be found and where the generalization ordering is quite clear. Instead of using another definition of generalization we introduced the equivalent following axioms which order some terms relative to generalization:

$$
\begin{array}{cc}
(3.1\mathrm{a}) & (3.1\mathrm{b}) \\
\exists x\, P(x, y) < P(x, z) & < \quad P(A, y) < \forall x\, P(x, y)
\end{array}
$$

3.2 The elementary rewriting steps

3.2.1 *Structural matching*

One says that t_1 structurally matches t_2 when t_1 becomes identical to t_2 (modulo a variable renaming) when the two terms t_1 and t_2 are represented by two trees which are identical except for their terminal nodes.

3.2.2 *Using idempotency*

This amounts to a use of idempotency in order to favour a structural matching of t_1 and t_2.

For instance, suppose that $t_1 = P\&Q$ and $t_2 = Q$: one then uses idempotency when one tries to find if Q can take the form $Q'\&Q''$ such that Q' structurally matches P. The term t_2 is then rewritten as $t_2' = Q'\&Q$ which is logically equivalent to t_2 but allows to atempt a matching of $t_2 = t_2'$ and t_1.

3.2.3 *Detecting a matching*

Given t_1 and t_2, one attempts to find substitutions such that $\sigma_1\, t_1 = t_2$ or $\sigma_2\, t_2 = t_1$.

3.2.4 *Using implication laws*

One uses the classical properties:

(3.2.4a)   if $x \Rightarrow y$ (x implies y)   then x and $x\,\&y$ are logically equivalent,
(3.2.4b)   if $x \Rightarrow y$ then y and $x \lor y$ are logically equivalent,

in order to favour a structural matching of t_1 and t_2.

For instance, let $t_1 = EQ(x, 1)\&EQ(y, 2)$ where EQ is a predicate which takes the value TRUE if its two terms are equal, and $t_2 = LOWER(x, y)$ where LOWER is the lower relationship of number theory.

Using (3.2.4a) several times on t_1 and t_2, one finds that

$$t_1 = t_1'' = EQ(x, 1)\&EQ(y, 2)\&LOWER(x, 2)\&LOWER(1, y) \quad \text{while}$$

$$t_2 = t_2'' = EQ(x_1, x_2)\&EQ(y_1, y_2)\&LOWER(x_1, y_2)\&LOWER(x_2, y_1).$$

Since the substitution $\sigma = (x_1 \leftarrow x, y_1 \leftarrow y, x_2 \leftarrow 1, y_2 \leftarrow 2)$ is such that $\sigma t_2'' = t_1''$, we say that t_2 is more general than t_1 because t_1'' is the learning canonical form of t_1 relative to t_2 obtained by using the implication laws and because t_2'' is the learning canonical form of t_2 relative to t_1 obtained by using the implication laws.

3.2.5 *Developing or reducing to TRUE or FALSE values*

One can also attempt to bring the structural match between t_1 and t_2 to success by using the tautologies:

$$A \& \text{TRUE} = A \quad \text{and} \quad A \lor \text{FALSE} = A,$$

in either direction depending on t_1 and t_2.

For instance, suppose that $t_1 = P(x) \& Q(x)$ and $t_2 = P(x)$, then one can try to prove that $Q(x) = \text{TRUE}$ so that t_1 *reduces to* t_2 or $Q(A) = \text{TRUE}$ so that the canonical form of t_2 is $t_{2'} = P(x) \& Q(A)$. In each case, the learning canonical forms of t_1 and t_2 are brought into a structural matching.

3.2.6 *Transformation of the representation*

One may bring t_1 and t_2 into a structural matching by considering that the 'missing operators' of, say, t_1 are actually variables of a more general operator which must be introduced into the representation (how to invent these new operators is not considered here: as the following examples show one needs a good knowledge of the universe's semantics).

For instance, suppose that one wishes to compare $t_1 = P(x) \& Q(x)$ and $t_2 = P(x)$.

Instead of using idempotency, it may be more useful to consider P and Q as instances of (functional) variables and find some more general operator G such that $G(P, x)$ and $G(Q, x)$ have the same interpretation as $P(x)$ and $Q(x)$. This is useful when one has some information about $G(y, x)$. For instance, consider the assertion $\text{RED}(x)$ (there are objects that can have the red hue), it may be useful to rewrite it as $\text{COLOUR}(\text{RED}, x)$ when, for instance, one knows that all the objects in our universe are coloured, i.e $\forall x \, \exists y \, \text{COLOUR}(y, x) = \text{TRUE}$, especially in view of applying 3.2.5.

In theory, this brings us to second order logics but in practice this may well reduce to a kind of hierarchy among operators which are considered as being part of the knowledge base describing our universe.

3.3 Computing a learning canonical form of two formulas t_1 and t_2

Our strategy follows:

Proc$_1$: Attempt to detect a matching and if this fails then try to use the generalization axioms.

Use idempotency and call Proc$_1$. If this fails then

use implication laws and call Proc$_1$. If this fails then

develop or reduce to TRUE or FALSE values and call Proc$_1$. If this fails then

transform the representation, develop or reduce TRUE or FALSE values and call Proc$_1$. If this fails then conclude that $t_1 <> t_2$.

4. EXAMPLES OF THE CONSEQUENCES OF OUR DEFINITIONS

We give examples into a universe of coloured shapes to that RED(A) can be rewritten as COLOUR(RED, A) and BLOCK(A) as SHAPE(BLOCK, A). Notice that we assume that it is impossible to learn from partial descriptions into universes where this kind of knowledge is not known.

The starred examples are more or less in contradiction with the usual definitions of generalization and they will be further commented on.

(4.1) RED(A) $<$ RED(A)& BLOCK(A)
*(4.2) RED(A) $<>$ RED(A)&BLUE(A)   (in general)
(4.3) RED(A) $<$ RED(A)&BLOCK(B)
*(4.4) RED(A) $<$ RED(A)&BLUE(B)
(4.5) RED(x) $<$ RED(y)&BLOCK(y)
*(4.6) RED(x) $<>$ RED(y)&BLUE(y)
(4.7) RED(x) $<$ RED(y)&BLOCK(z)
*(4.8) RED(y)&RED(z) $<$ RED(x)
(4.9) RED(A) $\vee$ BLOCK(A) $<$ RED(A)
*(4.10) RED(A) $\vee$ BLUE(A) $<$ RED(A)   (under some conditions)
(4.11) RED(A) $\vee$ BLOCK(B) $<$ RED(A)
(4.12) RED(y) $\vee$ BLOCK(y) $<$ RED(x)
*(4.13) RED(y) $\vee$ BLUE(y) $<$ RED(x)   (under some conditions).
(4.14) RED(y) $\vee$ BLOCK(z) $<$ RED(x)
(4.15) RED(y) $\vee$ RED(z) $<$ RED(x)

Proving (4.2)

In general, RED(A)&BLUE(A) is equivalent to another operator, either FALSE or REDBLUESPOTTED(A) or ROSY(A) etc. . . . .

Using a distance notion which is intuitively clear in this case (and altogether not defined in this paper), replacing RED(A)&BLUE(A) by one of an equivalent form leads to an expression 'nearer' to RED(A) (because a failure of matching with & is avoided), and therefore those equivalent forms are canonical and RED(A) is not comparable to any of them (unless it is so in a very specific universe).

Proving (4.4)

One changes the representation and t_1=RED(A) becomes $t_1{}'$=COLOUR(RED, A) and t_2 becomes $t_2{}'$=COLOUR(RED, A)&COLOUR(BLUE, B). In t_1 one has the knowledge that B has a colour (which is not valid with regard to t_2 but because one supposes that all objects of the universe are coloured, this may be untrue and t_1 and t_2 would the be non-comparable), i.e. $\exists x$ COLOUR(x, B)= TRUE.

$$t_1' \text{ becomes } t_2'' = t_1' \& \text{TRUE}$$
$$= \text{COLOUR(RED}, A)\& \ x\,\text{COLOUR}(x, B)$$
$$= \exists x\,(\text{COLOUR(RED}, A)\&\text{COLOUR}(x, B))$$

which is more general than t_2' by (3.1a).

Proving (4.8)

One uses idempotency and $t_1 = \text{RED}(y)\&\text{RED}(z)$ is more general than $t_2' = \text{RED}(x)$ $\&\text{RED}(x)$ because $\sigma t_1 = t_2$, where $\sigma = (y \leftarrow x, z \leftarrow x)$.

Proving (4.10)

Let $t_1 = \text{RED}(A) \vee \text{BLUE}(A)$ and $t_2 = \text{RED}(A)$. We change the representation and write: $t_1 = t_1' = \text{COLOUR(RED}, A) \vee \text{COLOUR(BLUE}, A)$ (which as opposed to (4.2), has generally no implication) and $t_2 = t_2' = \text{COLOUR(RED}, A)$.

There are two cases:

either A is the object which has all colours, i.e.

$$\forall x\,\text{COLOUR}(x, A) = \text{TRUE, then } t_1 <> t_2$$

or A is not spotted by all colours, i.e.

$$\forall x\,\text{COLOUR}(x, A) = \text{FALSE and it follows:}$$

$$t_2'' = t_2' \vee \text{FALSE}$$
$$= \text{COLOUR(RED}, A) \vee \forall x\,\text{COLOUR}(x, A)$$
$$= \forall x\,(\text{COLOUR(RED}, A) \vee \text{COLOUR}(x, A))$$

and $t_1' < t_2''$ because of (3.16).

Proving (4.13)

The same proof as in (4.10) applies, except that one must be in a universe where there is no object spotted by all colours, i.e. $\forall x\,\text{COLOUR}(x, y) = \text{FALSE}$, to be able to compare the two clauses.

NOTES

1. This example is drawn from Bongard 1970. For more details about it, see Claviéras *et al.* 1983 and Sallantin 1983. A hint about these descriptions is given in what follows.
2. See, for example, Hayes-Roth and McDermott 1978, Michalski 1980, Plotkin 1970, Vere 1980.
3. Hayes-Roth and McDermott 1978. Vere 1981.
4. Under the idempotency of logical AND, P, for example, is equivalent to P AND P.
5. Discussed in Hayes-Roth and McDermott 1978, Kodratoff 1982, and Vere 1980.

Bibliography

Letters in square brackets following bibliographical entries refer to chapters.
Key: I   —   Introduction
      S   —   Ch. 1 (Sloman)
      P   —   Ch. 2 (Palmer)
      E   —   Ch. 3 (Engel)
      J   —   Ch. 4 (Jacob)
      N   —   Ch. 5 (Narayanan)
      M   —   Ch. 6 (Mouloud)
      T   —   Ch. 7 (Tiercelin)
      H   —   Ch. 8 (Higginbotham)
      B   —   Ch. 9 (Boden)
      E-B   —   Ch. 10 (Ennals & Briggs)
      C   —   Ch. 11 (Chouraqui)
      Bu —   Ch. 12 (Bundy)
      K   —   Ch. 13 (Kayser)
      Y   —   Ch. 14 (Yazdani)
      K-G —   Ch. 15 (Kodratoff & Ganascia)

Ajsukiewicz 1955   K. Ajsukiewicz: 'Classification des Raisonnements' (in Polish). *Studia Logica* II, Warsaw. [C]

Amarel 1968   Saul Amarel: 'On Machine Representations of Problems of Reasoning about Actions: The Missionaries and Cannibals Problem'. In B. Meltzer and D. Michie (eds): *Machine Intelligence 3*. Edinburgh U.P. [B]

Anderson 1964 Alan Ross Anderson (ed): *Minds and Machines*. N.J.: Prentice-Hall. [I, T]

Arbib 1964 Michael Arbib: *Brains, Machines and Mathematics*. N.Y.: McGraw-Hill. [T]

Armstrong 1968 David Armstrong: *A Materialist Theory of Mind*. London: Routledge & Kegan Paul. [I]

Ashby 1961 W. Ross Ashby: *An Introduction to Cybernetics*. London: Chapman & Hall. [T]

Berkeley 1969. E. C. Berkeley: *Cerveaux Electroniques, Machines à Penser*. Paris: Gauthier Villars. [M]

Biro & Shahan 1982. N. Biro & P. Shahan (eds): *Mind, Brain and Function*. Brighton: Harvester Press. [I, E]

Blanche 1973 R. Blanche: *Le Raisonnement*. Paris: P.U.F. [C]

Bledsoe 1977 W. W. Bledsoe: 'Non-resolution Theorem Proving'. *Artificial Intelligence* 9(1). [C]

Block 1980a Ned Block (ed): *Readings in the Philosophy of Psychology*, Vols. 1 and 2. London: Methuen. [I, E]

Block 1980b Ned Block: 'What is Functionalism?' In Block 1980a, Vol. 1. [E]

Block 1980c Ned Block: 'Troubles with Functionalism'. In Block 1980a, Vol. 1. [I, E]

Bobrow & Collins 1975 D. G. Bobrow and A. Collins (eds): *Representation and Understanding: Studies in Cognitive Science*, N.Y.: Academic Press. [C, K]

Boden 1972 Margaret Boden: *Purposive Explanation in Psychology*. Brighton: Harvester Press. [I, B]

Boden 1977 Margaret Boden: *Artificial Intelligence and Natural Man*. Brighton: Harvester Press. [I, B, Y]

Boden 1981a Margaret Boden: *Minds and Mechanisms: Philosophy, Psychology and Computational Models*. Brighton: Harvester Press. [I, B]

Boden 1981b Margaret Boden: 'The Case for a Cognitive Biology'. In Boden 1981a. [B]

Boden 1981c Margaret Boden: 'Failure is not the Spur' Forthcoming in O. Selfridge *et al.* (eds): *Adaptive Control in Ill-Defined Systems*. Proceedings of a 1981 NATO workshop. [Y]

Boden 1982 Margaret Boden: 'Mechanisms of Creativity'. Inaugural Lecture, University of Sussex. [Y]

Bongard 1970 N. Bongard: *Pattern Recognition*. N.Y.; Spartan Books. [K-G]

Borillo *et al.* 1979. M. Borillo *et al.* (eds): *Représentation des Connaissances et Raisonnement dans les Sciences de l'Homme*. Colloque de St. Maximin. Marseille: I.N.R.I.A./Laboratoire d'Informatique pour les Sciences de l'Homme. [C]

Borillo *et al.* 1982. A. Borillo *et al.* (eds): *Approches Formelles de la Sémantique Naturelle*. Toulouse: C.N.R.S. – U.P.S., L.S.I. [C]

Bouveresse 1971 Jacques Bouveresse: 'Le Fantôme dans la Machine'. In *La Parole Malheureuse*. Paris: Minuit. [T]

Bramer 1980   M. A. Bramer: 'A Survey and Critical Review of Expert System Research'. Milton Keynes: Open University, Faculty of Mathematics. [C]

Brown & Sleeman 1982   J. S. Brown and D. Sleeman (eds): *Intelligent Tutoring Systems*. N.Y.: Academic Press. [B]

Bundy 1975   Alan Bundy: 'Analysing Mathematical Proofs (or Reading Between the Lines):. *Proceedings* of the 4th I.J.C.A.I. Expanded version available as D.A.I. Research Report no. 2. University of Edinburgh. [Bu]

Bundy *et al.* 1979   Alan Bundy, L. Byrd, G. Luger, C. Mellish, R. Milne & M. Palmer: 'Mecho: A Program to Solve Mechanics Problems'. Working Paper 50, Dept. of Artificial Intelligence, University of Edinburgh. [Bu]

Bundy & Sterling 1981   Alan Bundy & L. S. Sterling: 'Meta-level Inference in Algebra'. Research Paper 164. Dept of Artificial Intelligence, University of Edinburgh. Presented at the Workshop on Logic Programming for Intelligent Systems, Los Angeles 1981. [Bu]

Bundy & Welham 1981.   Alan Bundy & B. Welham: 'Using Meta-level Inference for Selective Application of Multiple Rewrite Rules in Algebraic Manipulation'. *Artificial Intelligence* 16(2). [Bu]

Bundy *et al.* 1982   Alan Bundy, L. Byrd & C. Mellish: 'Special Purpose, but Domain Independent Inference Mechanisms'. In ECAI 1982. Also available as Research Paper no. 179, Department of Artificial Intelligence, University of Edinburgh. [Bu]

Burge 1977   Tyler Burge: 'Belief *de re*'. *Journal of Philosophy*, LXXIV. [E]

Canguilhem 1972   Georges Canguilhem: *La Connaissance de la vie*. Paris: Vrin. [T]

Chang & Lee 1973   C. L. Chang & R. C-T. Lee: *Symbolic Logic and Mechanical Theorem Proving*. N.Y.: Academic Press. [C]

Chen & Findler 1979   D. T-W. Chen & N. V. Findler: 'Toward Analogical Reasoning in Problem Solving by Computers'. *Journal of Cybernetics*. [C]

Chomsky 1957   Noam Chomsky: *Syntactic Structures*. The Hague: Mouton. [H]

Chomsky 1959a   Noam Chomsky: 'On Certain Formal Properties of Grammars'. *Information and Control*, 2 (2). [N]

Chomsky 1959b   Noam Chomsky: 'Review of B. F. Skinner's *Verbal Behaviour*.' *Language*, 35. Reprinted in J. Fodor and J. Katz (eds): *The Structure of Language*. N.Y.: Prentice Hall, 1964. [I, H]

Chomsky 1965   Noam Chomsky: *Aspects of the Theory of Syntax*. M.I.T. Press. [H]

Chomsky 1966   Noam Chomsky: *Current Issues in Linguistic Theory*. The Hague: Mouton. [Y]

Chomsky 1975   Noam Chomsky: *Reflections on Language*. Pantheon. [J]

Chomsky 1980   Noam Chomsky: *Rules and Representations*. N.Y.: Columbia U.P. [J, H]

Chomsky 1981   Noam Chomsky: *Lectures on Government and Binding*. Dordrecht: Foris Publications. [H]

Chouraqui 1981   Eugene Chouraqui: *Contribution à l'Etude théorique de la*

Représentation des Connaissances: le système symbolique ARCHES. Thèse de doctorat d'état. Nancy: I.N.P.L. [C]

Chouraqui 1982   Eugene Chouraqui: 'Construction of a Model for Reasoning by Analogy'. Orsay: *Proceedings* of ECAI–82. [C]

Chouraqui 1983   Eugene Chouraqui: 'Formal Expression of the Evolution of Knowledge'. Cambridge, Mass.: *Proc.* 1983 International System Dynamics Conference. [C]

Churchland 1979   Paul Churchland: *Scientific Realism and the Plasticity of Mind.* Cambridge U.P. [B]

Churchland & Churchland 1982   Paul and Patricia Churchland: 'Functionalism, Qualia and Intentionality'. In Biro & Shahan 1982. [I, E]

Clark *et al.* 1981   K. L. Clark, J. R. Ennals & F. G. McCabe: *A micro-PROLOG Primer.* London: Logic Programming Associates. [E-B]

Clark & Gregory 1982   K. L. Clark & S. Gregory: 'PARLOG: A Parallel Implementation of PROLOG'. Imperial College. [E-B]

Clark & Tarnlund 1982   K. L. Clark & S.-A. Tarnlund (eds): *Logic Programming.* N.Y.: Academic Press. [E-B]

Clark *et al.* 1982   K. L. Clark, F. G. McCabe & P. Hammond: 'PROLOG: A Language for Implementing Expert Systems'. In Hayes *et al.* 1982 [E-B]

Clavieras *et al.* 1983   B. Clavieras, J.-G. Ganascia & R. Lemerle-Loisel: 'Généralisation de différences entre descriptions'. *Actes Journées sur les outils de l'apprentissage à partir d'exemples.* Orsay. [K-G]

Clocksin & Mellish 1981   W. Clocksin & C. Mellish: *Programming in PROLOG.* N.Y.: Springer-Verlag. [E-B]

Cohen & Perrault 1979   P. R. Cohen & C. R. Perrault: 'Elements of a plan-based theory of speech acts'. *Cognition Science* 3. [C]

Costa 1982   E. Costa: *Dérecursivation automatique en utilisant des systèmes de réécriture de termes.* Thèse de 3ème cycle, Paris 1981 Published by L.R.I. Bat. 490, F 91495 ORSAY CEDEX. [K-G]

Coulon *et al.* 1979   Daniel Coulon, Jacques Fuss, Francois Jakob, Daniel Kayser & Michel Monfils: 'Une experience de "comprehension" de texte en langage naturel R.A.I.R.O.'. *Informatique,* 13(4). [K]

Cresswell 1973   M. J. Cresswell: *Logics and Language.* London: Methuen. [C]

Dahl *et al.* 1972   D.-J. Dahl, C. A. M. Hoare & E. J. Dijkstra: *Structured Programming.* Academic Press 1972. [E]

Davidson 1974   Donald Davidson: 'Belief and the Basis of Meaning'. *Synthèse* **24.** [E]

Davidson 1980   Donald Davidson: *Essays on Actions and Events.* Oxford U.P. [E]

Davis 1979   M. Davis: 'The Prehistory of Automated Deduction'. *Proc. 4th Workshop on Automated Deduction.* Austin, Texas. Jan. 1979. [E-B]

Davis & King 1977   R. Davis & J. King: 'An Overview of Production Systems'. In E. W. Elcock & D. Michie (eds): *Machine Intelligence 8.* Chichester: Ellis Horwood [C] de Beaugrande 1979 R. A. de Beaugrande: 'Toeards a General Theory of Creativity'. *Poetics,* **8.** [Y]

de Beaugrande & Colby 1979 R. A. de Beaugrande and B. N. Colby: 'Narrative Models of Action and Interaction'. *Cognitive Science* **3,** 1. [Y]

Dennett 1978a Daniel Dennett: *Brainstorms.* Brighton: Harvester Press. [I, P, E, T]

Dennett 1978b Daniel Dennett: 'Intentional Systems'. In Dennett 1978a. [P, T, B]

Dennett 1978c Daniel Dennett: 'Current Issues in the Philosophy of Mind'. *American Philosophical Quarterly,* **15**(4). [I]

Dennett 1980 Daniel Dennett: 'Reply to Prof. Stich'. *Philosophical Books,* **21**(2). [E]

Dennett 1982a Daniel Dennett: 'Beyond belief'. In Woodfield 1982. [I, E, J]

Dennett 1982a Daniel Dennett: 'Making Sense of Ourselves'. In Biro & Shahan 1982. [E]

Dopp 1962 J. Dopp: *Logiques Construites par une Méthode de Déduction naturelle.* Paris: Gauthier-Villars. [C]

Dorolle 1949 M. Dorolle: *La Raisonnement par Analogie.* Paris: P.U.F. [C]

Dreyfus 1972 Hubert Dreyfus: *What Computers Can't Do: A Critique of Artificial Intelligence.* N.Y.: Harper & Row. [I, B]

Dreyfus 1980 Hubert Dreyfus: 'Les Ordinateurs, Peuvent-Ils être vraiment intelligents?'. *Critique,* **XXXVI.** [I, T]

Dreyfus 1981 Hubert Dreyfus: 'From Micro-Worlds to Knowledge Representation: AI at an Impasse'. Preface to second (1979) edition of Dreyfus 1972. Reprinted (with revisions) in Haugeland 1981. [I]

Dummett 1981 Michael Dummett: Review of N. Chomsky's *Rules and Representations. London Review of Books,* 3 September. [H]

ECAI 1982 European Conference on Artificial Intelligence: *Proceedings of the 5th European Conference on Artificial Intelligence,* Orsay [Bu, Y, K-G]

Ennals 1982a J. R. Ennals: *Beginning micro-PROLOG.* Chichester and London: Ellis Horwood and Heinemann. [E-B]

Ennals 1982b J. R. Ennals: 'Teaching Logic as a Computer Language in Schools'. *Proc. 1st International Logic Programming Conference,* Marseille 1982. reprinted, with additional material, in M. Yazdani (ed): *New Horizons in Educational Computing.* Ellis Horwood, 1984 and in D. Warren and M. van Caneghem (eds): *Logic Programming and its Applications.* Ablex 1983. [E-B]

Ennals 1983 J. R. Ennals: 'Artificial Intelligence' in N. J. Rushby (ed): *Computer-Based Learning.* Pergamon Infotech. [E-B]

Ennals forthcoming J. R. Ennals: 'Computers and History Teaching'. In Y. Larsson, Sydney: Allen & Unwin. Forthcoming. [E-B]

Esposito 1973 J. Esposito: 'Synechism, Socialism and Cybernetics'. *Transactions of the C. S. Peirce Society,* **IX,** 2. [T]

Farinas del Cerro 1981 L. Farinas del Carro: *Déduction automatique et Logique*

Modale. Thèse d'Etat, Université de Paris. [C]

Feigenbaum & Feldman 1963 E. A. Feigenbaum and J. Feldman (eds): *Computers and Thought.* N.Y.: McGraw-Hill. [I]

Field 1978 Hartry Field: 'Mental Representation'. *Erkenntnis* **13.** Reprinted in Block 1980a, vol. II. [E]

Findler & Chen 1973. N. V. Findler & D. T.-W. Chen: 'On the Problems of Times, Retrieval of Temporal Relations, Causality and Coexistence'. *International Journal of Computer and Information Sciences,* 2(3) [C]

Fodor *et al.* 1974 J. A. Fodor, T. G. Bever & M. F. Garrett: *The Psychology of Language.* N.Y.: McGraw-Hill. [H]

Fodor 1975 Jerry Fodor: *The Language of Thought.* M.I.T. Press. [I, E, J]

Fodor 1980 Jerry Fodor: 'Methodological Solipsism Considered as a Research Strategy'. *The Behavioural and Brain Sciences,* **3.** Reprinted in Haugeland 1981 and in Fodor 1981. [I, E, J]

Fodor 1981 Jerry Fodor: *RePresentations.* Brighton: Harvester Press. [I, E, J, B]

Fodor 1983 Jerry Fodor: *The Modularity of Mind.* M.I.T. Press. [I]

Fuchi 1981 N. Fuchi: *Aiming for Knowledge Information Processing.* Electrotechnical Laboratory, Ibaraki, Japan. [E-B]

Gauld & Shotter 1977 A. Gauld & J. Shotter: *Human Action and its Psychological Investigation.* London: Routledge & Kegan Paul. [B]

Gick & Holyoak 1980 M. L. Gick and K. J. Holyoak: 'Analogical Problem Solving'. *Cognitive Psychology* **12.** [C]

Gödel 1946 Kurt Gödel: 'Russell's Mathematical Logic'. In P. A. Schilpp (ed): *The Philosophy of Bertrand Russell.* Evanston: Northern U.P. [E-B]

Grize 1979 J. B. Grize: 'Le Discours Analogique'. In *Représentation des connaissances et raisonnement dans les sciences de l'Homme.* Colloque de Saint-Maximin. Marseille: I.N.R.I.A./Laboratoire d'Informatique pour les Sciences de l'Homme. [C]

Gross & Lentin 1967 M. Gross & A. Lentin: *Notions sur les Grammaires Formelles.* Paris: Gauthier Villars. [M]

Gunderson 1971 Keith Gunderson: *Mentality and Machines.* N.Y.: Doubleday Anchor. [E]

Hammond 1982 P. Hammond: 'A PROLOG Expert System Shell (APES)'. Imperial College. [E-B]

Harman 1973 Gilbert Harman: *Thought.* Princeton U.P. [E]

Haugeland 1978 John Haugeland: 'The Nature and Plausibility of Cognitivism', *The Behavioural and Brain Sciences,* **1.** Reprinted in Haugeland 1981, ch. 9. [I]

Haugeland 1979 John Haugeland: 'Understanding a Natural Language'. *Journal of Philosophy,* **LXXVI,** 11. [E]

Haugeland 1981 John Haugeland: (ed): *Mind Design.* Vermont: Bradford Books. [I, E]

Hayes 1979 P. J. Hayes: 'The Naive Physics Manifesto'. In D. Michie (ed):

Expert Systems in the Micro-Electronic Age. Edinburgh U.P. [B]

Hayes *et al.* 1982   P. J. Hayes, D. Michie & Y-H. Pao (eds): *Machine Intelligence 10: Intelligent Systems – Practice and Perspective.* Chichester: Ellis Horwood. [E-B]

Hayes-Roth & McDermott 1978   F. Hayes-Roth & J. McDermott: 'An Interference Matching Technique for Inducing Abstractions'. *Communications of A.C.M.,* **21.** [K-G]

Hayes-Roth *et al.* 1983   F. Hayes-Roth *et al.* (eds): *Building Expert Systems.* London: Addison-Wesley. [C]

Heidegger 1962   M. Heidegger: *Being and Time.* N.Y.: Harper & Row [I]

Heil 1981   J. Heil: 'Does Cognitive Psychology rest on a Mistake?'. *Mind,* **XC.** [I, E]

Hintikka 1980   J. J. Hintikka: 'C. S. Peirce's First Real Discovery and its Contemporary Significance'. *The Monist,* **63**(3). [T]

Hinton 1981   G. E. Hinton: 'Shape Representation in Parallel Systems'. In IJCAI 1981. [B]

Hofstadter 1979   Douglas W. Hofstadter: *Godel, Escher, Bach: An Eternal Golden Braid.* Brighton: Harvester Press. [I]

Hofstadter & Dennett 1982   Douglas W. Hofstadter & D. C, Dennett (eds): *The Mind's I: Fantasies and Reflections on Self and Soul.* Brighton: Harvester Press. [I]

Holmes 1966   L. Holmes: 'Peirce on Self-Control'. *Transactions of the C.S. Peirce Society,* **II** (2). [T]

Hook 1960   Sidney Hook (ed): *Dimensions of Mind: A Symposium.* N.Y.: University Press. [T]

Hsiang 1982   J. Hsiang: *Topics in Automated Theorem Proving and Program Generation.* Ph.D. thesis, Dept. of Computer Science, University of Illinois. [K-G]

Hume 1955   David Hume: *A Treatise of Human Nature.* ed. L. A. Selby-Bigge. Oxford. [P]

IJCAI 1977   International Joint Conference on Artificial Intelligence: *Proceedings of the Fifth Int. Joint Conference,* August 1977. (2 vols.). W. Kaufmann. [C, Y]

IJCAI 1981   International Joint Conference on Artificial Intelligence: *Proceedings of the Seventh Int. Joint Conference,* August 1981. (2 vols.) W. Kaufmann. [B, K]

Inhelder & Karmiloff-Smith 1975   B. Inhelder & A. Karmiloff-Smith: 'If you Want to Get Ahead, Get a Theory'. *Cognition,* **3.** [B]

Jeffrey 1967   R. Jeffrey: *Formal Logic: Its Scope and Limits.* N.Y.: McGraw-Hill. [C]

Kaplan unpublished David Kaplan: 'Demonstratives'. Unpublished. [J]

Karmiloff-Smith 1979   A Karmiloff-Smith: 'Micro- and Macro-Developmental Changes in Language Acquisition and Other Representational Systems'. *Cognitive Science,* **3.** [B]

Kayser 1980 Daniel Kayser: 'Vers une modelisation du raisonnement approximatif': *Actes du Colloque sur la representation des connaissances et du raisonnement.* Institut National de Recherche en Informatique et Automatique. [C, K]

Kayser & Coulon 1981 Daniel Kayser & Daniel Coulon: 'Variable-depth Natural Language Understanding'. In IJCAI 1981. [K]

Kayser forthcoming. Daniel Kayser: 'Apport de différentes méthodes au problème de la représentation des connaissances'. [K]

Klein 1975 S. Klein: 'Meta-Compiling Text Grammars as a Mode for Human Behaviour'. In R. C. Schank & B. N. Nash-Webber (eds): *Theoretical Issues in Natural Language Processing.* Proceedings of Workshop of Assoc. of Computational Linguistics, June 1975. [Y]

Kling 1971 R. E. Kling: 'A Paradigm for Reasoning by Analogy'. *Artificial Intelligence,* **22.** [C]

Kodratoff 1982 Yves Kodratoff: 'Generalizing and Particularizing as the techniques of learning'. *Proc. International Conference on A.I. and Information-control of Robots,* Bratislava. Forthcoming in *Computers and Artificial Intelligence.* [K-G]

Kowalski 1979 Robert A. Kowalski: *Logic for Problem Solving.* N.Y.: North-Holland. [E-B, C]

Kowalski 1982 Robert A. Kowalski: 'Logic Programming and the Fifth Generation'. In *State of the Art Report on Fifth Generation Computing.* Pergamon Infotech. [E-B]

Kripke 1982 Saul Kripke: *Wittgenstein on Rules and Private Language.* Oxford: Blackwell. [E]

Kuhn 1970 Thomas Kuhn: *The Structure of Scientific Revolutions.* Chicago U.P. [I]

Ladrière 1952 Jean Ladrière: *Les Limitations internes des Formalismes: Etude sur la signification du Théorème de Gödel.* Paris: Gauthier-Villars. [C]

Ladrière 1970 Jean Ladrière: *L'Articulation du Sens.* Paris: Aubier Montagne. [M]

Laurière 1982 Jean-Louis Laurière: 'Représentation et utilisation des connaissances'. *Revue R.A.I.R.O.: Technique et Sciences Informatiques,* I(1), (2). [C, K]

Lenat 1977 D. B. Lenat: 'Automated Theory Formation in Mathematics'. In IJCAI 1977. [Y]

Lewin 1952a K. Lewin: *Field Theory in Social Sciences.* London: Cartwright. [M]

Lewin 1952b K. Lewin: 'Comportement et Développement Comme fonction de la Situation Totale'. In L. Carmichael: *Manuel de Psychologie de l'Enfant.* Paris: P.U.F. [M]

Lewis 1966 David Lewis: 'An Argument for the Identity Theory'. *Journal of Philosophy,* 1963. [I]

Lewis 1972 David Lewis: 'Psychophysical and Theoretical Identifications'.

Australasian Journal of Philosophy, **50.** [I]

Lucas 1961   J. R. Lucas: 'Minds, Machines and Gödel'. *Philosophy,* **XXXVI.** Reprinted in Anderson 1964. [I, N]

Lycan 1979   William G. Lycan: 'A New Lilliputian Argument against Machine Functionalism'. *Philosophical Studies,* **35.** [I]

Lycan 1981   William G. Lycan: 'Form, Function and Feel'. *Journal of Philosophy,* **LXXVIII.** [I, E]

Lyons 1968   John Lyons: *Introduction to Theoretical Linguistics.* Cambridge U.P. [K]

McCarthy & Hayes 1969   J. McCarthy & P. J. Hayes: 'Some Philosophical Problems from the Standpoint of Artificial Intelligence'. In B. Meltzer & D. Michie (eds): *Machine Intelligence 4.* Edinburgh U.P. [C]

McCarthy 1977   J. McCarthy: 'Epistemological Problems of Artificial Intelligence'. In IJCAI 1977. [C]

McCarthy 1980   J. McCarthy: 'Circumscription: a Form of Non-monotonic Reasoning'. *Artificial Intelligence,* **13.** [C]

McDermott 1981   Drew McDermott: 'Artificial Intelligence meets Natural Stupidity'. in Haugeland 1981. [I]

McGinn 1982   Colin McGinn: 'The Structure of Content'. In Woodfield 1982. [E]

Mangold 1983   Tom Mangold: 'Beyond Deterrence'. *The Listener,* 8 September. [I]

Marr 1982 David Marr: *Vision.* M.I.T. Press. [I, B]

Meehan 1976   J. R. Meehan: *The Metanovel: Writing Stories by Computer.* Research Report no. 74. Yale University. [Y]

Melden 1961 A. I. Melden: *Free Action.* London: Routledge & Kegan Paul. [P]

Mellor 1974 David Mellor: 'In Defence of Dispositions'. *Philosophical Review,* **LXXXIII.** [E]

Mellor 1980a   David Mellor: 'Consciousness and Degrees of Belief'. In Mellor 1980b. [E]

Mellor 1980b David Mellor: *Prospects for Pragmatism.* Cambridge U.P. [E]

Merleau-Ponty 1962   Maurice Merleau-Ponty: *The Phenomenology of Perception.* London: Routledge & Kegan Paul. [I]

Merleau-Ponty 1972   Maurice Merleau-Ponty: *La Psychologie du Comportment.* Paris: Gallimard. [M]

Michalski 1980 R. S. Michalski: 'Inductive Learning as rule-guided Transformtion of Symbolic Descriptions: a Theory and Implementation'. *Proc. International Workshop on Program Construction, Bonas.* Forthcoming in A. Biermann *et al.* (eds): *Automatic Program Construction Techniques.* London: Macmillan. [K-G]

Miller & Johnson-Laird 1976   G. A. Miller & P. Johnson-Laird: *Language and Perception.* Cambridge, Mass.: Belknap Press. [B]

Minsky 1968 Marvin Minsky: 'Matter, Mind and Models' in M. Minsky (ed): *Semantic Information Processing.* M.I.T. Press. [Bu, Y]

Minsky 1974   Marvin Minsky: *A Framework for Representing Knowledge.* M.I.T. AI Lab Memo 306. Reprinted (in part) in Haugeland 1981. [I, K]

Moore 1977   R. C. Moore: 'Reasoning about Knowledge and Action'. In IJCAI 1977.

Morton 1980   Adam Morton: *Frames of Mind.* Oxford U.P. [E]

Mouloud 1964   Noël Mouloud: *Formes Structures et Modes Productifs.* Paris: S.E.D.E.S. [M]

Mouloud 1964   Noël Mouloud: *L'Analyse du Sens.* Paris: Payot. [M]

Nagel 1974   Thomas Nagel: 'What is it like to be a Bat?'. *Philosophical Review,* LXXXIII. Reprinted in T. Nagel: *Mortal Questions,* Cambridge U.P. 1979, and in Block 1980a, Vol. 1. [I, E, N]

Newell & Simon 1972   Allen Newell & Herbert Simon: *Human Problem Solving.* N. J.: Prentice-Hall. [B]

Newell & Simon   Allen Newell & Herbert Simon: 'Computer Science as Empirical Enquiry: Symbols and Search'. *Communications of the A.C.M.,* **14**(3). Also in Haugeland 1981. [C]

Oleron 1977   Pierre Oleron: *Le Raisonnement.* Paris: P.U.F. [C]

Papert 1980   Seymour Papert: *Mindstorms: Children, Computers and Powerful Ideas.* Brighton: Harvester Press. [B]

Parkinson 1966   G. H. R. Parkinson (ed): Leibniz — Logical Papers. Oxford U.P. [E-B]

Peirce 1868   Charles Sanders Peirce: 'Questions concerning Certain Faculties Claimed for Man'; 'Consequences of Four Incapacities'; 'Grounds of Validity of the Laws of Logic'. All in *Journal of Speculative Philosophy,* 1868. [T]

Peirce 1877   Charles Sanders Peirce: 'Logical Machines'. *Amsterdam Journal of Psychology,* November 1877. Reprinted in Peirce 1976 [T]

Peirce 1910   Charles Sanders Peirce: 'On Definition and Classification'. Catalogued in Robin 1967 as: A.Ms., G–1910–1. pp. 19–21, np. [T]

Peirce 1913   Charles Sanders Peirce: 'An Essay toward Improving our Reasoning in Security and Uberty'. Catalogued in Robin 1967 as: Ms., np. late (c. 1913). [T]

Peirce 1958   Charles Sanders Peirce: *Collected Papers.* Vols. I–VI, eds. C. Hartshorne and P. Weiss. Vols. VII–VIII. ed. A. Burks. Cambridge, Mass.: Belknap Press. [T]

Peirce 1976   Charles Sanders Peirce: *The New Elements of Mathematics.* (ed): C. Eisele. (4 vols). The Hague: Mouton. [T]

Pereira *et al.* 1979   L. M. Pereiera & D. H. D. Warren: *User's Guide to DEC-system-10 PROLOG.* Occasional Paper 15, Department of Artificial Intelligence, University of Edinburgh. [Bu]

Perelman & Olbrechts-Tyteca 1970   Ch. Perelman & L. Olbrechts-Tyteca: *Traité de l'Argumentation.* Editions de l'Institut de Sociologie, Université de Bruxelles. [C]

Perry 1977   J. Perry: 'Frege on Demonstratives'. *Philosophical Review,* **86**. [J]

Perry 1979 J. Perry: 'The Problem of the Essential Indexical'. *Nous*, **13**. [I]

Pitts & McCulloch 1943 W. Pitts & W. S. McCulloch: 'A Logical Calculus of the ideas immanent in Nervous Activities'. *Bulletin de Mathématique et Biophysique.* [M]

Plotkin 1970 G. D. Plotkin: 'A Note on Inductive Generalization', in B. Meltzer & D. Michie (eds): *Machine Intelligence 5.* American Elsevier. [K-G]

Polya 1945 G. Polya: *How to Solve It.* Princeton U.P. [Y]

Polya 1962 G. Polya: *Mathematics and Plausible Reasoning.* Vols. I & II. Princeton U.P. [C]

Porte 1965 J. Porte: *Recherches sur la Théorie Générale des Systèmes formels.* Paris: Gauthier Villars. [C]

Prade 1982 H. Prade: *Modèles Mathématiques de l'Imprécis et de l'Incertain en vue de l'Application au Raisonnement naturel.* Thèse d'état, Université Paul Sabatier, Toulouse. [C]

Pradines 1946 M. Pradines: *Traité de Psychologie Generale: Tome II B: Le Génie Humain, ses Instruments.* Paris: P.U.F. [M]

Prigogine & Stencers 1979 J. Prigogine & J. Stencers: *La Nouvelle Alliance.* Paris: Gallimard. [M]

Putnam 1960 Hilary Putnam: 'Minds and Machines'. In Hook 1960; Reprinted in Putnam 1975b. [I, M, T]

Putnam 1964 Hilary Putnam: 'Robots: Machines or Artificially Created Life?'. *Journal of Philosophy,* **61**. [I, M]

Putnam 1867a Hilary Putnam: 'Psychological Predicates'. In W. H. Capitan & D. D. Merrill (eds): *Art, Mind and Religion.* Pittsburgh U.P. Reprinted as 'The Nature of Mental States', in Putnam 1975b and in Block 1980a, vol. I. [I, M]

Putnam 1867b Hilary Putnam: 'The Mental Life of Some Machines', in H.-N. Castañeda (ed): *Intentionality, Minds and Perception.* Wayne State U.P. Reprinted in Putnam 1975b. [I, M]

Putnam 1975a Hilary Putnam: 'The Meaning of "Meaning"'. In Putnam 1975b [J]

Putnam 1975b Hilary Putnam: *Mind, Language and Reality: Philosophical Papers Vol. II.* Cambridge U.P. [M]

Putnam 1975c Hilary Putnam: 'Philosophy and our Mental Life'. In Putnam 1975b. Reprinted in Block 1980a Vol. I. [I, M]

Putnam 1979 Hilary Putnam: 'Ce qui est inné et pourquoi'. In M. Piattelli-Palmarini (ed): *Théories du Langage, Théories de l'Apprentissage.* Paris: Le Seuil. [J]

Putnam 1981 Hilary Putnam: *Reason, Truth and History.* Cambridge U.P. [J, M]

Quine 1960 W. V. O. Quine: *Word and Object.* M.I.T. Press. [I]

Quine 1975 W. V. O. Quine: 'Mind and Verbal Dispositions'. In Samuel D. Guttenplan (ed): *Mind and Language.* Oxford U.P. [H]

Ramsey 1978 F. P. Ramsey: 'Facts and Propositions'. In F. P. Ramsey: *Founda-*

tions, ed. D. H. Mellor. London: Routledge & Kegan Paul. [E]

Ransdell 1977   Joseph Ransdell: 'Some Leading Ideas of Peirce's Semiotic'. *Semiotica*, **19** (3/4). [T]

Reiter 1980   R. Reiter: 'A Logic for Default Reasoning'. *Artificial Intelligence*, **13** [C]

Rieger 1975   Charles J. Rieger: 'Conceptual Memory and Inference'. In Schank 1975. [K]

Riesbeck 1975   Christopher K. Riesbeck: 'Conceptual Analysis'. In Schank 1975. [K]

Ringle 1979   Martin Ringle (ed): *Philosophical Perspectives in Artificial Intelligence*. Brighton: Harvester Press. [I]

Robin 1967   Richard S. Robin (ed): *Annotated Catalogue of the Papers of C. S. Peirce*. M.I.T. Press. [T]

Robinson 1965   J. Alan Robinson: 'A Machine Oriented Logic Based on the Resolution Principle'. *Journal of A.C.M.*, **12**(1). [E-B, C]

Robinson 1979   J. Alan Robinson: *Logic: Form and Function. The Mechanisation of Deductive Reasoning*. Edinburgh U.P. [E-B]

Robinson 1982   J. Alan Robinson: 'Logical Reasoning in Machines'. Syracuse University. [E-B]

Robinson & Sibert 1982a   J. A. Robinson & E. E. Sibert: LOGLISP: An Alternative to PROLOG'. In Hayes *et al.* 1982. [E-B]

Robinson & Sibert 1982b   J. A. Robinson & E. E. Sibert: LOGLISP' Motivation, Design and Implementation'. In Clark & Tarnlund 1982. [E-B]

Rorty 1980   Richard Rorty: *Philosophy and the Mirror of Nature*. Oxford: Blackwell. [I]

Roussel 1975   P. Roussel: *PROLOG: Manuelle d'Utilisation*. Groupe d'Intelligence Artificielle. Univ. d'Aix-Marseille, Luminy. [E-B, C]

Rumelhart & Norman 1975   D. E. Rumelhart & D. A. Norman: *Exploration in Cognition*. San Francisco: Freeman & Co. [C]

Russell & Whitehead 1913   Bertrand Russell & A. N. Whitehead: *Principia Mathematica*, Vol. I. Cambridge U.P. [C]

Ruyer 1952   Raymond Ruyer: *La Cybernétique et les Origines de L'Information*. Paris: Flammarion. [M]

Ryle 1949   Gilbert Ryle: *The Concept of Mind*. London: Hutchinson [I, F, M]

Ryle 1973   Gilbert Ryle: 'Review of Anthony Quinton: *The Nature of Things.'* *New Statesman*, April 6. [P]

Sallantin 1983   J. Sallantin: 'Méthodologie pour la construction de règles à partir de données binaires'. *Actes Journées sur les Outils de l'Apprentissage à partir d'Exemples*. Orsay. [K-G]

Santane-Toth & Szeredi 1982   E. Santane-Toth & P. Szeredi: 'PROLOG Applications in Hungary'. In Clark & Tarnlund 1982. [E-B]

Sato & Sakurai 1983   M. Sato & T. Sakurai: 'Qute: A Prolog/Lisp type Language for Logic Programming'. University of Tokyo. [E-B]

Schank 1973   R. C. Schank: *Causality and Reasoning*. Instituto per gli studi semantici e cognitivi. Castagnola, Switzerland. [C]

Schank 1975   R. C. Schank (ed): *Conceptual Information Processing*. N.Y.: American Elsevier. [K]

Schank 1982 R. C. Schank: 'Looking at Learning'. In ECAI 1982. [K-G]

Schiffer 1978 S. Schiffer: 'The Basis of Reference'. *Erkenntnis* **13**, 1978 [E]

Schwind 1980   C. Schwind: 'A Completeness Proof for the Logic of Action'. Internal Report 172. Marseille: C.N.R.S. Labaratoire d'Informatique pour les Sciences de l'Homme. [C]

Searle 1980   John Searle: 'Minds, Brains and Programs', with Peer Commentaries. In *The Behavioural and Brain Sciences, 3*. Reprinted (without commentaries) in Haugeland 1981a. [I, E, J, N, B]

Searle 1981 John Searle: 'Analytic Philosophy and Mental Phenomena'. In P. A. French *et al.* (eds): *Mid-West Studies in Philosophy*. Vol. 6. U. of Minnesota Press. [E]

Sergot 1983   M. Sergot: 'A Query-User Facility for Logic Programming'. In P. Degano & E. Sandewall (eds): Integrated Interactive Computing Systems. N.Y.: North-Holland. [E-B]

Shoemaker 1982 Sidney Shoemaker: 'Some Varieties of Functionalism'. In Biro & Shahan 1982. [E]

Short 1981a   T. L. Short: 'Peirce's Concept of Final Causation'. *Transactions of the C. S. Peirce Society,* Summer 1981. [T]

Short 1981b   T. L. Short: 'Semeiosis and Intentionality'. *Transactions of the C. S. Peirce Society,* Fall 1981. [T]

Shortliffe 1976   E. H. Shortliffe: *Computer-based Medical Consultations: MYCIN.* N.Y.: American Elsevier. [C]

Siegel & Bossu 1981   P. Siegel & G. Bossu: *La Saturation au Secours de la Non-monotonie.* Thèse de 3ième cycle. Groupe d'Intelligence Artificielle. Université d'Aix-Marseille II. [C]

Sloman 1978a Aaron Sloman: *The Computer Revolution in Philosophy: Philosophy, Science and Models of Mind.* Brighton: Harvester Press. [I, B, Bu]

Sloman 1978b Aaron Sloman: 'Intuition and Analogical Reasoning', in Sloman 1978a. [B]

Sober 1982 Eliot Sober: 'Why must Homunculi be so Stupid?'. *Mind,* **XCI.** [P]

Sterling *et al.*, 1982   L. Sterling, A. Bundy, L. Byrd, R. O'Keefe & B. Silver: 'Solving Symbolic Equations with PRESS'. In J. Calmet (ed): *Computer Algebra, Lecture Notes in Computer Science,* no. 144. Springer Verlag. Longer version available as Research Paper no. 171. Department of Artificial Intelligence, University of Edinburgh. [Bu]

Stich 1978   Stephen Stich: 'Beliefs and Subdoxastic States'. *Philosophy of Science,* **45**. [E]

Stich 1979 Stephen Stich: 'Do Animals have Beliefs?'. *Australasian Journal of Philosophy,* **57**. [E]

Stich 1982a   Stephen Stich: 'On the Ascription of Content'. In Woodfield 1982. [E]

Stich 1982b Stephen Stich: 'Dennett on Intentional Systems'. In Biro & Shahan 1982. [E]

Stickel 1981 M. E. Stickel: 'A Unification Algorithm for Associative-commutative Functions'. *Journal of A.C.M.*, **28**. [K-G]

Takeuchi *et al.*, 1982 I. Takeuchi *et al.*: *New Unified Environment*. Nippon Telegram and Telephone Public Corporation. [E-B]

Tarski 1969 A. Tarski: 'The Establishment of Scientific Semantics'. In A. Tarski: *Logic, Semantics, Metamathematics.*. Oxford U.P. [M]

Tiercelin-Engel 1982 Claudine Tiercelin-Engel: *Intuition et Inférence: La Critique peircéènne de la Métaphysique (1867–1868)*. Doctorat de troisième cycle, Université de Paris I. [T]

Travis forthcoming Charles Travis: 'Objects of Belief'. French translation to appear in P. Jacob (ed): *Grammaire Générative et Sémantique*, forthcoming issue of *Communication*. 1984. [J]

Turing 1937 Alan M. Turing: 'On Computable Numbers with an Application to the *Entscheidungsproblem*'. *Proc. London Mathematical Society*, **42**. [I, M]

Turing 1950 Alan M. Turing: 'Computing Machinery and Intelligence'. *Mind*, **LIX**. Reprinted in Anderson 1964. [I]

Unger 1981 P. Unger: 'Toward a Psychology of Common Sense'. Unpublished. [E]

Valéry 1910 Paul Valéry: *Cahier B 1910*. Paris: Gallimard. [T]

van Caneghem 1982 M. van Caneghem (ed): *Proceedings of the First International Logic Programming Conference*, Marseille. [C]

van Heijenoort 1967 J. van Heijenoort (ed): *From Frege to Gödel*. Harvard U.P. [E-B]

Vere 1980 S. A. Vere: 'Multilevel Counterfactuals for Generalizations of Relational Concepts and Productions'. *Artificial Intelligence*, **14**. [K-G]

Vere 1981 S. A. Vere: 'Constrained N-to-1 Generalizations'. Unpublished draft, Feb. 1981. [K-G]

Warren & Pereira 1981 D. H. D. Warren & F. L. N. Pereira: 'An Efficient, Easily Adaptable System for Interpreting Natural Language Queries'. D.A.I. Research Paper no. 155. University of Edinburgh. [E-B]

Waterman & Hayes-Roth 1978 D. A. Waterman & F. Hayes-Roth: *Pattern-directed Inference Systems*. N.Y.: Academic Press. [C]

Weizenbaum 1966 Joseph Weizenbaum: 'ELIZA – A Computer Program for the Study of Natural Language Communication between Man and Machine'. *Comm. A.C.M.*, **9**(1). [E-B]

Weizenbaum 1976 Joseph Weizenbaum: *Computer Power and Human Reason: From Judgement to Calculation*. N.Y.: W. H. Freeman. [I]

Whiteley 1962 C. H. Whiteley: 'Minds, Machines and Gödel: A Reply to Mr. Lucas'. *Philosophy*, **37**. [I]

Wiener 1965 Norber Wiener: *Cybernetics*, Second Edition. M.I.T. Press. [T]

Wilks forthcoming Yorick Wilks: 'Machines and Consciousness'. In C. Hookway (ed): *Minds, Machines and Evolution*. Forthcoming, 1984. Cambridge U.P.

[Bu]

Winograd 1972   Terry Winograd: *Understanding Natural Language*. N.Y.: Academic Press. [I, M]

Winograd 1975   Terry Winograd: 'Frames and the Declarative–Procedural Controversy'. In Bobrow and Collins 1975. [K]

Winograd 1976 Terry Winograd: 'Toward a Procedural Understanding of Semantics'. *Revue Internationale de Philosophie*, 117–118. [I]

Winston 1975 P. H. Winston: *The Psychology of Computer Vision*. N.Y.: McGraw-Hill. [I]

Winston 1977 P. H. Winston: *Artificial Intelligence*. Reading, Mass.: Addision-Wesley. [I]

Winston 1980 P. H. Winston: 'Learning and Reasoning by Analogy'. *Communications of A.C.M.*, 23(12). [C]

Wittgenstein 1953   Ludwig Wittgenstein: *Philosophical Investigations*. Edited with English translation, by G. E. M. Anscombe and R. Rhees. (Third Edition 1968). Oxford: Basil Blackwell. [P, M]

Woodfield 1982 Andrew Woodfield, ed. *Thought and Object: Essays on Intentionality*. Oxford U.P. [E]

Yazdani 1982 Masoud Yazdani: 'How to Write a Story'. In ECAI 1982. [Y]

Zadeh 1977 L. A. Zadeh: 'Theory of Fuzzy Sets'. In J. Belzer *et al.* (eds): *Encyclopaedia of Computer Science and Technology*, Vol. 8. N.Y.: M. Dekker. [C]

Index